C.S.PACAT  JOHANNA THE MAD  JOANA LAFUENTE

FENCE ™

# VOLUME ONE

BOOM! BOX ™

ROSS RICHIE.................................................CEO & Founder
JOY HUFFMAN.....................................................................CFO
MATT GAGNON.............................................Editor-in-Chief
FILIP SABLIK................President, Publishing & Marketing
STEPHEN CHRISTY.....................President, Development
LANCE KREITER............Vice President, Licensing & Merchandising
PHIL BARBARO..........Vice President, Finance & Human Resources
ARUNE SINGH.................................Vice President, Marketing
BRYCE CARLSON......Vice President, Editorial & Creative Strategy
SCOTT NEWMAN.............................Manager, Production Design
KATE HENNING.................................Manager, Operations
SPENCER SIMPSON.................................Manager, Sales
SIERRA HAHN..............................................Executive Editor
JEANINE SCHAEFER....................................Executive Editor
DAFNA PLEBAN.................................................Senior Editor
SHANNON WATTERS..........................................Senior Editor
ERIC HARBURN....................................................Senior Editor
WHITNEY LEOPARD.......................................................Editor
CAMERON CHITTOCK..................................................Editor
CHRIS ROSA........................................................................Editor
MATTHEW LEVINE............................................................Editor

SOPHIE PHILIPS-ROBERTS.........................Assistant Editor
GAVIN GRONENTHAL....................................Assistant Editor
MICHAEL MOCCIO..........................................Assistant Editor
AMANDA LaFRANCO....................................Executive Assistant
JILLIAN CRAB......................................................Design Coordinator
MICHELLE ANKLEY.............................................Design Coordinator
KARA LEOPARD.................................................Production Designer
MARIE KRUPINA...................................................Production Designer
GRACE PARK.....................................Production Design Assistant
CHELSEA ROBERTS.....................Production Design Assistant
SAMANTHA KNAPP.......................Prduction Design Assistant
ELIZABETH LOUGHRIDGE......................Accounting Coordinator
STEPHANIE HOCUTT.....................Social Media Coordinator
JOSÉ MEZA...............................................................Event Coordinator
HOLLY AITCHISON.......................................Operations Coordinator
MEGAN CHRISTOPHER.................................Operations Assistant
RODRIGO HERNANDEZ....................................Mailroom Assistant
MORGAN PERRY.................Direct Market Representative
CAT O'GRADY.................................................Marketing Assistant
BREANNA SARPY.......................................Executive Assistant

# BOOm! BOX™

**FENCE Volume One, October 2018.** Published by BOOM! Box, a division of Boom Entertainment, Inc. Fence is ™ & © 2018 C.S. Pacat. Originally published in single magazine form as FENCE No. 1-4. ™ & © 2017, 2018 C.S. Pacat. All rights reserved. BOOM! Box™ and the BOOM! Box logo are trademarks of Boom Entertainment, Inc., registered in various countries and categories. All characters, events, and institutions depicted herein are fictional. Any similarity between any of the names, characters, persons, events, and/or institutions in this publication to actual names, characters, and persons, whether living or dead, events, and/or institutions is unintended and purely coincidental. BOOM! Box does not read or accept unsolicited submissions of ideas, stories, or artwork.

For information regarding the CPSIA on this printed material, call: (203) 595-3636 and provide reference #RICH – 819684.

BOOM! Studios, 5670 Wilshire Boulevard, Suite 400, Los Angeles, CA 90036-5679. Printed in USA. Second Printing.

ISBN: 978-1-68415-192-9, eISBN: 978-1-64144-007-3

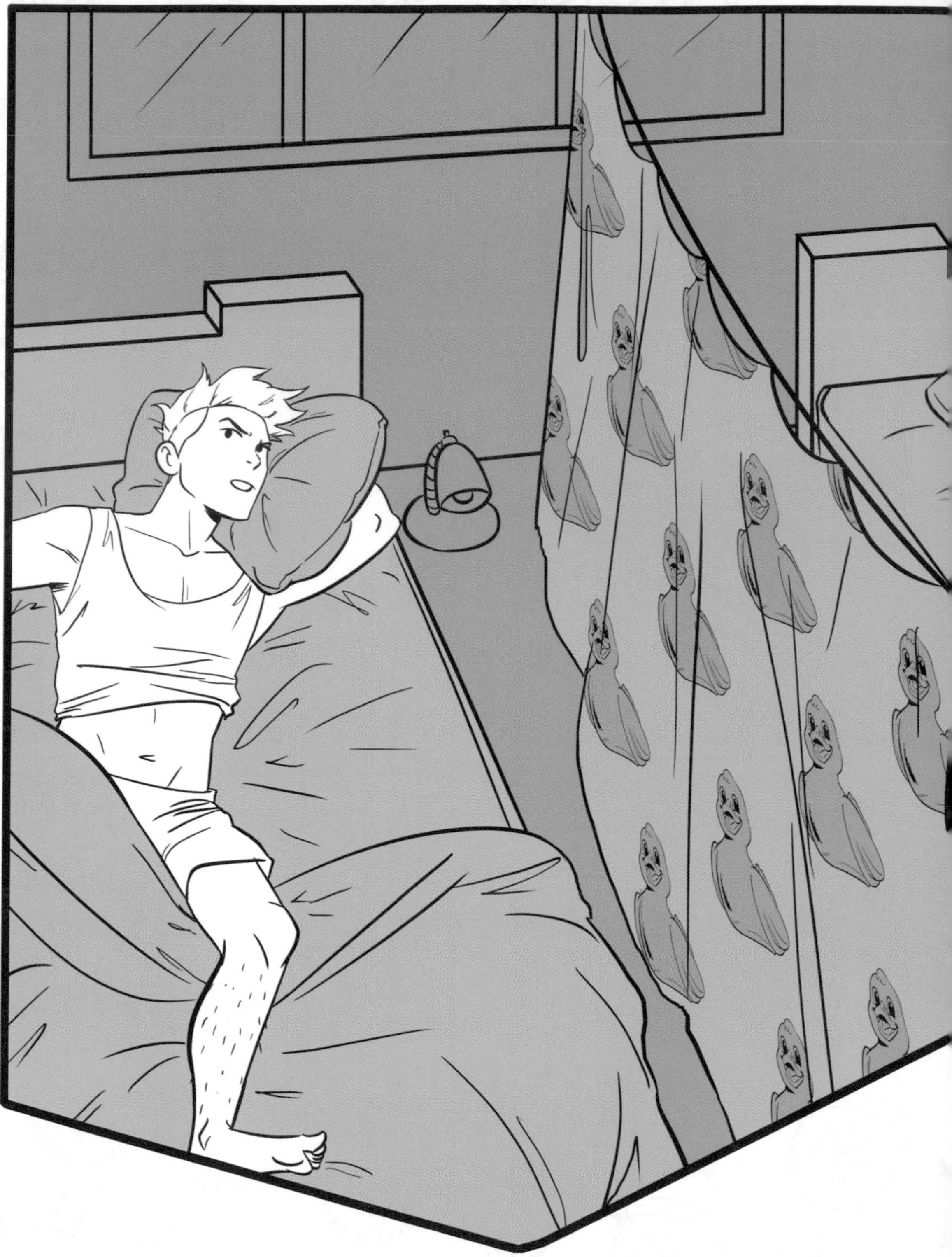

WRITTEN BY
# C.S. Pacat

ILLUSTRATED BY
# Johanna the Mad

COLORS BY
# Joana LaFuente

LETTERS BY
# Jim Campbell

TECHNICAL CONSULTANT
## Pieter Leeuwenburgh

SCHOOL LOGO DESIGNS
## Fawn Lau

COVER BY
## Johanna the Mad

SERIES DESIGNER
### Marie Krupina

COLLECTION DESIGNER
### Kara Leopard

EDITORS
### Shannon Watters & Dafna Pleban

CREATED BY
## C.S. Pacat & Johanna the Mad

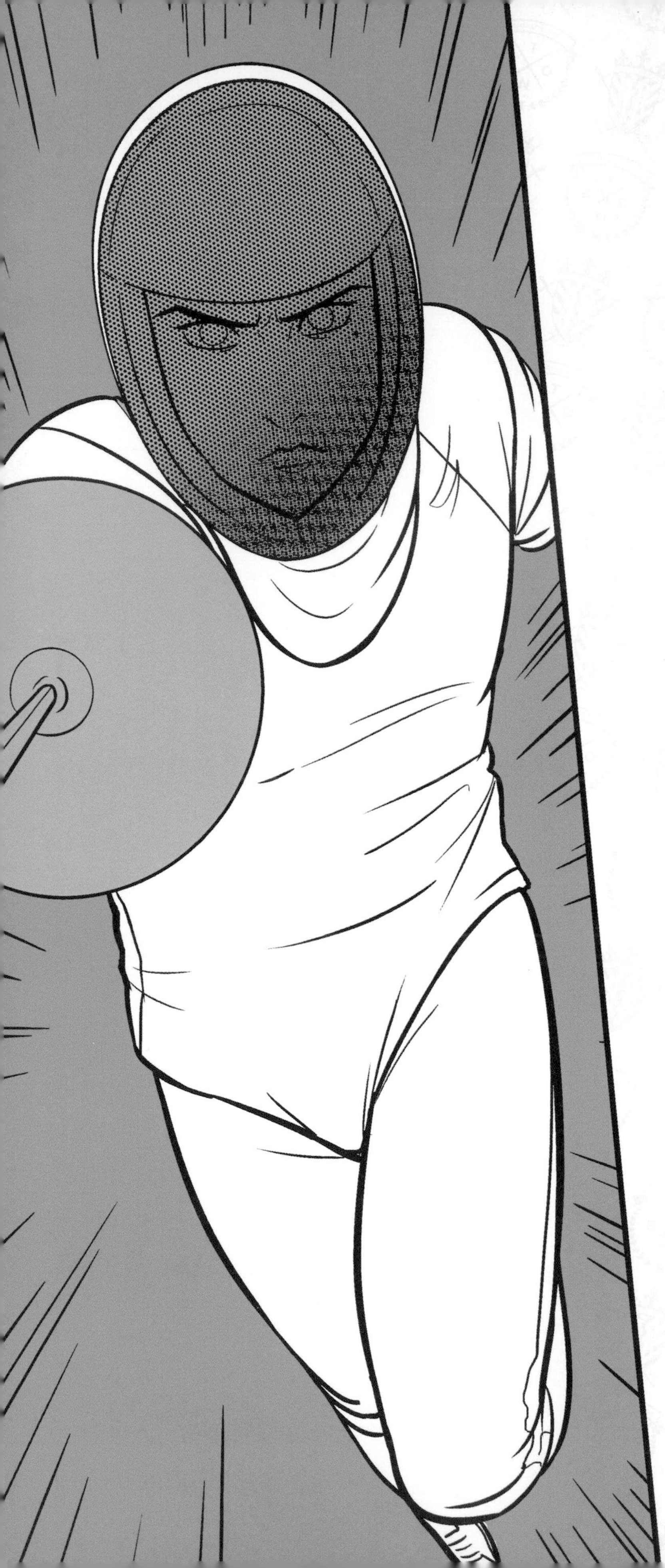

# CHAPTER One

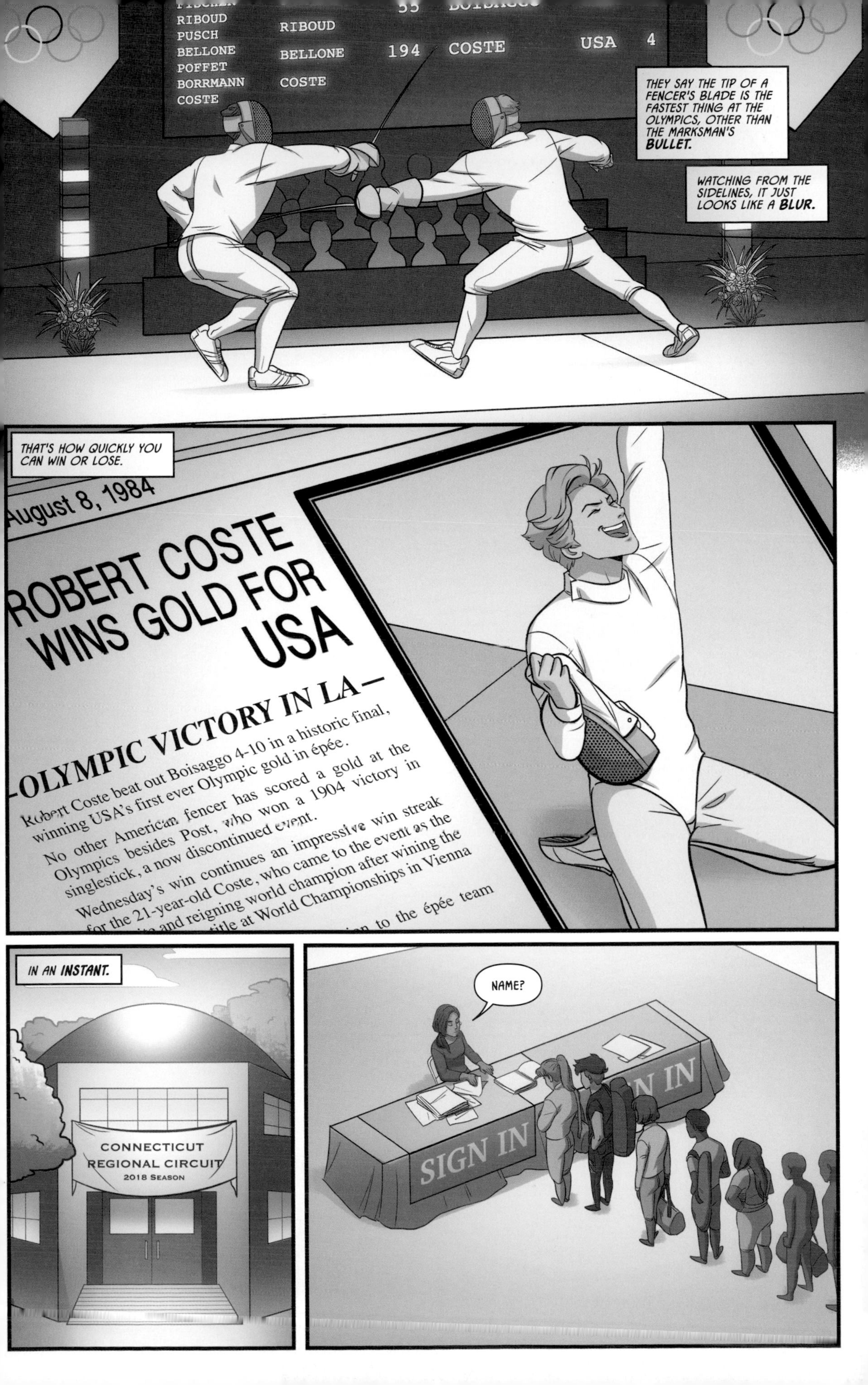

RIBOUD
PUSCH
BELLONE
POFFET
BORRMANN
COSTE
RIBOUD
BELLONE
COSTE
194 COSTE
USA 4
THEY SAY THE TIP OF A FENCER'S BLADE IS THE FASTEST THING AT THE OLYMPICS, OTHER THAN THE MARKSMAN'S BULLET.
WATCHING FROM THE SIDELINES, IT JUST LOOKS LIKE A BLUR.
THAT'S HOW QUICKLY YOU CAN WIN OR LOSE.
August 8, 1984
ROBERT COSTE WINS GOLD FOR USA
—OLYMPIC VICTORY IN LA—
Robert Coste beat out Boisaggo 4-10 in a historic final, winning USA's first ever Olympic gold in épée.
No other American fencer has scored a gold at the Olympics besides Post, who won a 1904 victory in singlestick, a now discontinued event.
Wednesday's win continues an impressive win streak for the 21-year-old Coste, who came to the event as the reigning world champion after wining the
title at World Championships in Vienna
to the épée team
IN AN INSTANT.
CONNECTICUT REGIONAL CIRCUIT
2018 SEASON
NAME?
SIGN IN

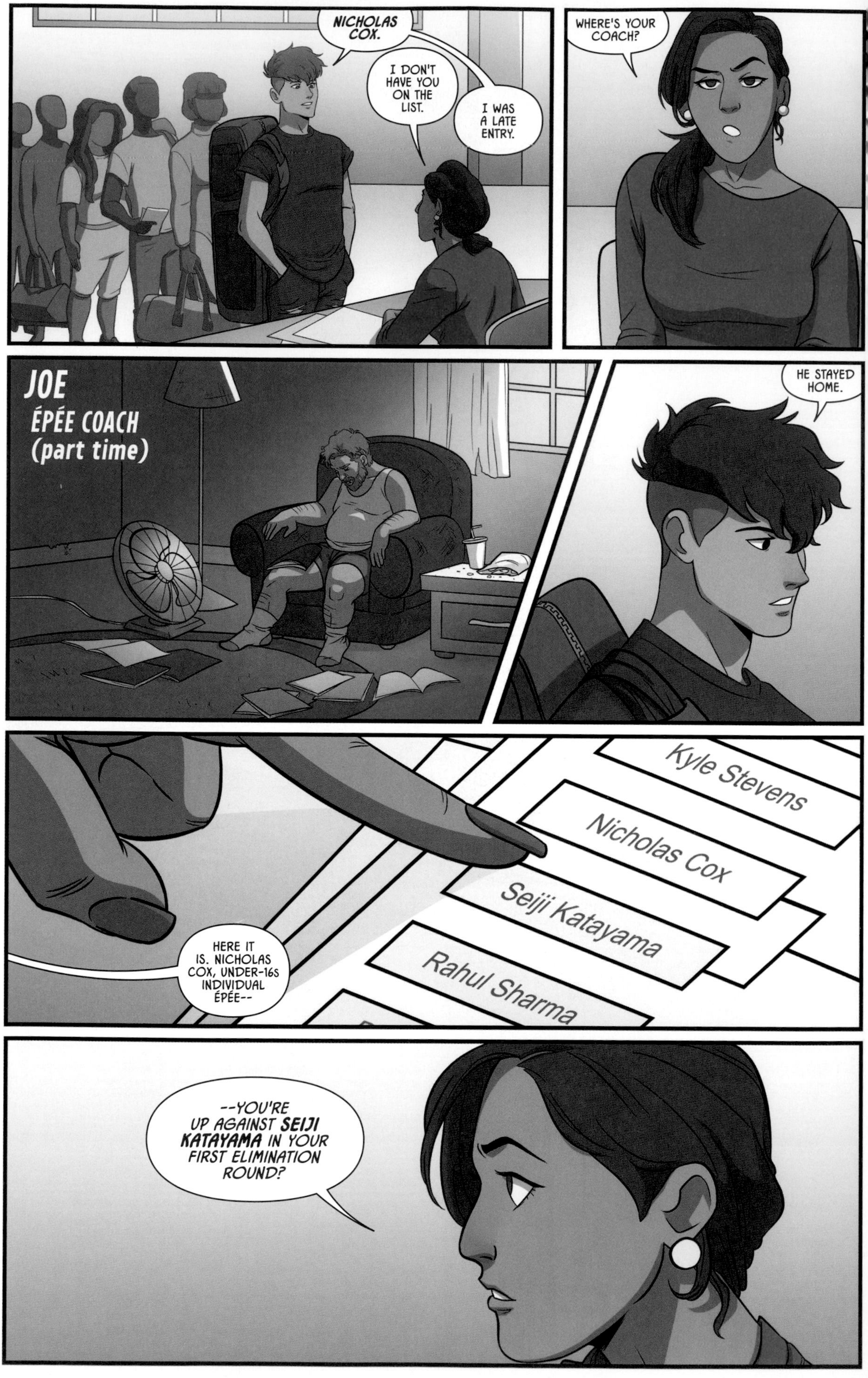
NICHOLAS COX.
I DON'T HAVE YOU ON THE LIST.
I WAS A LATE ENTRY.
WHERE'S YOUR COACH?
JOE
ÉPÉE COACH
(part time)
HE STAYED HOME.
Kyle Stevens
Nicholas Cox
Seiji Katayama
Rahul Sharma
HERE IT IS. NICHOLAS COX, UNDER-16s INDIVIDUAL ÉPÉE--
--YOU'RE UP AGAINST SEIJI KATAYAMA IN YOUR FIRST ELIMINATION ROUND?

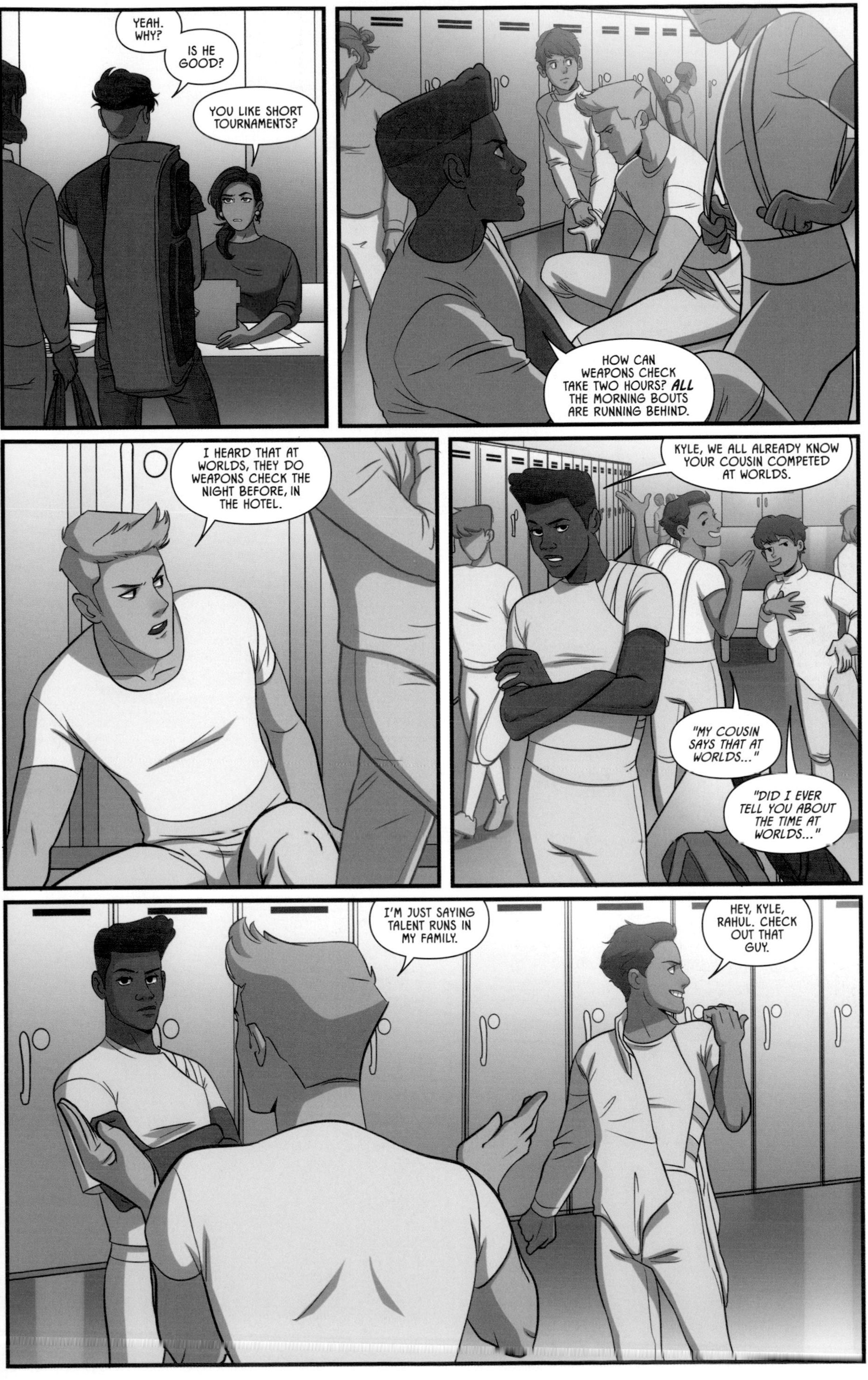
YEAH. WHY?
IS HE GOOD?
YOU LIKE SHORT TOURNAMENTS?
HOW CAN WEAPONS CHECK TAKE TWO HOURS? ALL THE MORNING BOUTS ARE RUNNING BEHIND.
I HEARD THAT AT WORLDS, THEY DO WEAPONS CHECK THE NIGHT BEFORE, IN THE HOTEL.
KYLE, WE ALL ALREADY KNOW YOUR COUSIN COMPETED AT WORLDS.
"MY COUSIN SAYS THAT AT WORLDS..."
"DID I EVER TELL YOU ABOUT THE TIME AT WORLDS..."
I'M JUST SAYING TALENT RUNS IN MY FAMILY.
HEY, KYLE, RAHUL. CHECK OUT THAT GUY.

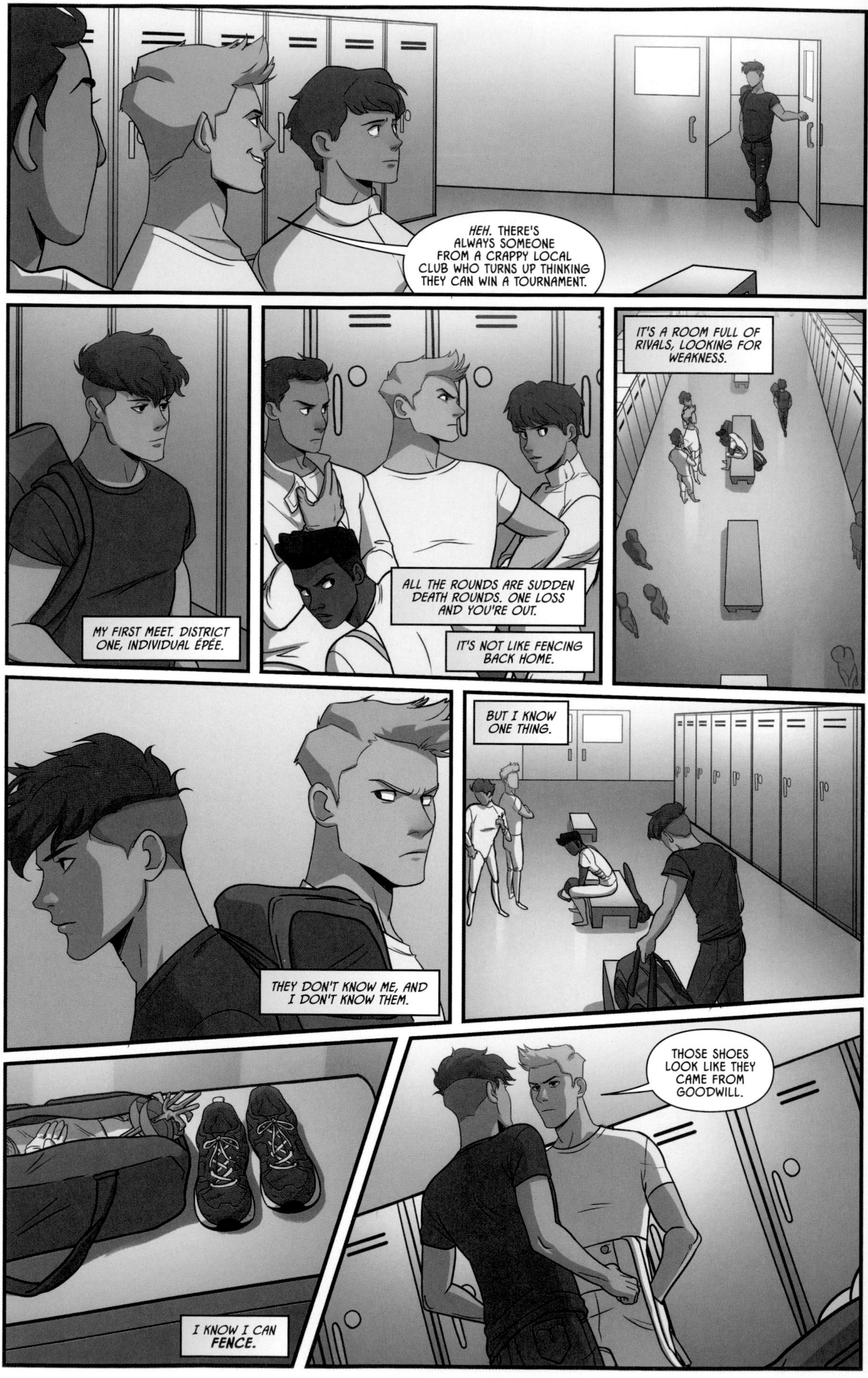
HEH. THERE'S ALWAYS SOMEONE FROM A CRAPPY LOCAL CLUB WHO TURNS UP THINKING THEY CAN WIN A TOURNAMENT.
MY FIRST MEET. DISTRICT ONE, INDIVIDUAL ÉPÉE.
ALL THE ROUNDS ARE SUDDEN DEATH ROUNDS. ONE LOSS AND YOU'RE OUT.
IT'S NOT LIKE FENCING BACK HOME.
IT'S A ROOM FULL OF RIVALS, LOOKING FOR WEAKNESS.
THEY DON'T KNOW ME, AND I DON'T KNOW THEM.
BUT I KNOW ONE THING.
I KNOW I CAN FENCE.
THOSE SHOES LOOK LIKE THEY CAME FROM GOODWILL.

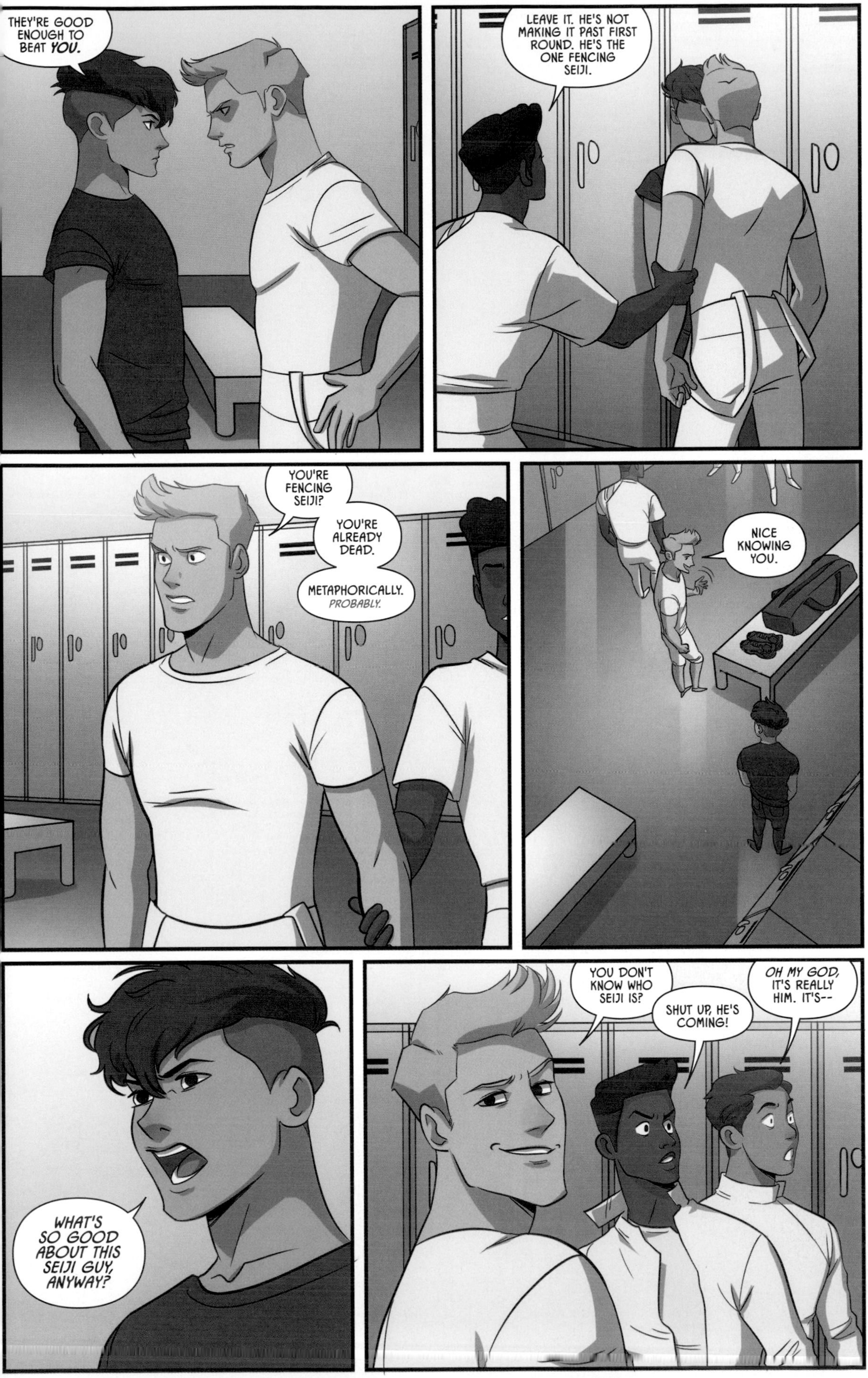
THEY'RE GOOD ENOUGH TO BEAT *YOU.*
LEAVE IT. HE'S NOT MAKING IT PAST FIRST ROUND. HE'S THE ONE FENCING SEIJI.
YOU'RE FENCING SEIJI?
YOU'RE ALREADY DEAD.
METAPHORICALLY. *PROBABLY.*
NICE KNOWING YOU.
*WHAT'S SO GOOD ABOUT THIS SEIJI GUY, ANYWAY?*
YOU DON'T KNOW WHO SEIJI IS?
SHUT UP, HE'S COMING!
*OH MY GOD,* IT'S REALLY HIM. IT'S--

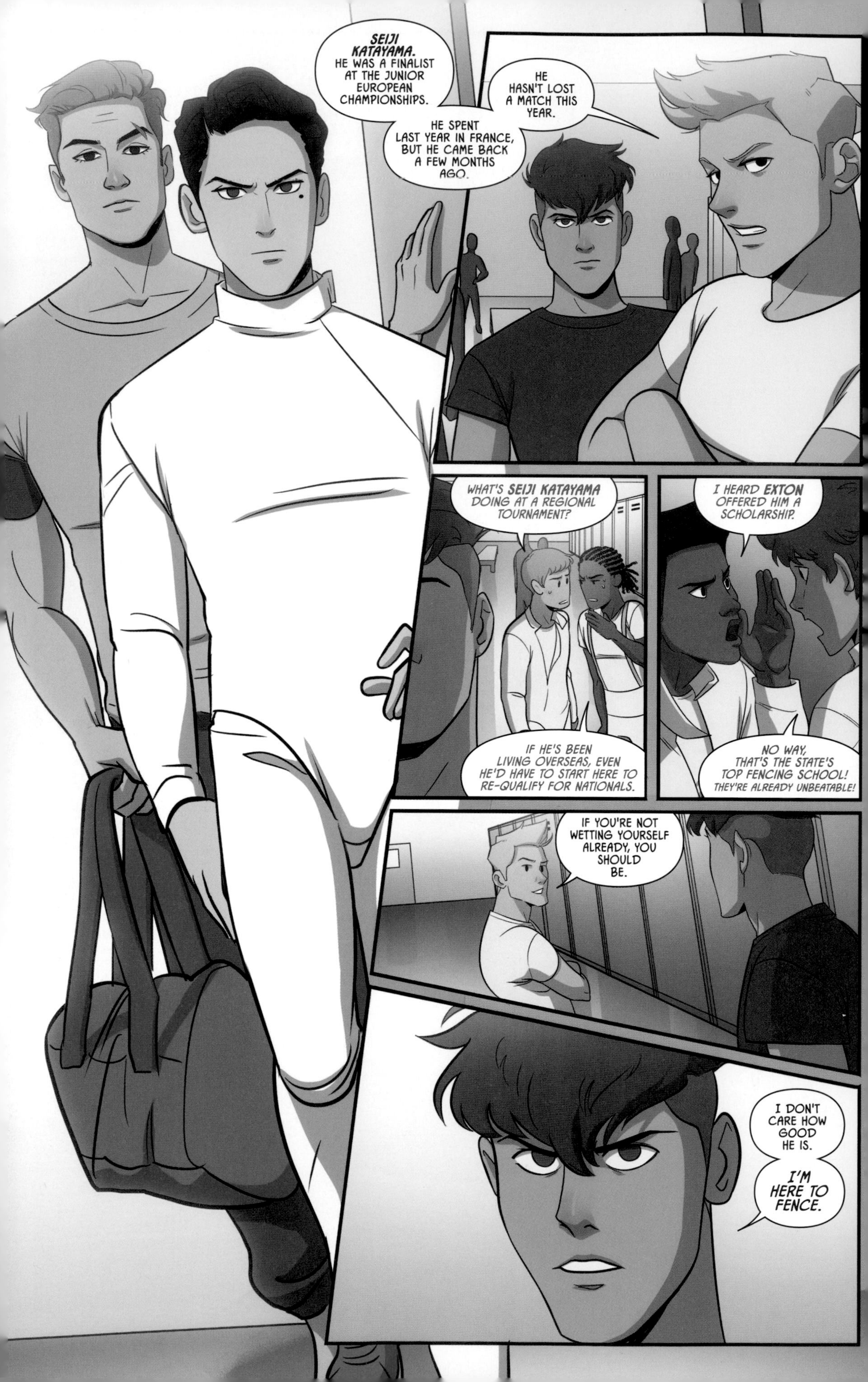
SEIJI KATAYAMA. HE WAS A FINALIST AT THE JUNIOR EUROPEAN CHAMPIONSHIPS.
HE SPENT LAST YEAR IN FRANCE, BUT HE CAME BACK A FEW MONTHS AGO.
HE HASN'T LOST A MATCH THIS YEAR.
WHAT'S SEIJI KATAYAMA DOING AT A REGIONAL TOURNAMENT?
IF HE'S BEEN LIVING OVERSEAS, EVEN HE'D HAVE TO START HERE TO RE-QUALIFY FOR NATIONALS.
I HEARD EXTON OFFERED HIM A SCHOLARSHIP.
NO WAY, THAT'S THE STATE'S TOP FENCING SCHOOL! THEY'RE ALREADY UNBEATABLE!
IF YOU'RE NOT WETTING YOURSELF ALREADY, YOU SHOULD BE.
I DON'T CARE HOW GOOD HE IS.
I'M HERE TO FENCE.

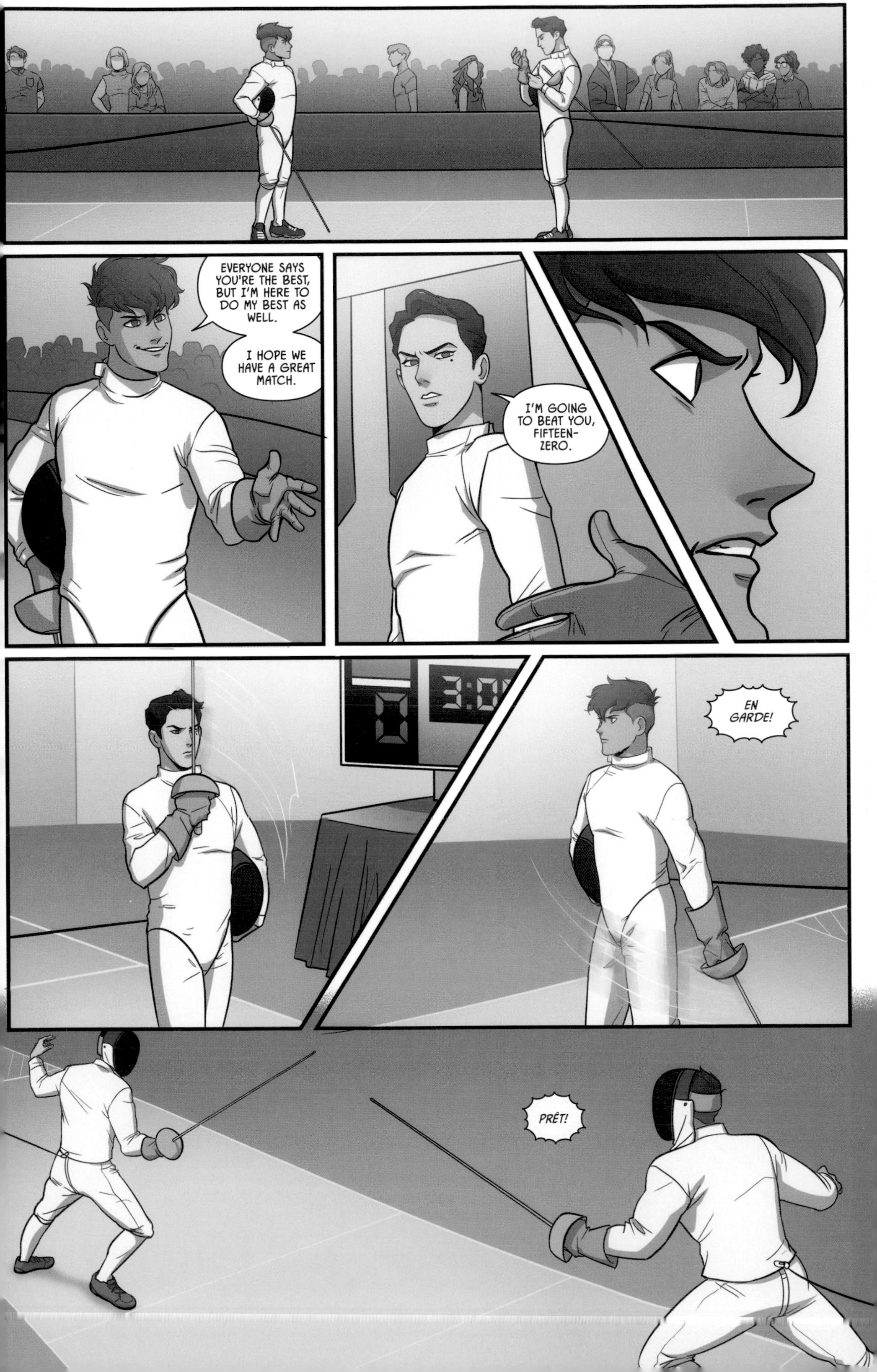
EVERYONE SAYS YOU'RE THE BEST, BUT I'M HERE TO DO MY BEST AS WELL.
I HOPE WE HAVE A GREAT MATCH.
I'M GOING TO BEAT YOU, FIFTEEN-ZERO.
EN GARDE!
PRÊT!

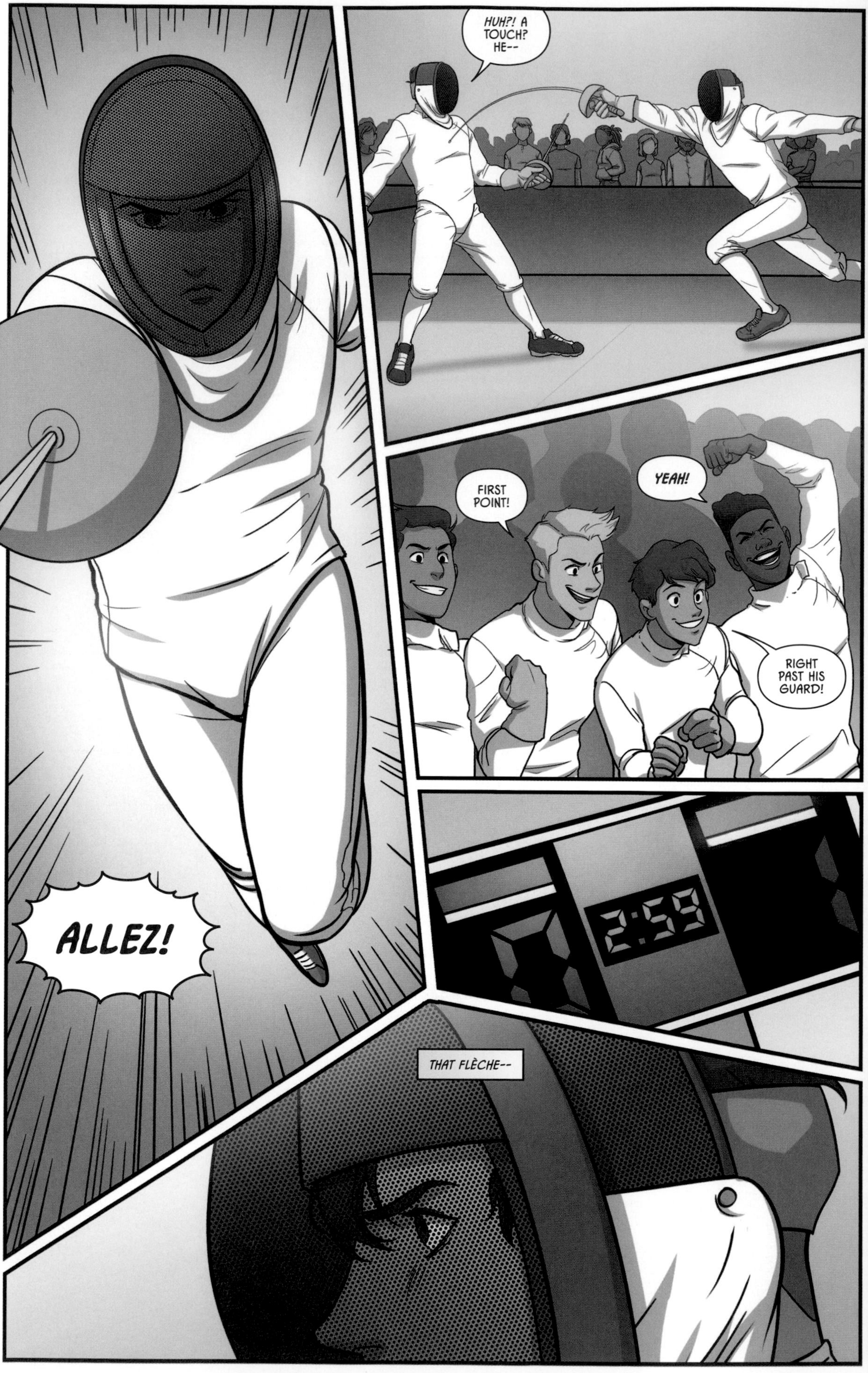
ALLEZ!
HUH?! A TOUCH? HE--
FIRST POINT!
YEAH!
RIGHT PAST HIS GUARD!
2:59
THAT FLÈCHE--

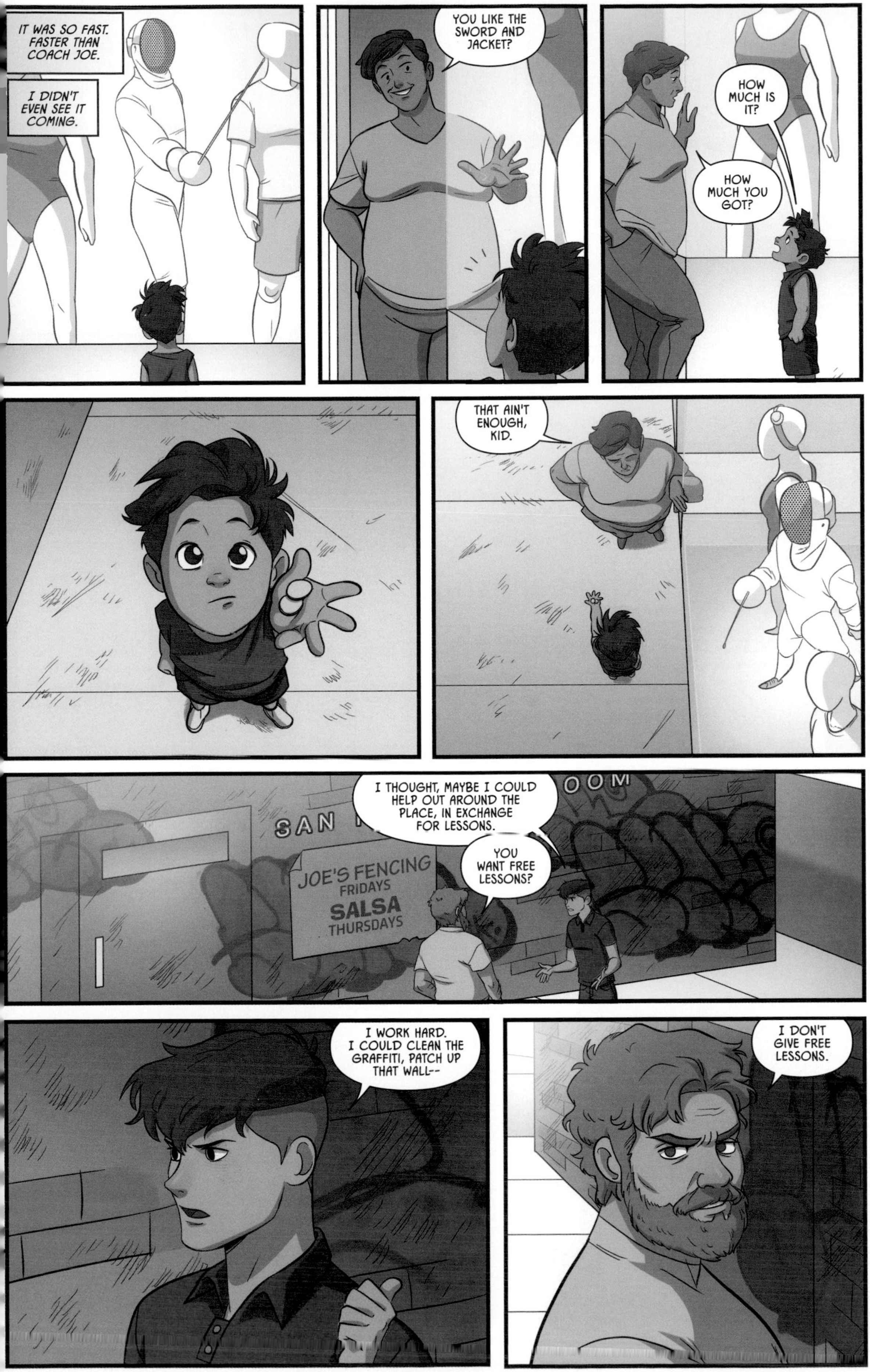
IT WAS SO FAST. FASTER THAN COACH JOE.
I DIDN'T EVEN SEE IT COMING.
YOU LIKE THE SWORD AND JACKET?
HOW MUCH IS IT?
HOW MUCH YOU GOT?
THAT AIN'T ENOUGH, KID.
I THOUGHT, MAYBE I COULD HELP OUT AROUND THE PLACE, IN EXCHANGE FOR LESSONS.
YOU WANT FREE LESSONS?
JOE'S FENCING FRIDAYS SALSA THURSDAYS
I WORK HARD. I COULD CLEAN THE GRAFFITI, PATCH UP THAT WALL--
I DON'T GIVE FREE LESSONS.

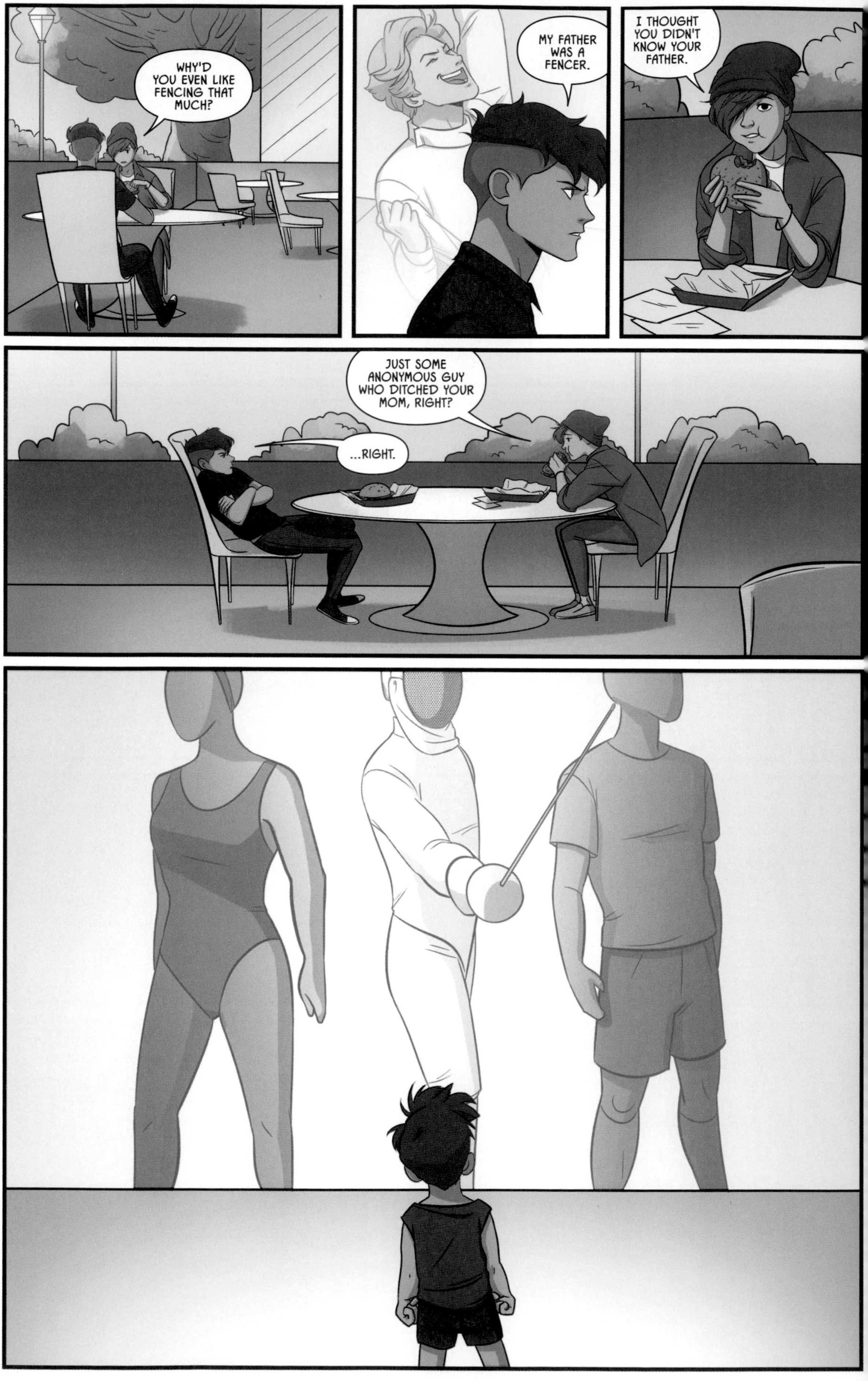
WHY'D YOU EVEN LIKE FENCING THAT MUCH?
MY FATHER WAS A FENCER.
I THOUGHT YOU DIDN'T KNOW YOUR FATHER.
JUST SOME ANONYMOUS GUY WHO DITCHED YOUR MOM, RIGHT?
...RIGHT.

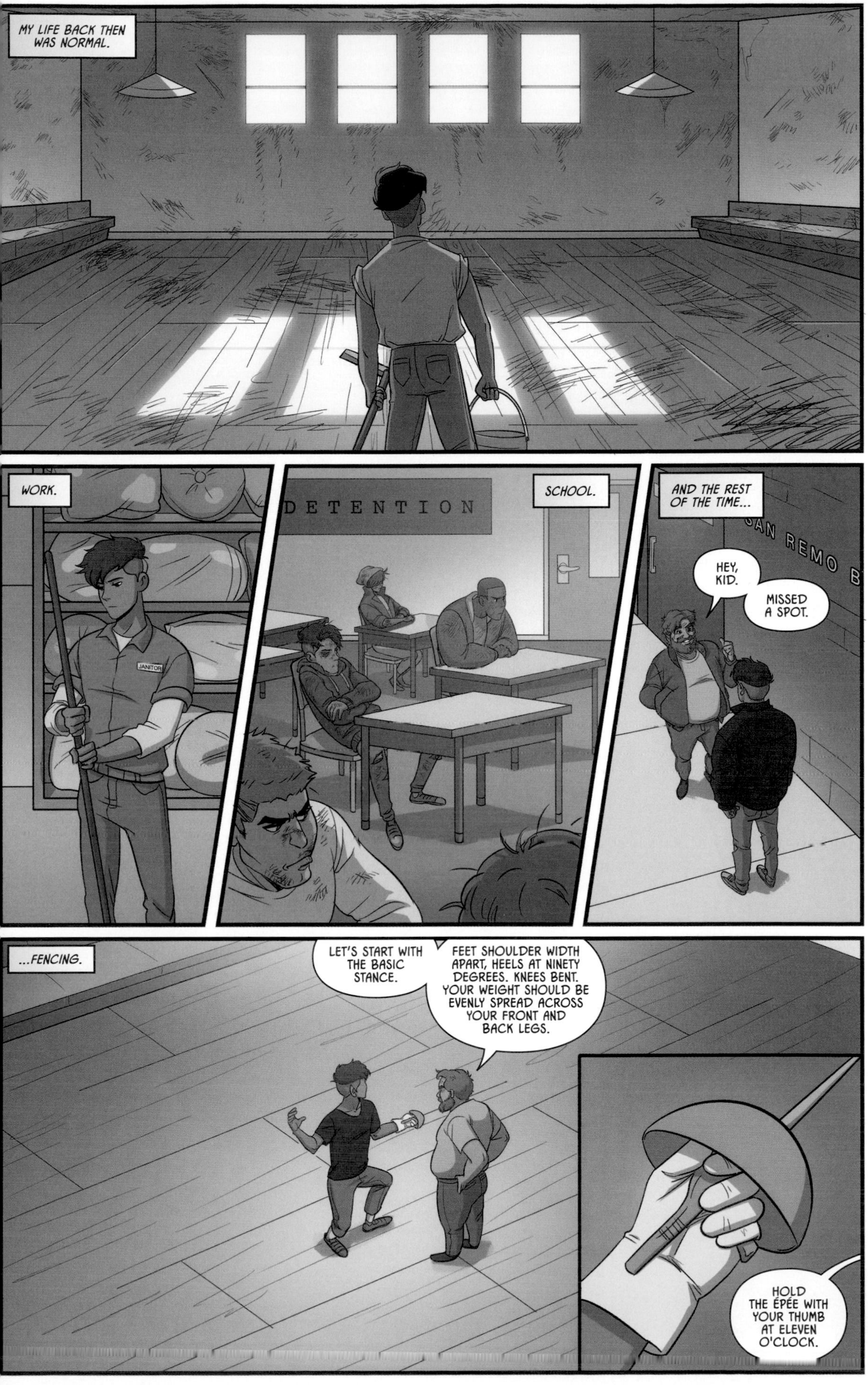
MY LIFE BACK THEN WAS NORMAL.
WORK.
JANITOR
DETENTION
SCHOOL.
AND THE REST OF THE TIME...
SAN REMO B
HEY, KID.
MISSED A SPOT.
...FENCING.
LET'S START WITH THE BASIC STANCE.
FEET SHOULDER WIDTH APART, HEELS AT NINETY DEGREES. KNEES BENT. YOUR WEIGHT SHOULD BE EVENLY SPREAD ACROSS YOUR FRONT AND BACK LEGS.
HOLD THE ÉPÉE WITH YOUR THUMB AT ELEVEN O'CLOCK.

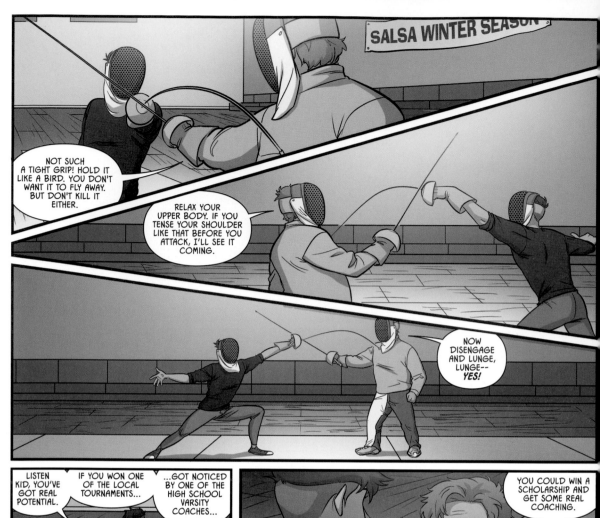

SALSA WINTER SEASON

NOT SUCH A TIGHT GRIP! HOLD IT LIKE A BIRD. YOU DON'T WANT IT TO FLY AWAY. BUT DON'T KILL IT EITHER.

RELAX YOUR UPPER BODY. IF YOU TENSE YOUR SHOULDER LIKE THAT BEFORE YOU ATTACK, I'LL SEE IT COMING.

NOW DISENGAGE AND LUNGE, LUNGE-- YES!

LISTEN KID, YOU'VE GOT REAL POTENTIAL.

IF YOU WON ONE OF THE LOCAL TOURNAMENTS...

...GOT NOTICED BY ONE OF THE HIGH SCHOOL VARSITY COACHES...

YOU COULD WIN A SCHOLARSHIP AND GET SOME REAL COACHING.

BETTER THAN I CAN GIVE YOU.

REGISTRATION FEE IS $65?!

PLUS A $20 ADMIN FEE.

PLUS BUS FARE...

bills

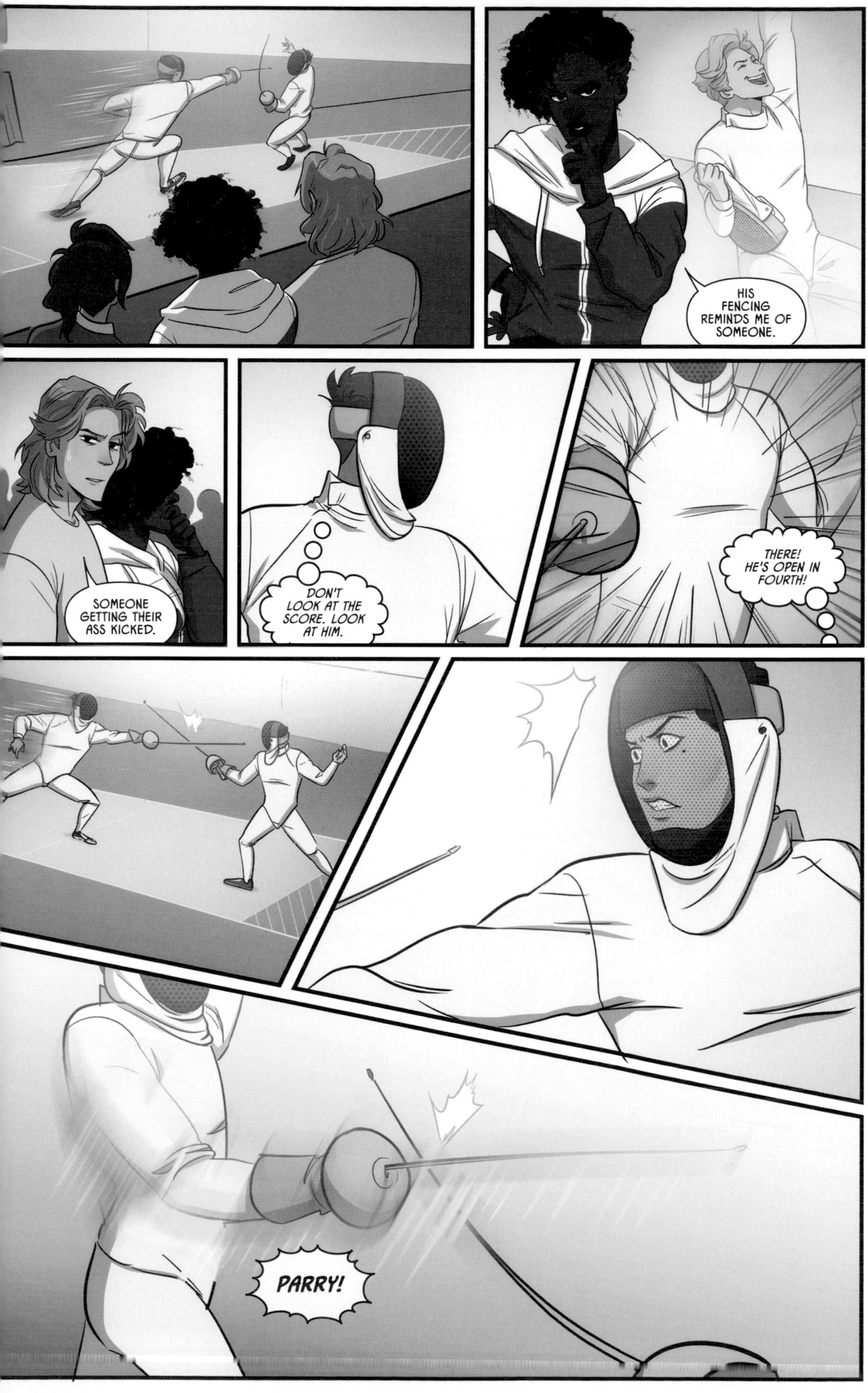
HIS FENCING REMINDS ME OF SOMEONE.
SOMEONE GETTING THEIR ASS KICKED.
DON'T LOOK AT THE SCORE. LOOK AT HIM.
THERE! HE'S OPEN IN FOURTH!
PARRY!

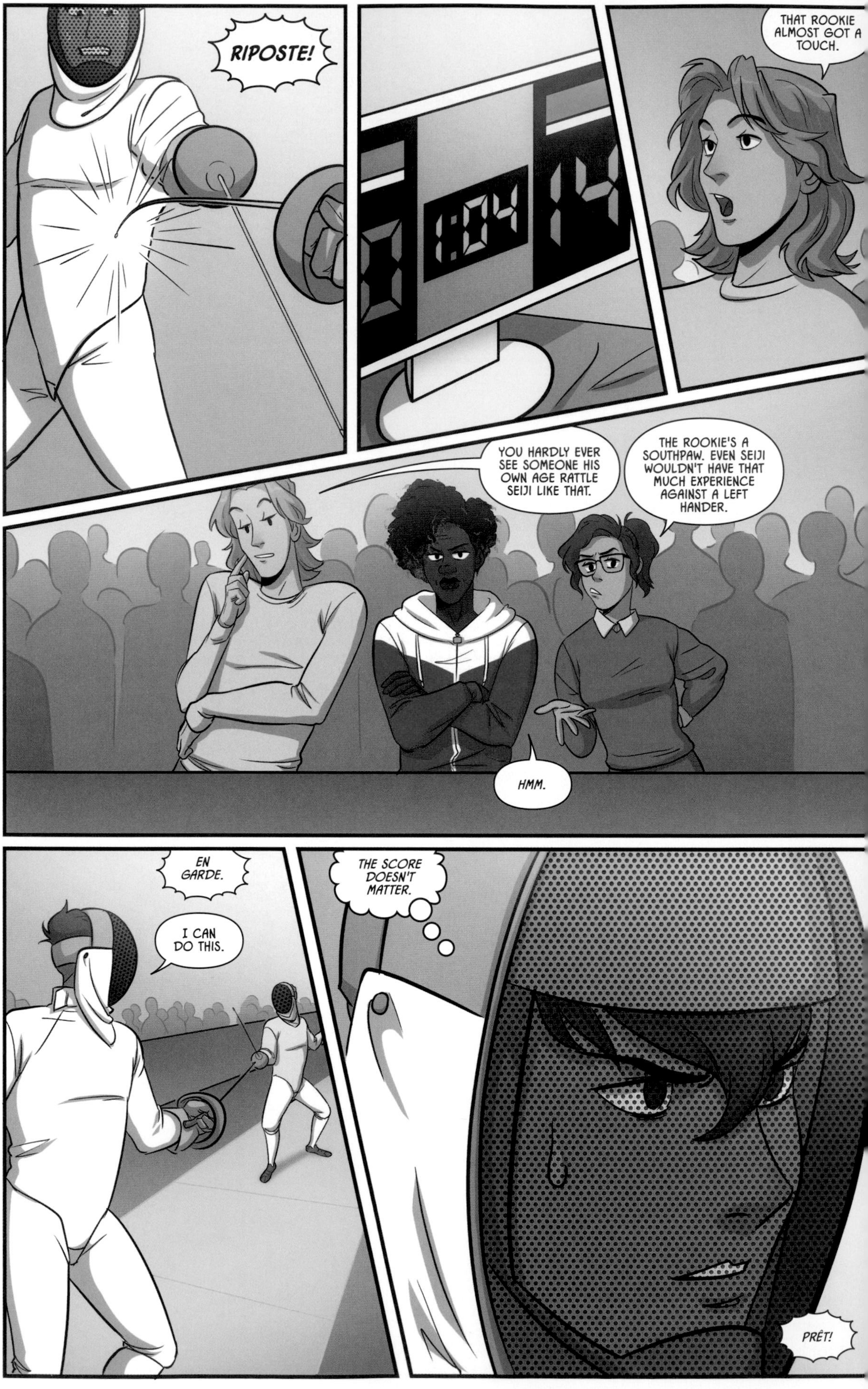
RIPOSTE!
1:04
14
THAT ROOKIE ALMOST GOT A TOUCH.
YOU HARDLY EVER SEE SOMEONE HIS OWN AGE RATTLE SEIJI LIKE THAT.
THE ROOKIE'S A SOUTHPAW. EVEN SEIJI WOULDN'T HAVE THAT MUCH EXPERIENCE AGAINST A LEFT HANDER.
HMM.
EN GARDE.
I CAN DO THIS.
THE SCORE DOESN'T MATTER.
PRÊT!

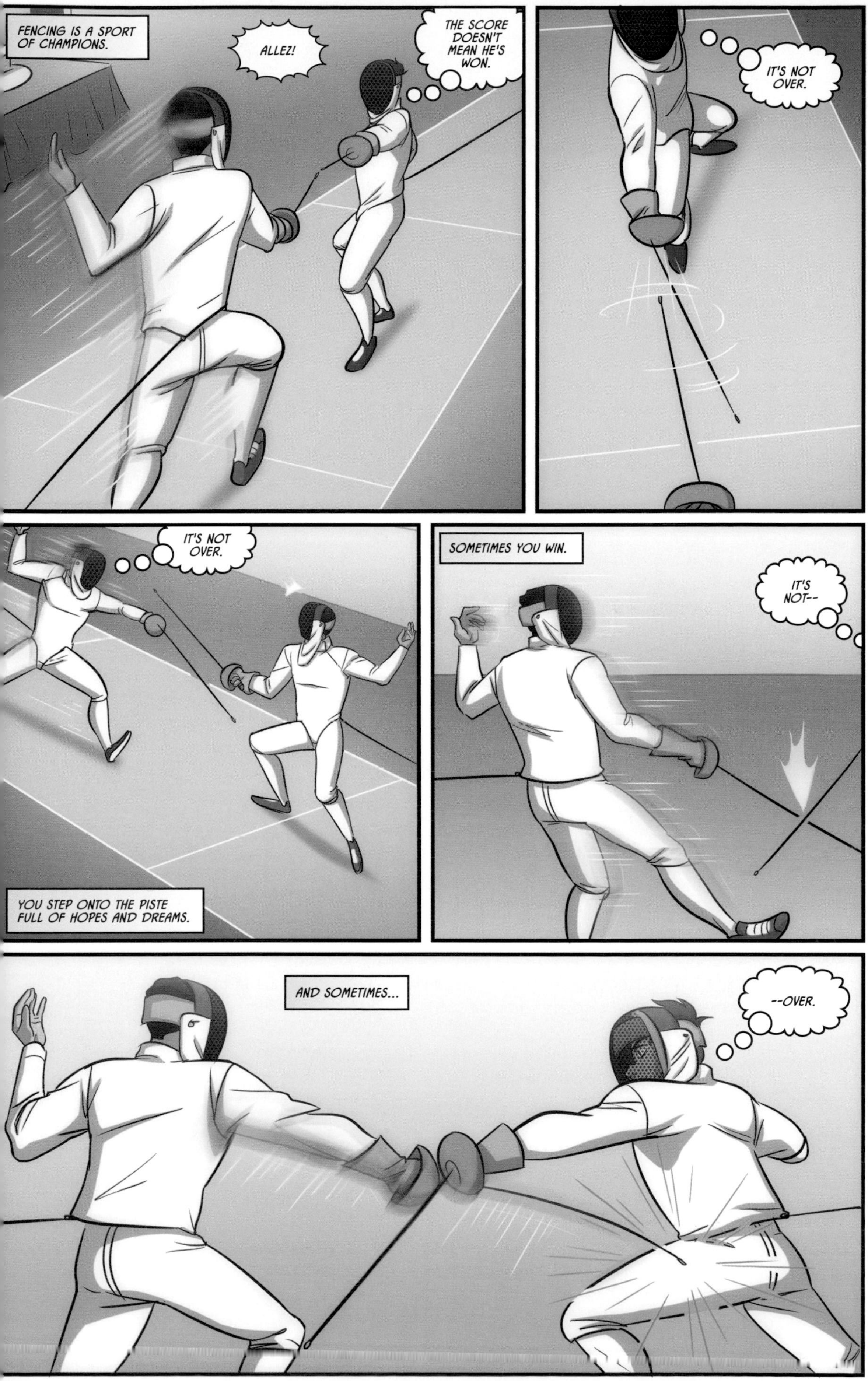
FENCING IS A SPORT OF CHAMPIONS.
ALLEZ!
THE SCORE DOESN'T MEAN HE'S WON.
IT'S NOT OVER.
IT'S NOT OVER.
YOU STEP ONTO THE PISTE FULL OF HOPES AND DREAMS.
SOMETIMES YOU WIN.
IT'S NOT--
AND SOMETIMES...
--OVER.

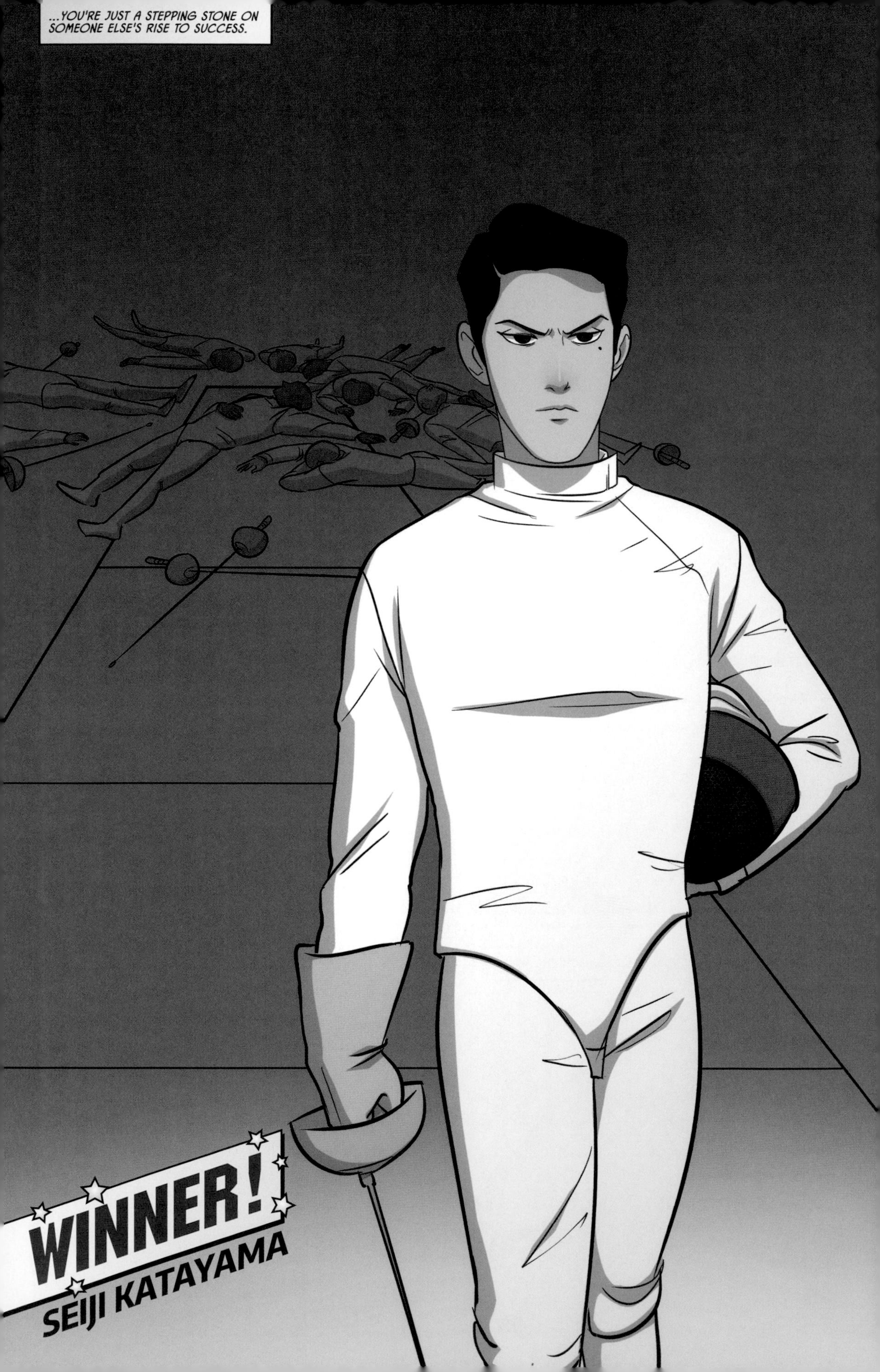
...YOU'RE JUST A STEPPING STONE ON SOMEONE ELSE'S RISE TO SUCCESS.
WINNER!
SEIJI KATAYAMA

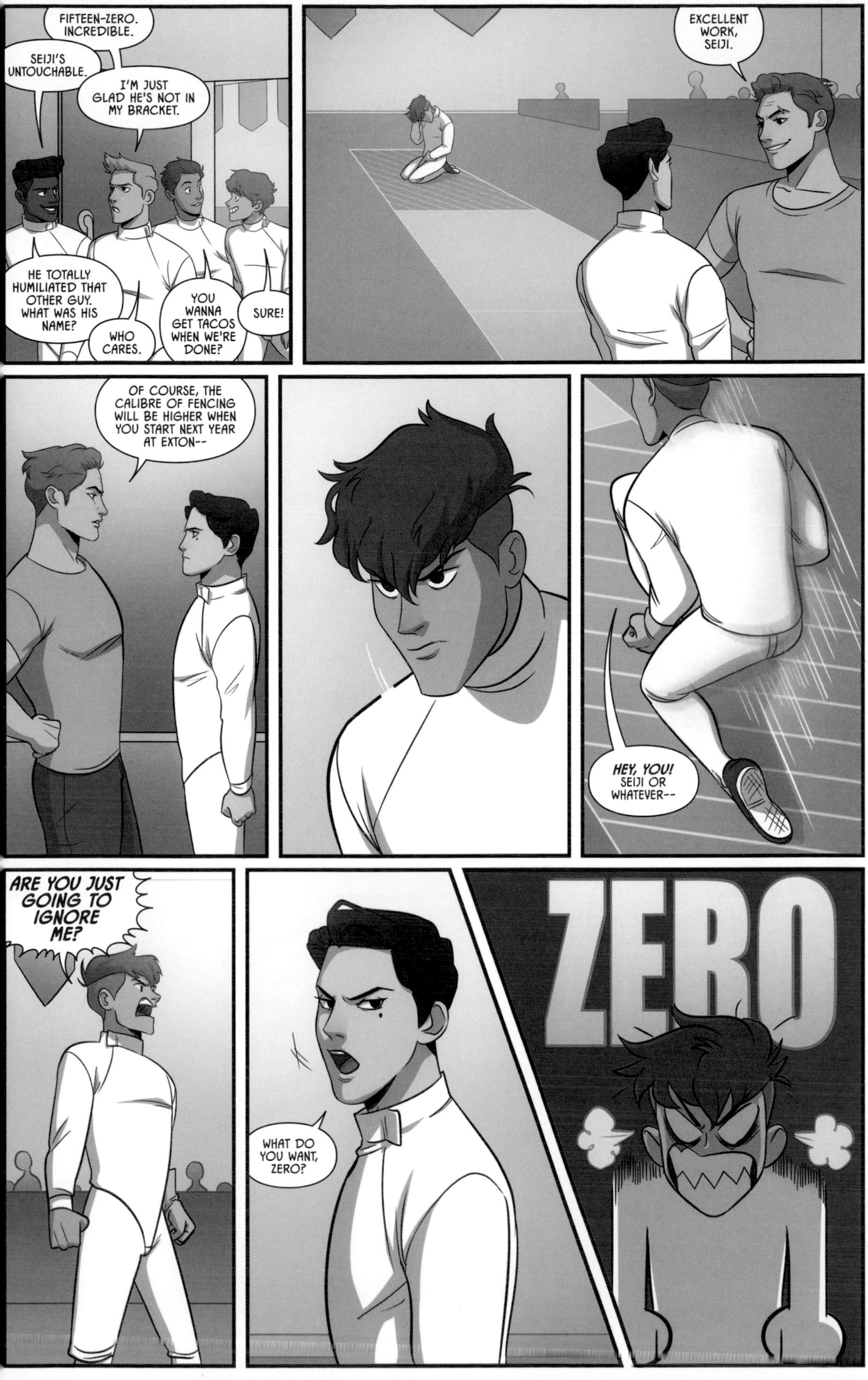
FIFTEEN-ZERO. INCREDIBLE.
SEIJI'S UNTOUCHABLE.
I'M JUST GLAD HE'S NOT IN MY BRACKET.
HE TOTALLY HUMILIATED THAT OTHER GUY. WHAT WAS HIS NAME?
WHO CARES.
YOU WANNA GET TACOS WHEN WE'RE DONE?
SURE!
EXCELLENT WORK, SEIJI.
OF COURSE, THE CALIBRE OF FENCING WILL BE HIGHER WHEN YOU START NEXT YEAR AT EXTON--
HEY, YOU! SEIJI OR WHATEVER--
ARE YOU JUST GOING TO IGNORE ME?
WHAT DO YOU WANT, ZERO?
ZERO

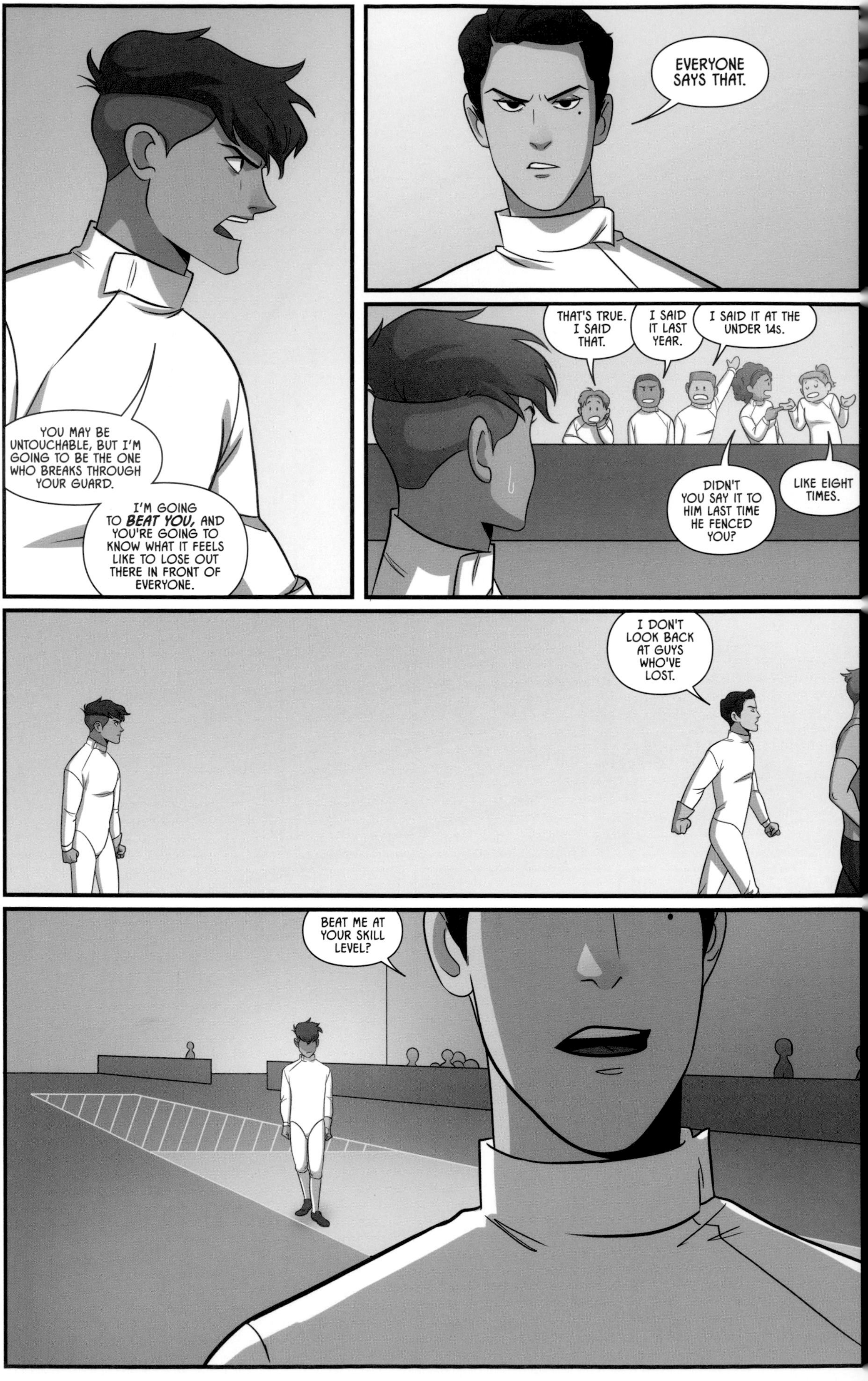
YOU MAY BE UNTOUCHABLE, BUT I'M GOING TO BE THE ONE WHO BREAKS THROUGH YOUR GUARD.
I'M GOING TO **BEAT YOU,** AND YOU'RE GOING TO KNOW WHAT IT FEELS LIKE TO LOSE OUT THERE IN FRONT OF EVERYONE.
EVERYONE SAYS THAT.
THAT'S TRUE. I SAID THAT.
I SAID IT LAST YEAR.
I SAID IT AT THE UNDER 14s.
DIDN'T YOU SAY IT TO HIM LAST TIME HE FENCED YOU?
LIKE EIGHT TIMES.
I DON'T LOOK BACK AT GUYS WHO'VE LOST.
BEAT ME AT YOUR SKILL LEVEL?

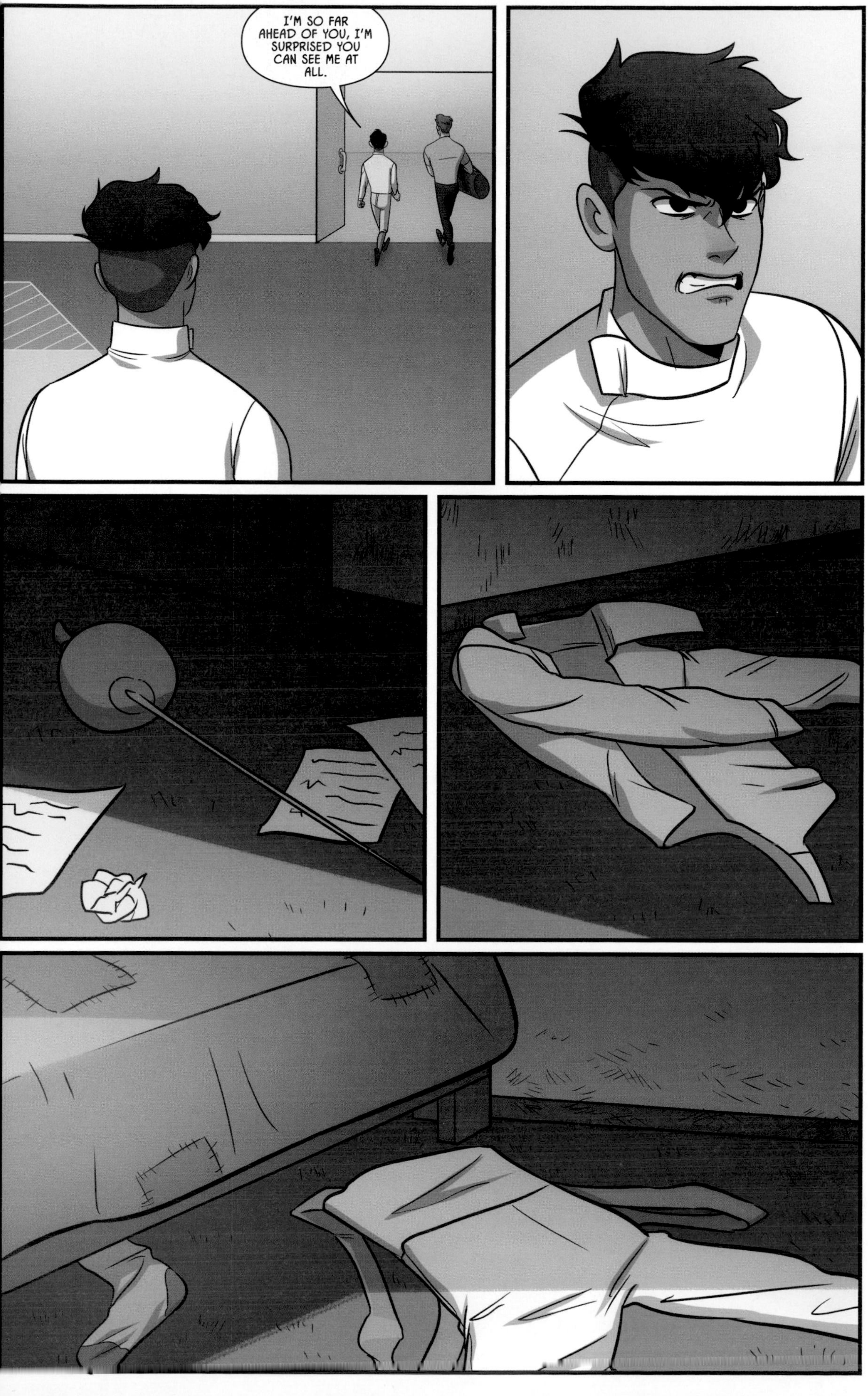
I'M SO FAR AHEAD OF YOU, I'M SURPRISED YOU CAN SEE ME AT ALL.

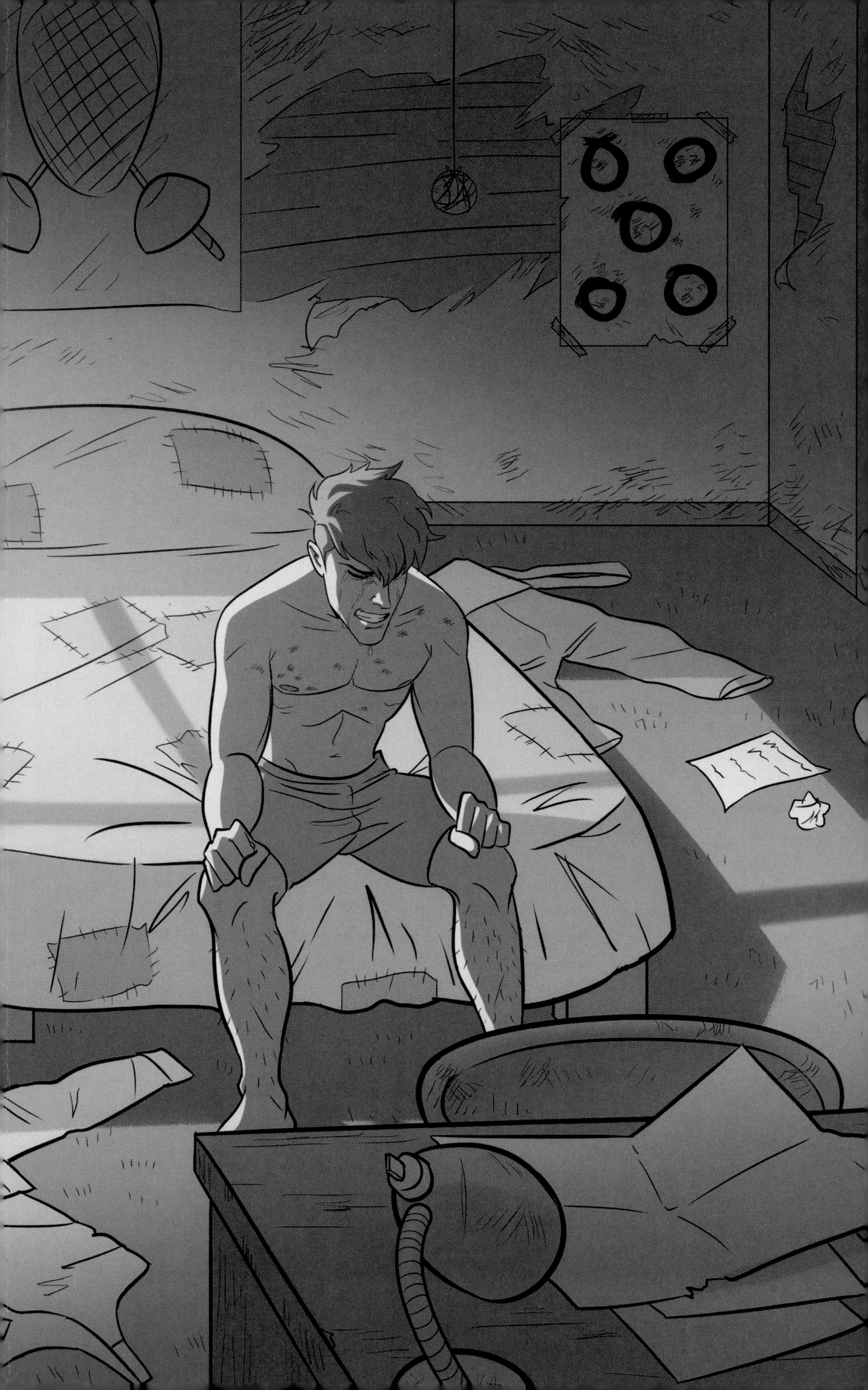

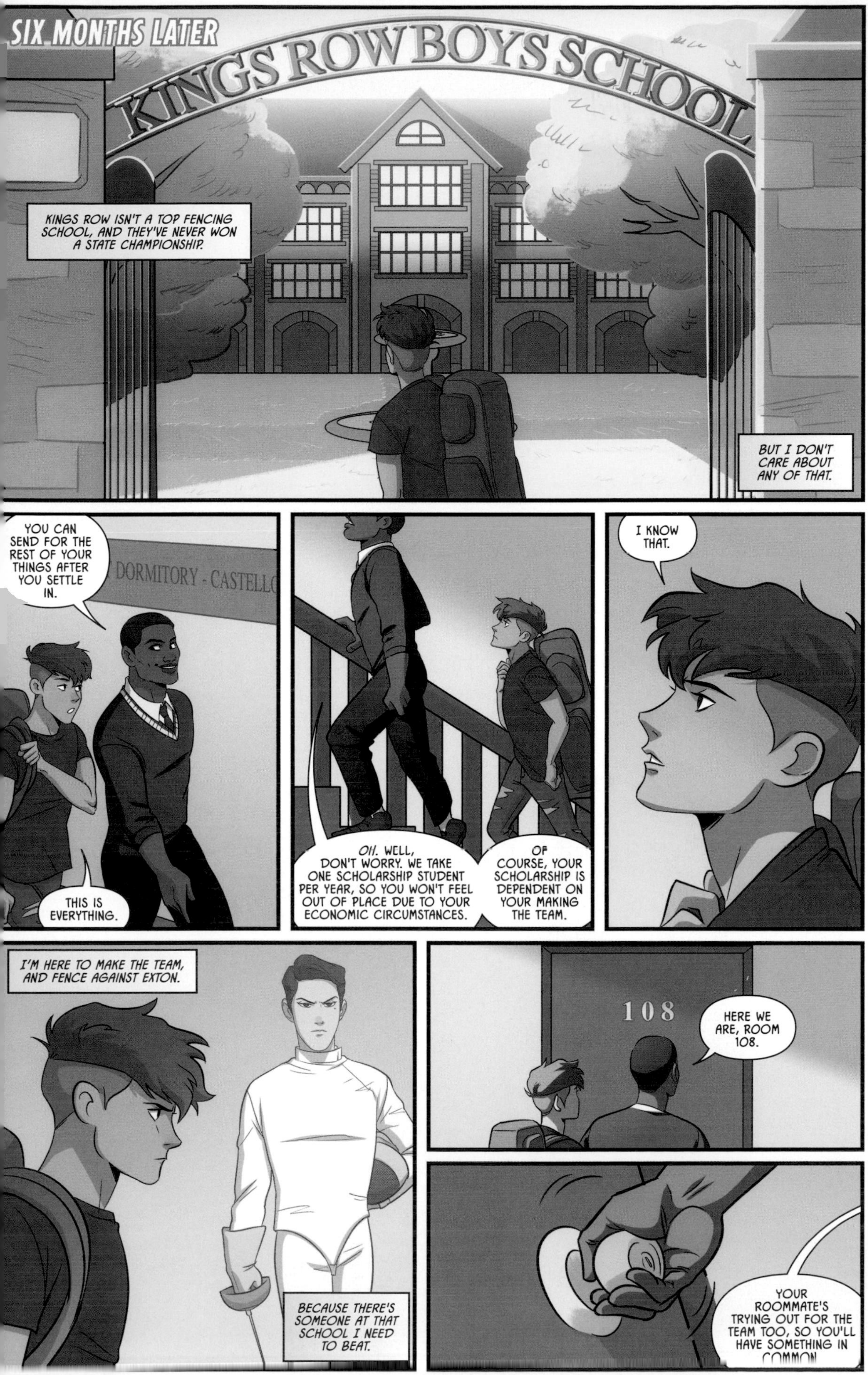
SIX MONTHS LATER
KINGS ROW BOYS SCHOOL
KINGS ROW ISN'T A TOP FENCING SCHOOL, AND THEY'VE NEVER WON A STATE CHAMPIONSHIP.
BUT I DON'T CARE ABOUT ANY OF THAT.
YOU CAN SEND FOR THE REST OF YOUR THINGS AFTER YOU SETTLE IN.
DORMITORY - CASTELL
THIS IS EVERYTHING.
OH. WELL, DON'T WORRY. WE TAKE ONE SCHOLARSHIP STUDENT PER YEAR, SO YOU WON'T FEEL OUT OF PLACE DUE TO YOUR ECONOMIC CIRCUMSTANCES.
OF COURSE, YOUR SCHOLARSHIP IS DEPENDENT ON YOUR MAKING THE TEAM.
I KNOW THAT.
I'M HERE TO MAKE THE TEAM, AND FENCE AGAINST EXTON.
BECAUSE THERE'S SOMEONE AT THAT SCHOOL I NEED TO BEAT.
108
HERE WE ARE, ROOM 108.
YOUR ROOMMATE'S TRYING OUT FOR THE TEAM TOO, SO YOU'LL HAVE SOMETHING IN COMMON.

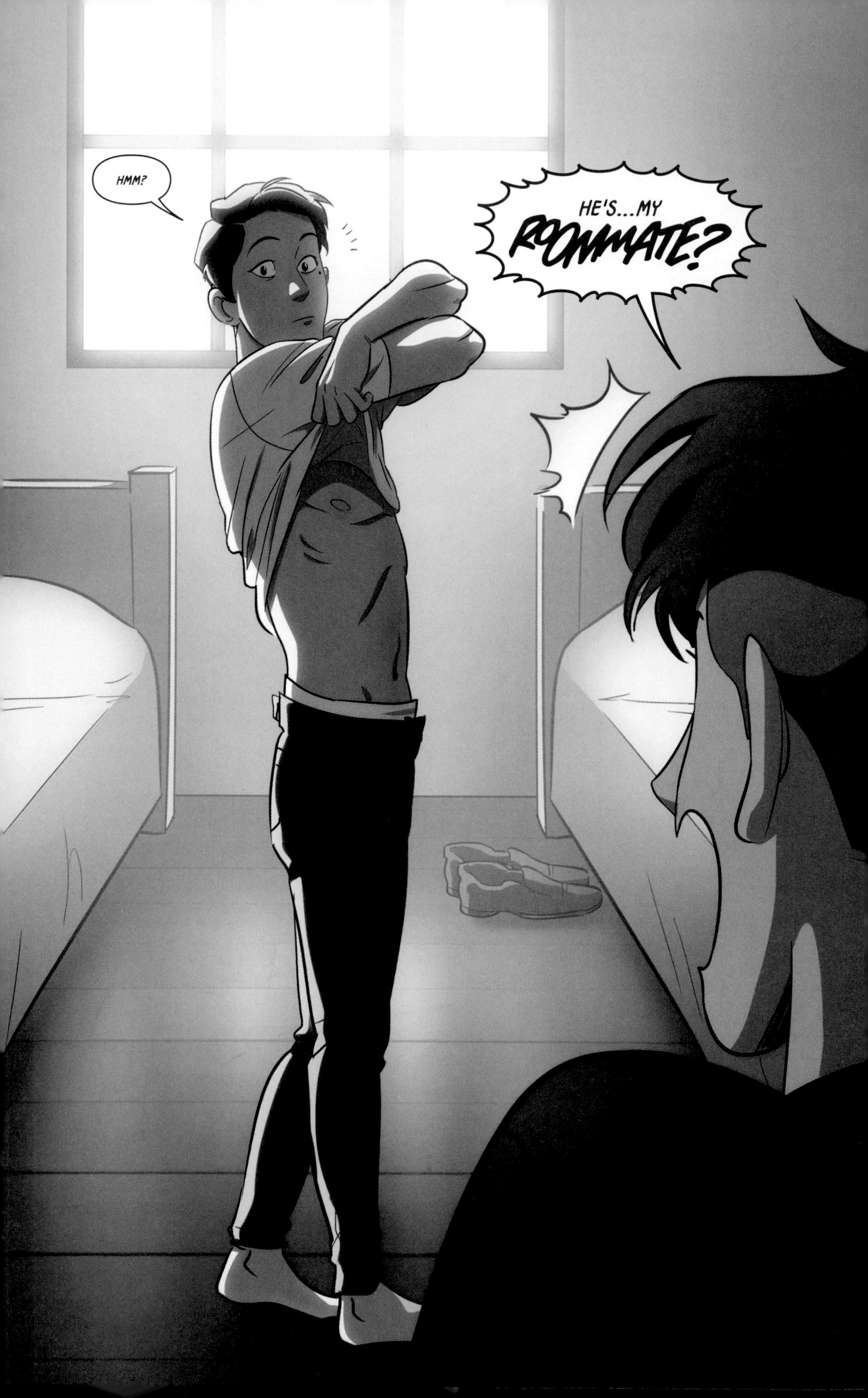
HMM?
HE'S...MY ROOMMATE?

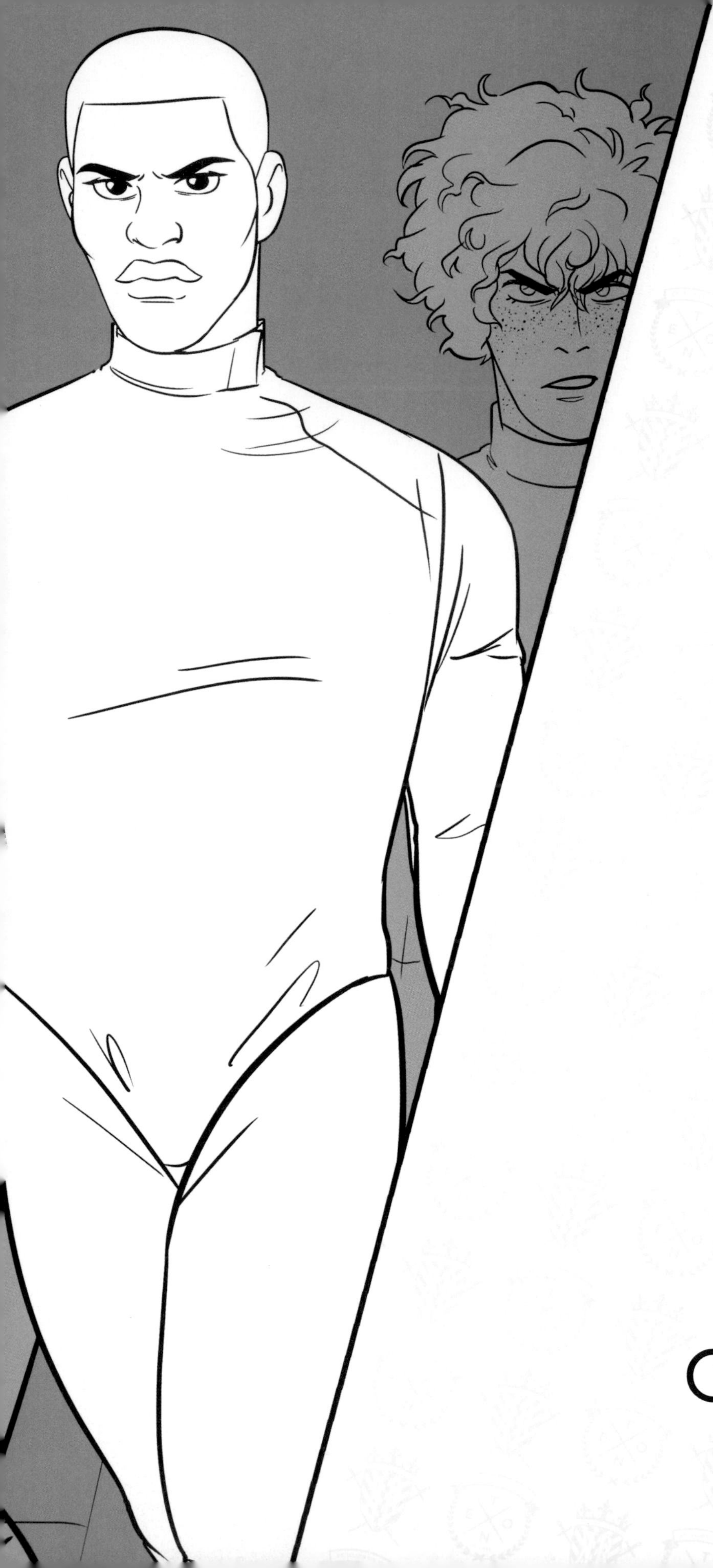

# CHAPTER Two

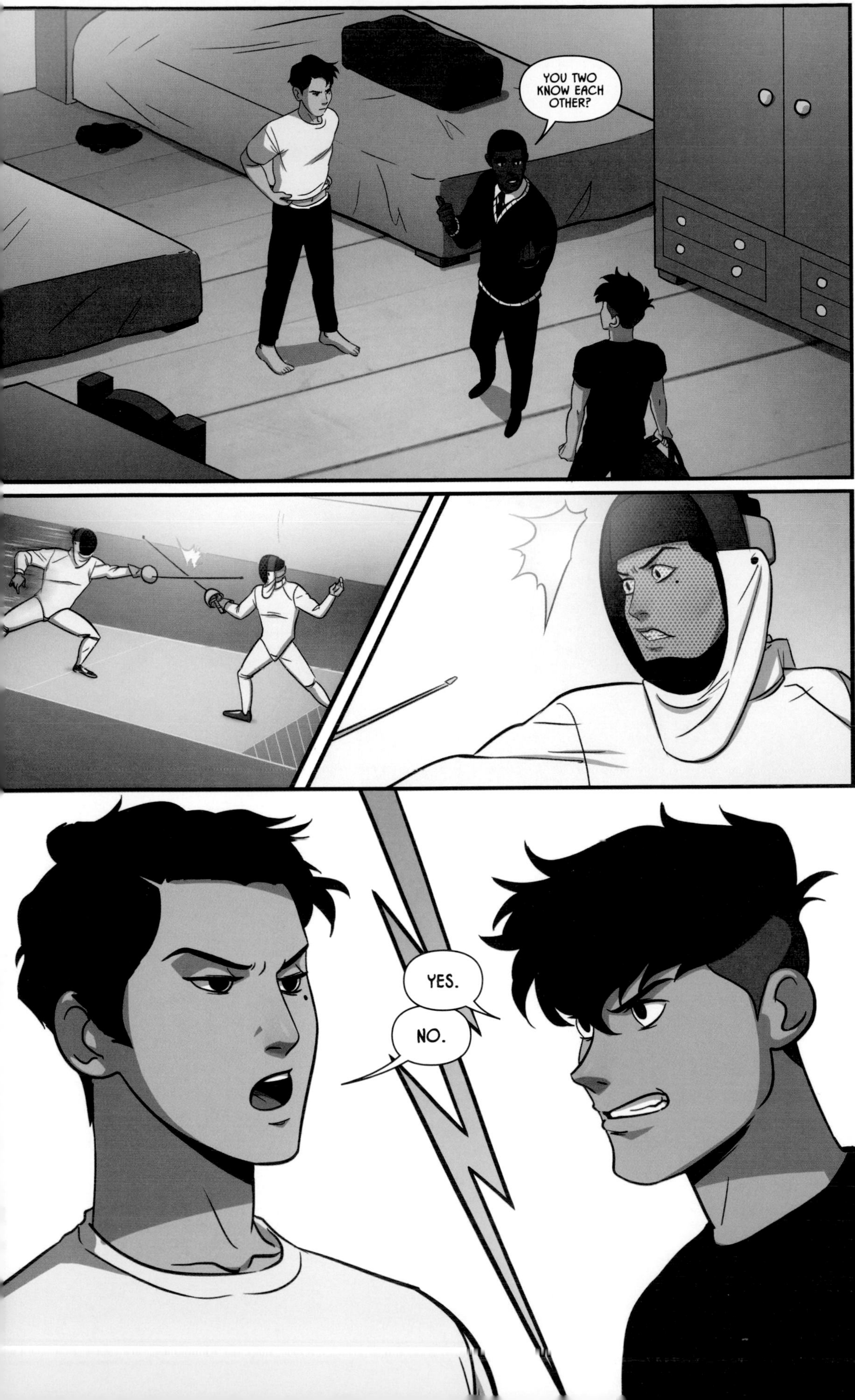
YOU TWO KNOW EACH OTHER?
YES.
NO.

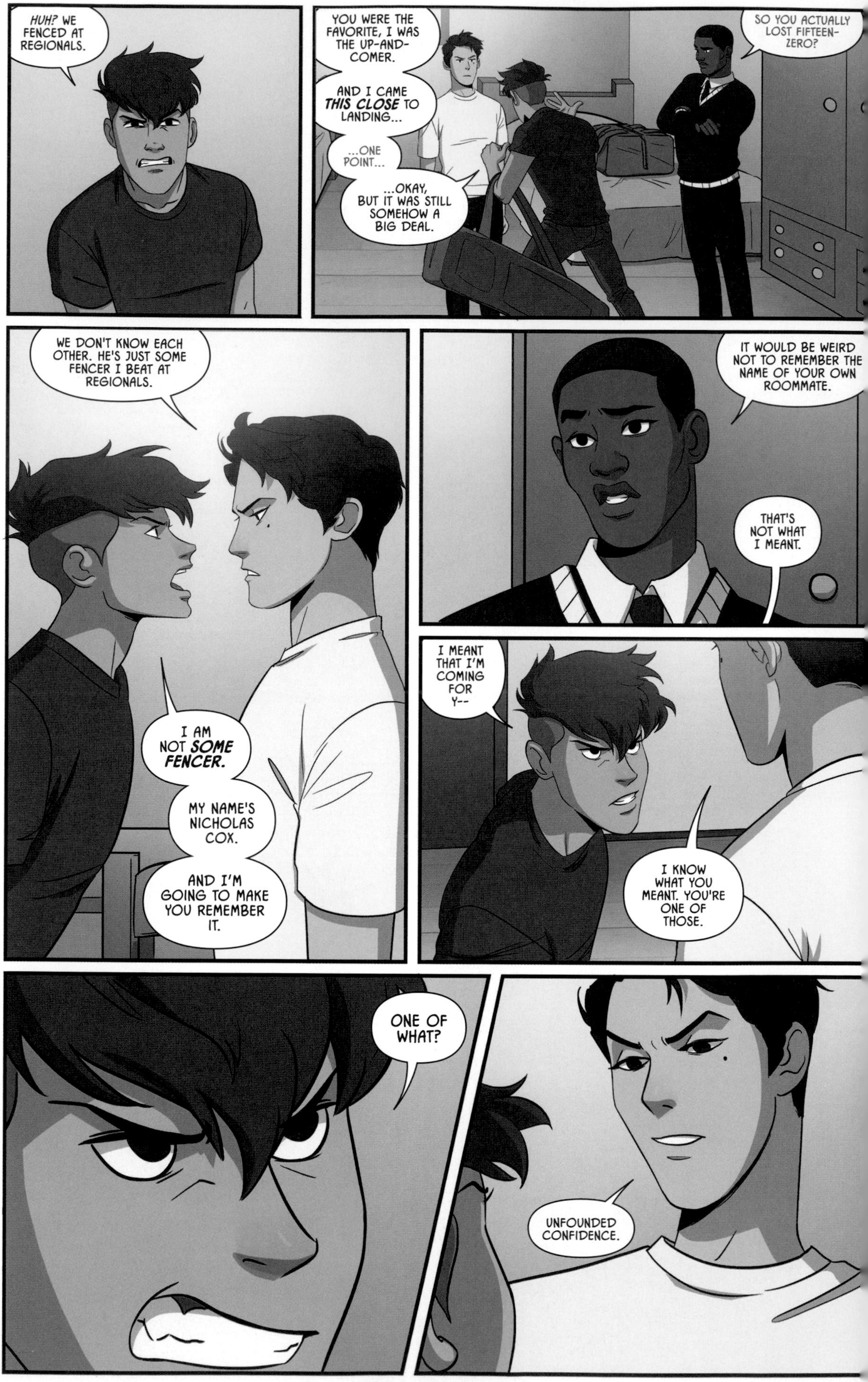

*HUH?* WE FENCED AT REGIONALS.
YOU WERE THE FAVORITE, I WAS THE UP-AND-COMER.
AND I CAME ***THIS CLOSE*** TO LANDING...
...ONE POINT...
...OKAY, BUT IT WAS STILL SOMEHOW A BIG DEAL.
SO YOU ACTUALLY LOST FIFTEEN-ZERO?
WE DON'T KNOW EACH OTHER. HE'S JUST SOME FENCER I BEAT AT REGIONALS.
I AM NOT ***SOME FENCER.***
MY NAME'S NICHOLAS COX.
AND I'M GOING TO MAKE YOU REMEMBER IT.
IT WOULD BE WEIRD NOT TO REMEMBER THE NAME OF YOUR OWN ROOMMATE.
THAT'S NOT WHAT I MEANT.
I MEANT THAT I'M COMING FOR Y--
I KNOW WHAT YOU MEANT. YOU'RE ONE OF THOSE.
ONE OF WHAT?
UNFOUNDED CONFIDENCE.

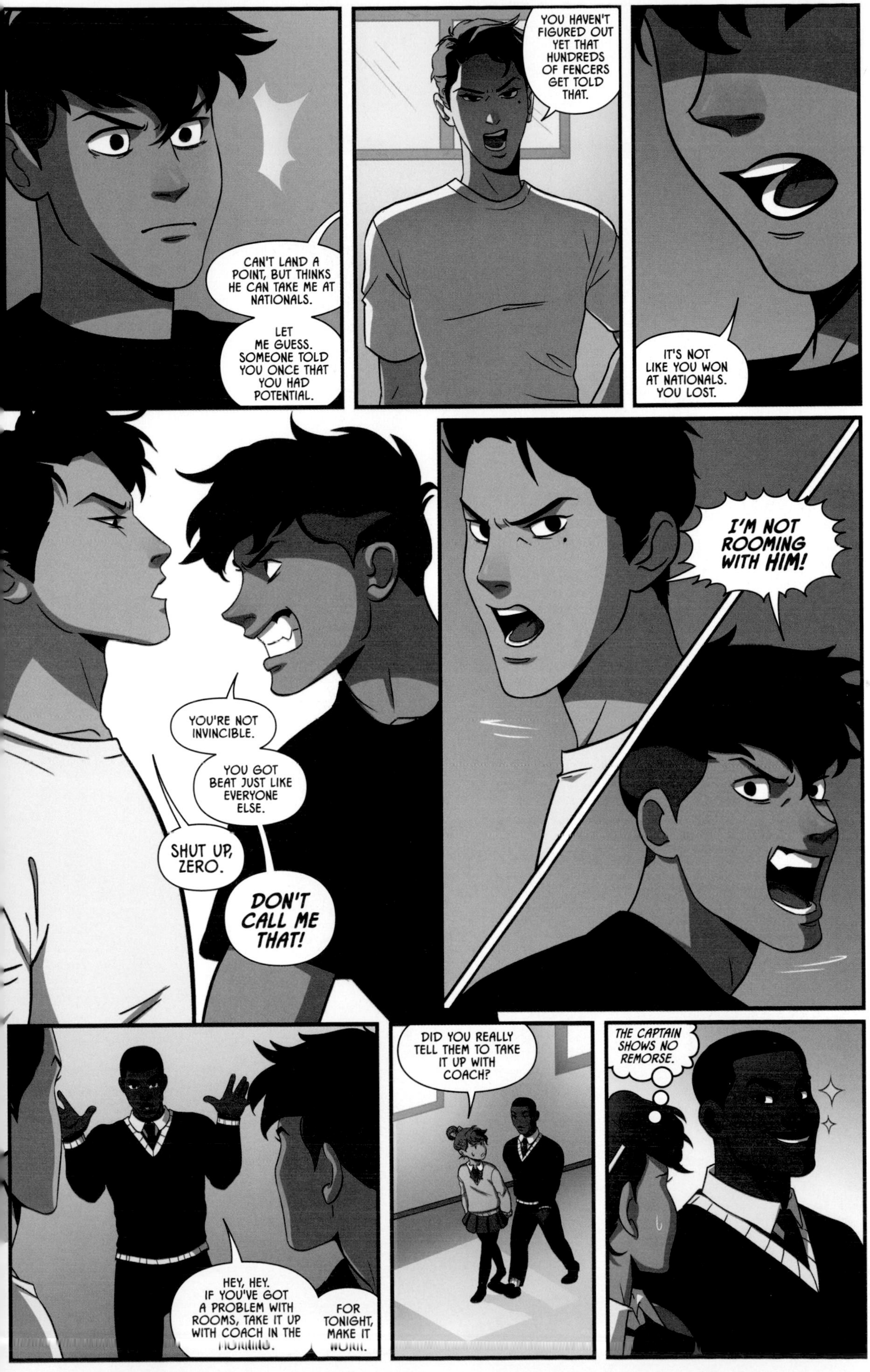
CAN'T LAND A POINT, BUT THINKS HE CAN TAKE ME AT NATIONALS.
LET ME GUESS. SOMEONE TOLD YOU ONCE THAT YOU HAD POTENTIAL.
YOU HAVEN'T FIGURED OUT YET THAT HUNDREDS OF FENCERS GET TOLD THAT.
IT'S NOT LIKE YOU WON AT NATIONALS. YOU LOST.
YOU'RE NOT INVINCIBLE.
YOU GOT BEAT JUST LIKE EVERYONE ELSE.
SHUT UP, ZERO.
DON'T CALL ME THAT!
I'M NOT ROOMING WITH HIM!
HEY, HEY. IF YOU'VE GOT A PROBLEM WITH ROOMS, TAKE IT UP WITH COACH IN THE
FOR TONIGHT, MAKE IT
DID YOU REALLY TELL THEM TO TAKE IT UP WITH COACH?
THE CAPTAIN SHOWS NO REMORSE.

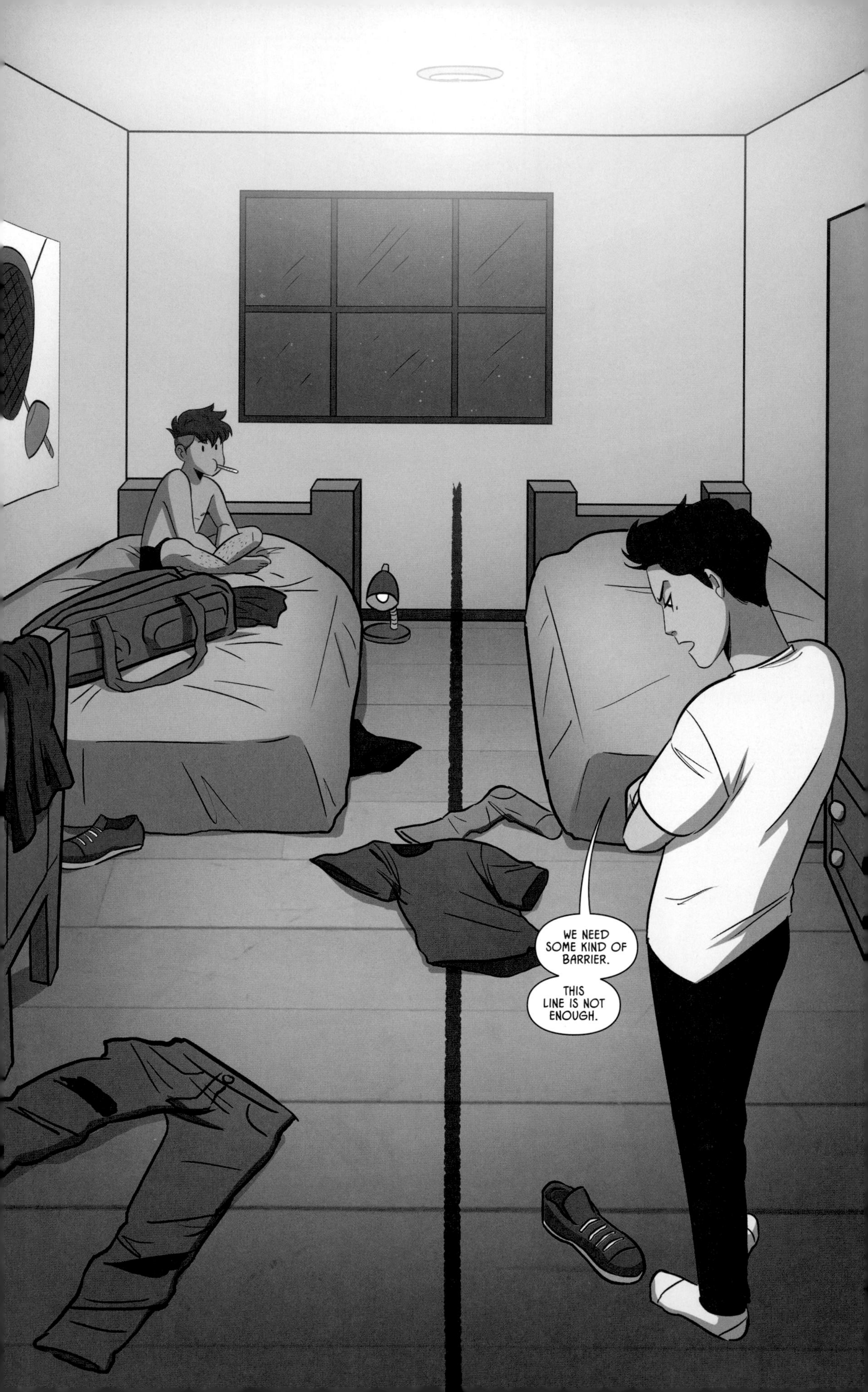
WE NEED SOME KIND OF BARRIER.
THIS LINE IS NOT ENOUGH.

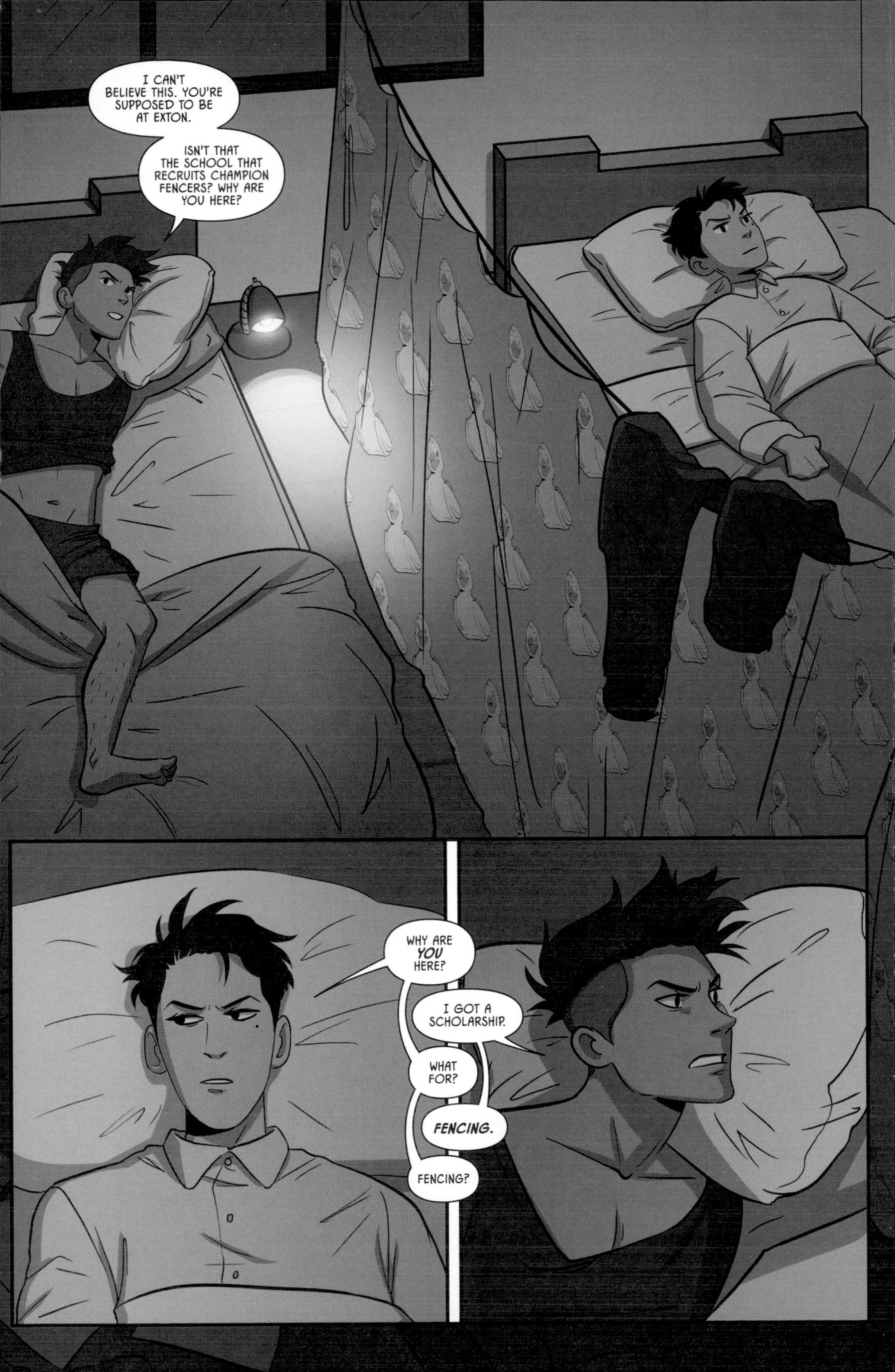
I CAN'T BELIEVE THIS. YOU'RE SUPPOSED TO BE AT EXTON.
ISN'T THAT THE SCHOOL THAT RECRUITS CHAMPION FENCERS? WHY ARE YOU HERE?
WHY ARE *YOU* HERE?
I GOT A SCHOLARSHIP.
WHAT FOR?
***FENCING.***
FENCING?

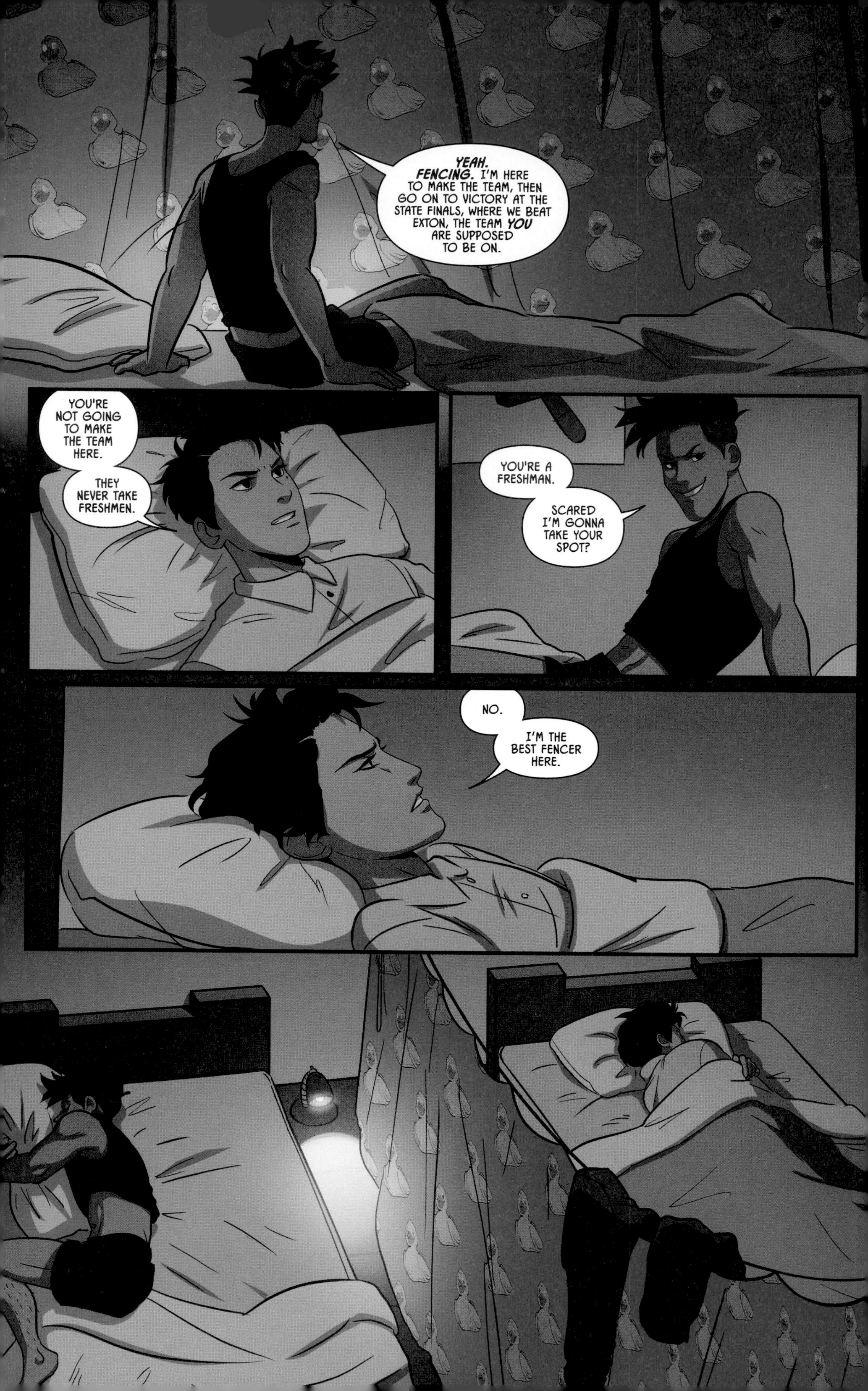
YEAH. FENCING. I'M HERE TO MAKE THE TEAM, THEN GO ON TO VICTORY AT THE STATE FINALS, WHERE WE BEAT EXTON, THE TEAM YOU ARE SUPPOSED TO BE ON.
YOU'RE NOT GOING TO MAKE THE TEAM HERE.
THEY NEVER TAKE FRESHMEN.
YOU'RE A FRESHMAN.
SCARED I'M GONNA TAKE YOUR SPOT?
NO.
I'M THE BEST FENCER HERE.

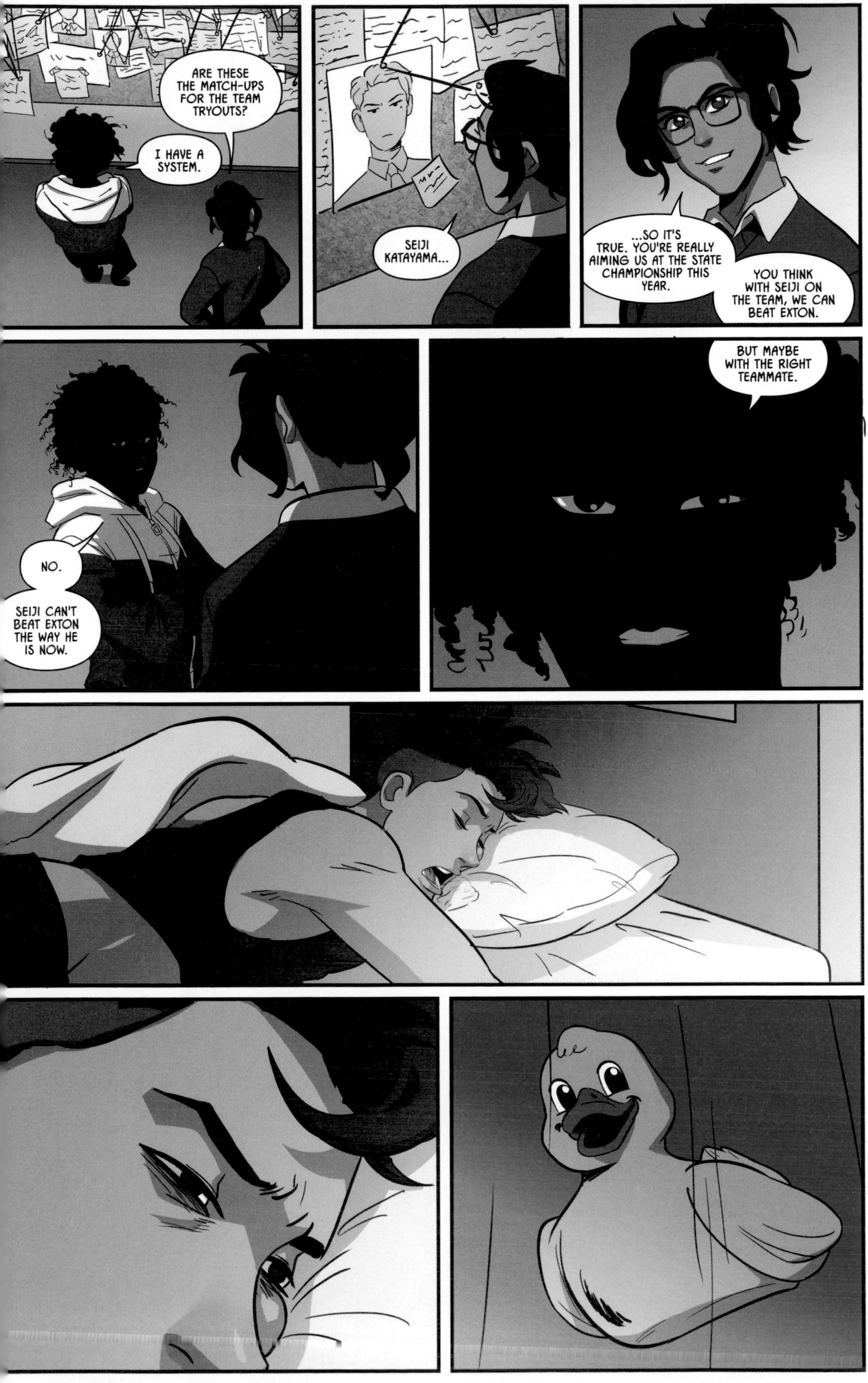
ARE THESE THE MATCH-UPS FOR THE TEAM TRYOUTS?
I HAVE A SYSTEM.
SEIJI KATAYAMA...
...SO IT'S TRUE. YOU'RE REALLY AIMING US AT THE STATE CHAMPIONSHIP THIS YEAR.
YOU THINK WITH SEIJI ON THE TEAM, WE CAN BEAT EXTON.
NO.
SEIJI CAN'T BEAT EXTON THE WAY HE IS NOW.
BUT MAYBE WITH THE RIGHT TEAMMATE.

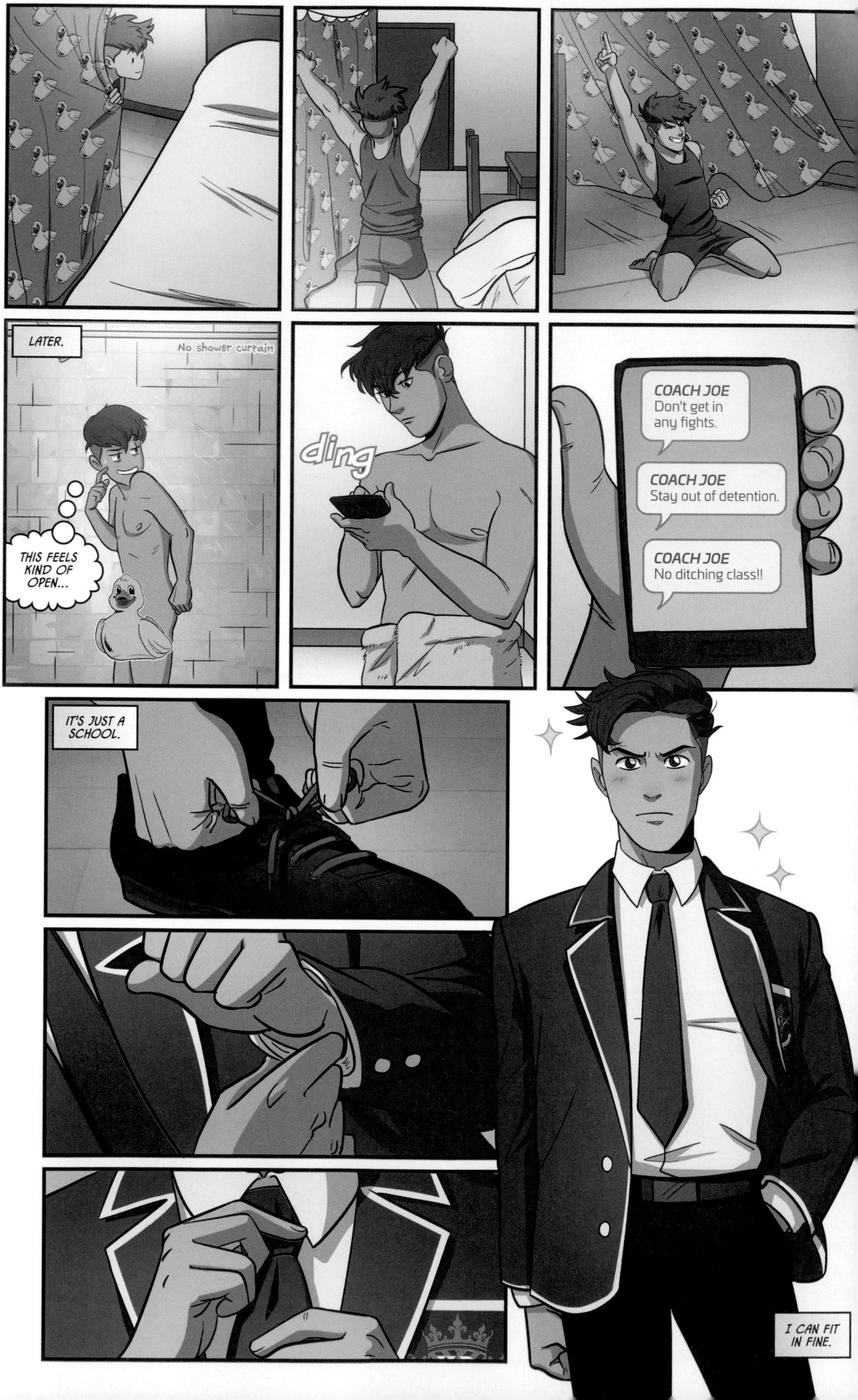

LATER.
No shower curtain
THIS FEELS KIND OF OPEN...
ding
COACH JOE
Don't get in any fights.
COACH JOE
Stay out of detention.
COACH JOE
No ditching class!!
IT'S JUST A SCHOOL.
I CAN FIT IN FINE.

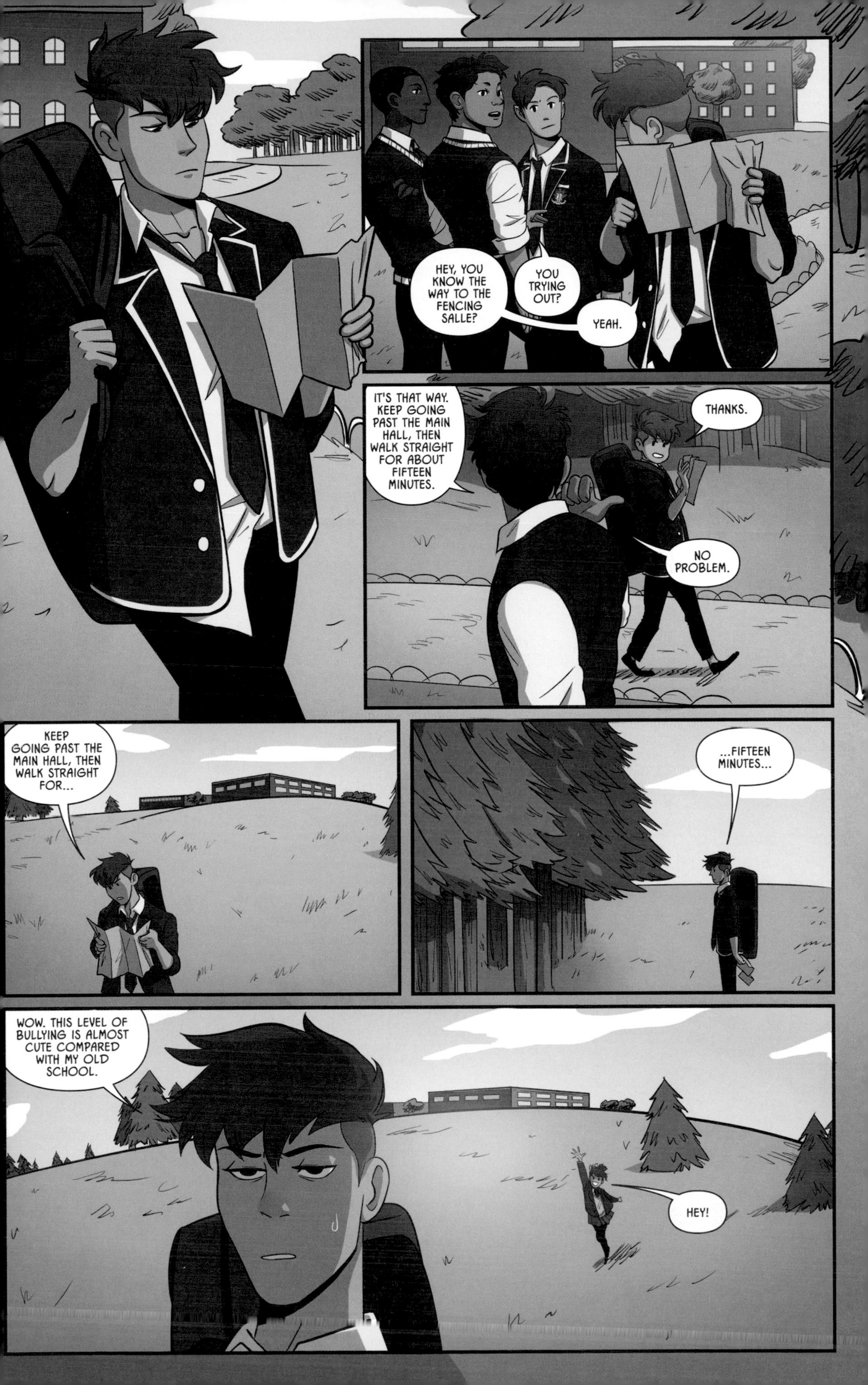
HEY, YOU KNOW THE WAY TO THE FENCING SALLE?
YOU TRYING OUT?
YEAH.
IT'S THAT WAY. KEEP GOING PAST THE MAIN HALL, THEN WALK STRAIGHT FOR ABOUT FIFTEEN MINUTES.
THANKS.
NO PROBLEM.
KEEP GOING PAST THE MAIN HALL, THEN WALK STRAIGHT FOR...
...FIFTEEN MINUTES...
WOW. THIS LEVEL OF BULLYING IS ALMOST CUTE COMPARED WITH MY OLD SCHOOL.
HEY!

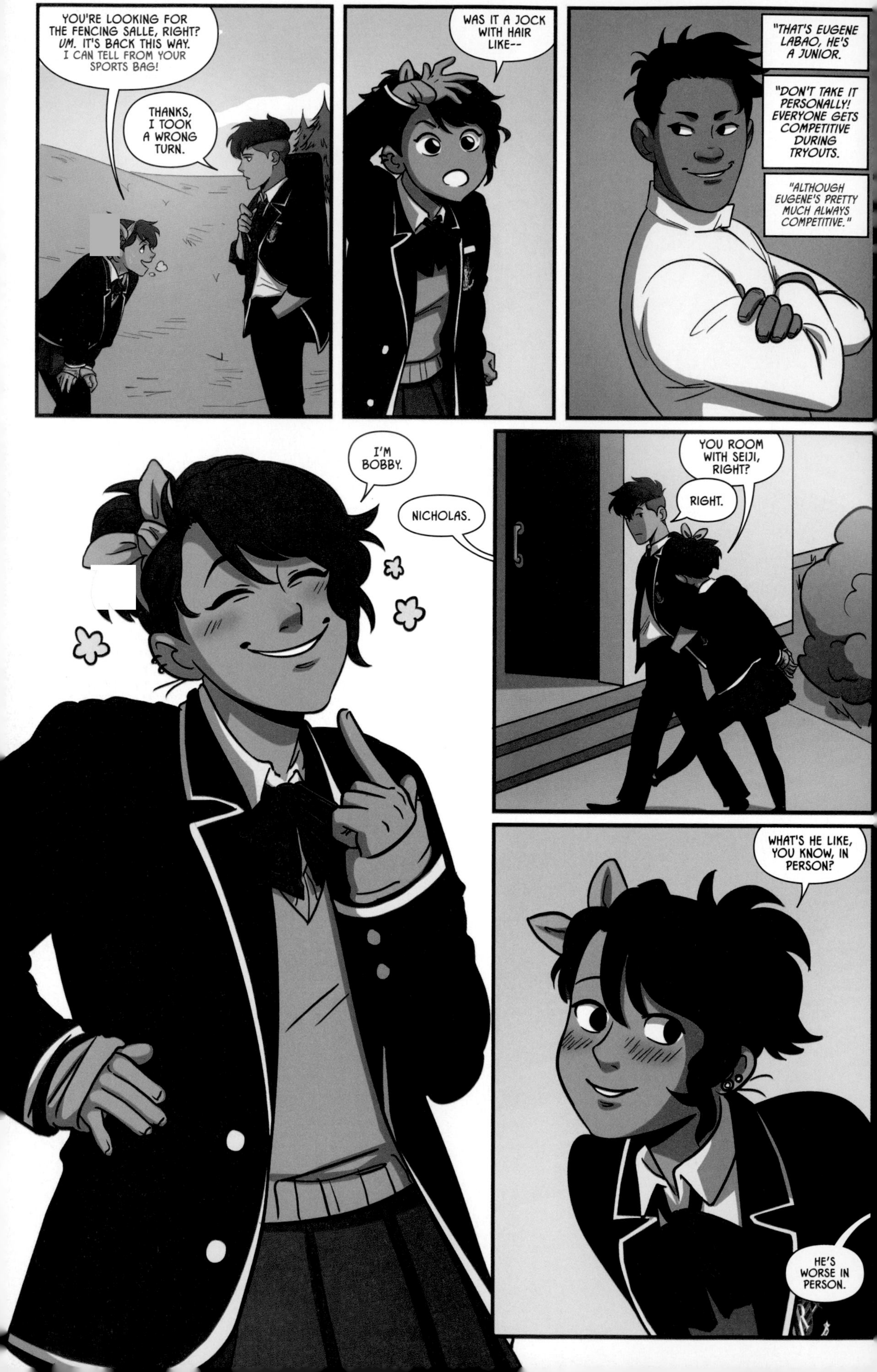
YOU'RE LOOKING FOR THE FENCING SALLE, RIGHT? UM. IT'S BACK THIS WAY. I CAN TELL FROM YOUR SPORTS BAG!
THANKS, I TOOK A WRONG TURN.
WAS IT A JOCK WITH HAIR LIKE--
"THAT'S EUGENE LABAO, HE'S A JUNIOR.
"DON'T TAKE IT PERSONALLY! EVERYONE GETS COMPETITIVE DURING TRYOUTS.
"ALTHOUGH EUGENE'S PRETTY MUCH ALWAYS COMPETITIVE."
I'M BOBBY.
NICHOLAS.
YOU ROOM WITH SEIJI, RIGHT?
RIGHT.
WHAT'S HE LIKE, YOU KNOW, IN PERSON?
HE'S WORSE IN PERSON.

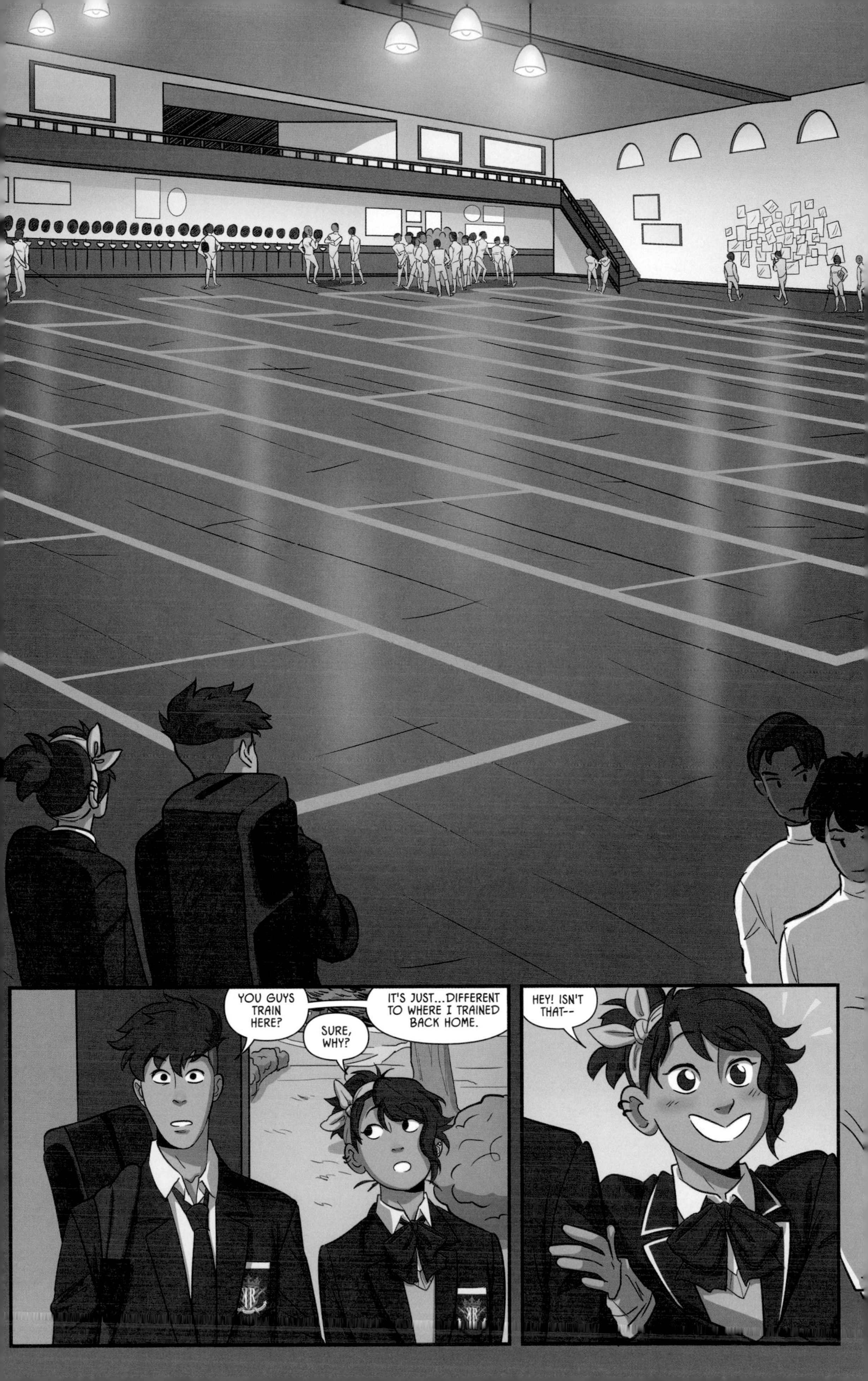
YOU GUYS TRAIN HERE?
SURE, WHY?
IT'S JUST...DIFFERENT TO WHERE I TRAINED BACK HOME.
HEY! ISN'T THAT--

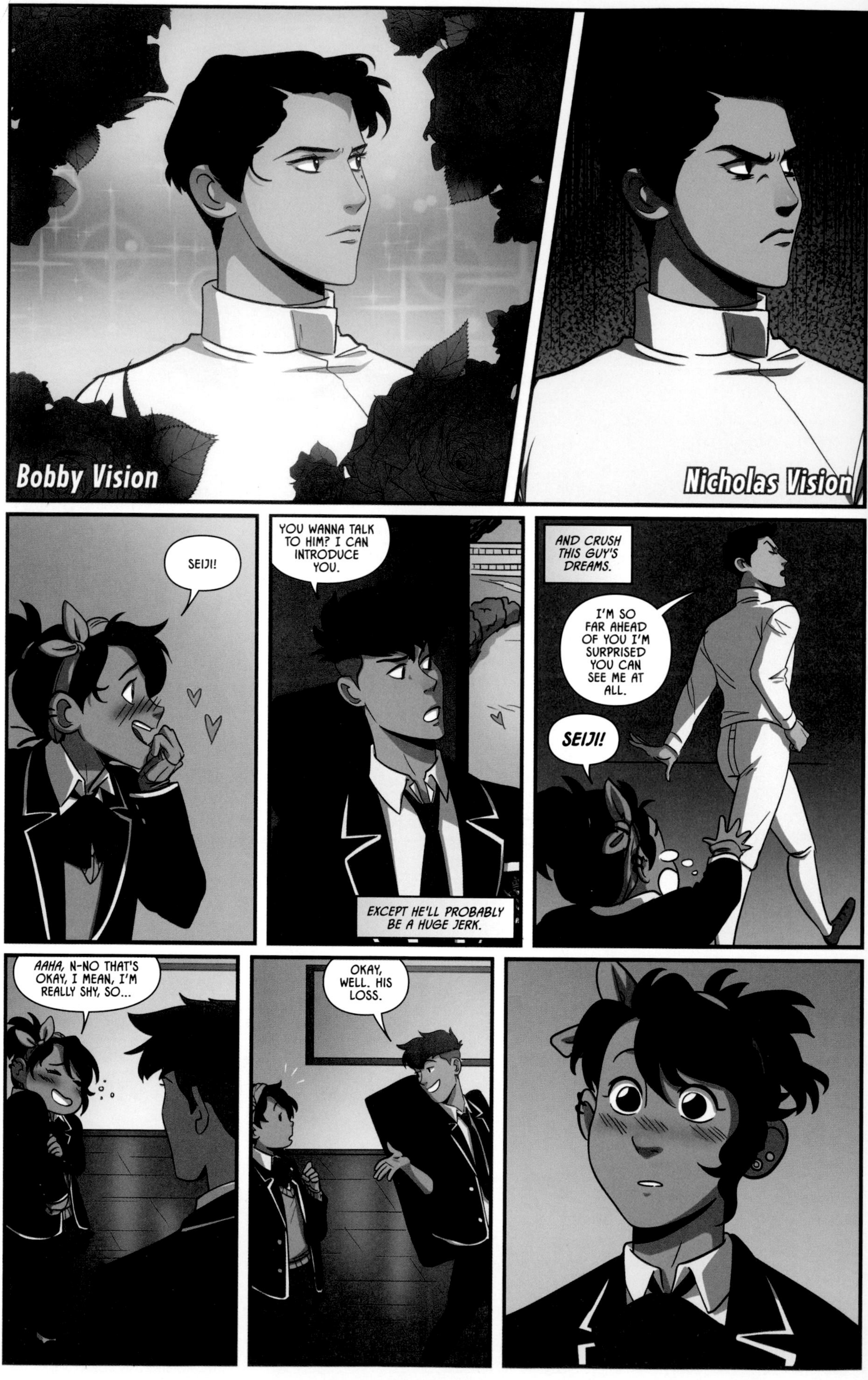
Bobby Vision
Nicholas Vision
SEIJI!
YOU WANNA TALK TO HIM? I CAN INTRODUCE YOU.
EXCEPT HE'LL PROBABLY BE A HUGE JERK.
AND CRUSH THIS GUY'S DREAMS.
I'M SO FAR AHEAD OF YOU I'M SURPRISED YOU CAN SEE ME AT ALL.
SEIJI!
AAHA, N-NO THAT'S OKAY, I MEAN, I'M REALLY SHY, SO...
OKAY, WELL. HIS LOSS.

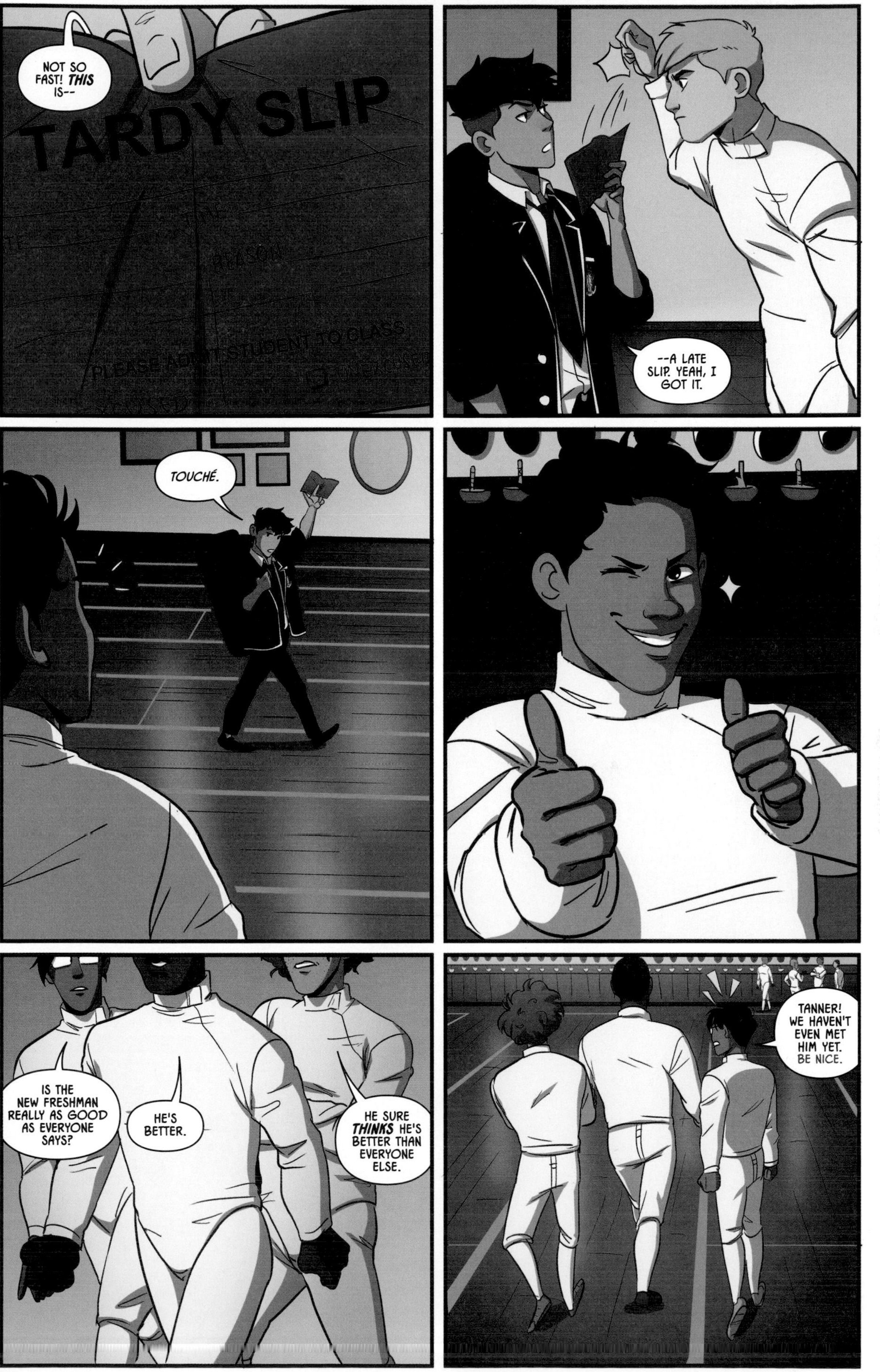
NOT SO FAST! ***THIS*** IS--
TARDY SLIP
REASON
PLEASE ADMIT STUDENT TO CLASS
--A LATE SLIP. YEAH, I GOT IT.
*TOUCHÉ.*
IS THE NEW FRESHMAN REALLY AS GOOD AS EVERYONE SAYS?
HE'S BETTER.
HE SURE ***THINKS*** HE'S BETTER THAN EVERYONE ELSE.
TANNER! WE HAVEN'T EVEN MET HIM YET. BE NICE.

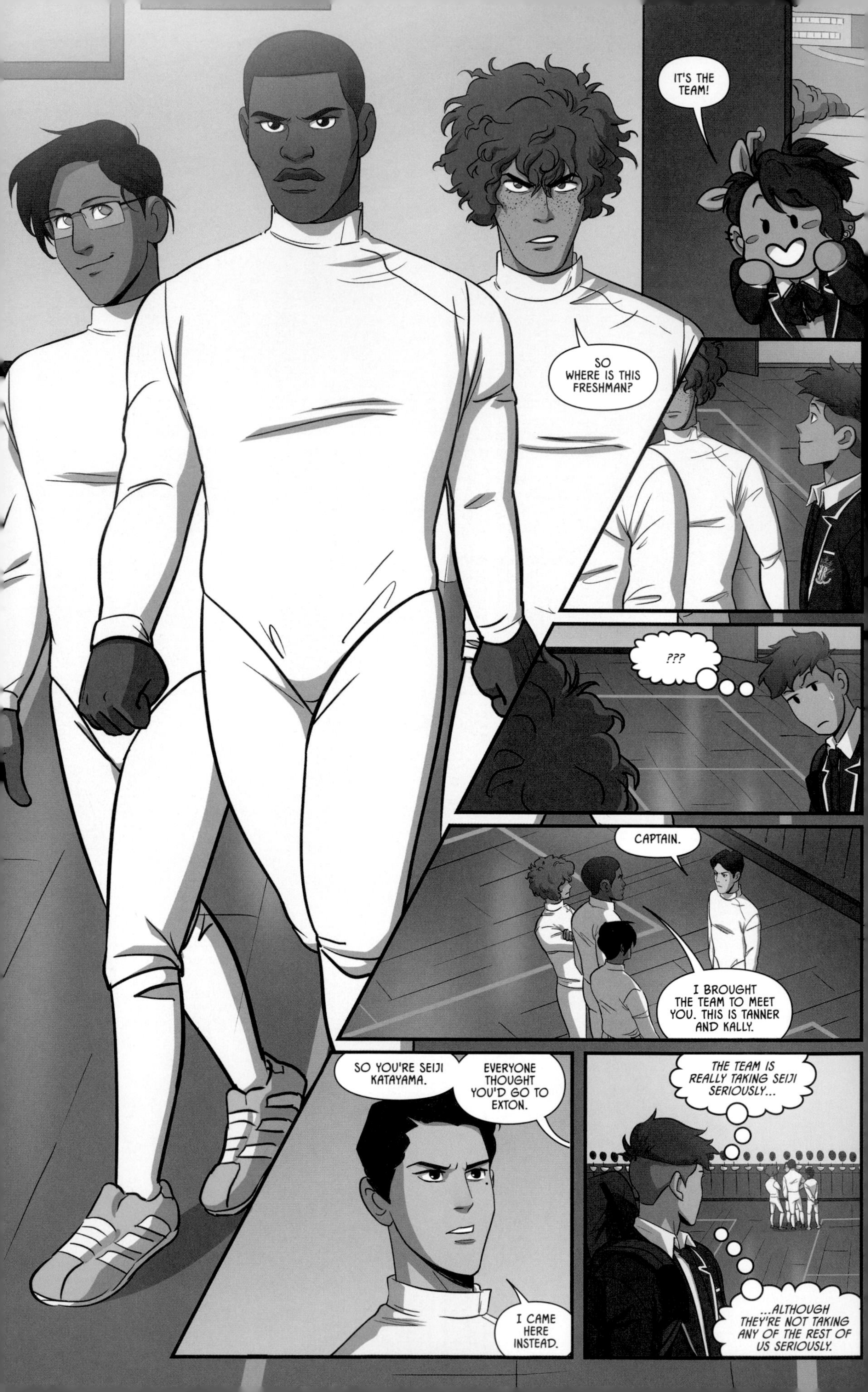
IT'S THE TEAM!
SO WHERE IS THIS FRESHMAN?
???
CAPTAIN.
I BROUGHT THE TEAM TO MEET YOU. THIS IS TANNER AND KALLY.
SO YOU'RE SEIJI KATAYAMA.
EVERYONE THOUGHT YOU'D GO TO EXTON.
I CAME HERE INSTEAD.
THE TEAM IS REALLY TAKING SEIJI SERIOUSLY...
...ALTHOUGH THEY'RE NOT TAKING ANY OF THE REST OF US SERIOUSLY.

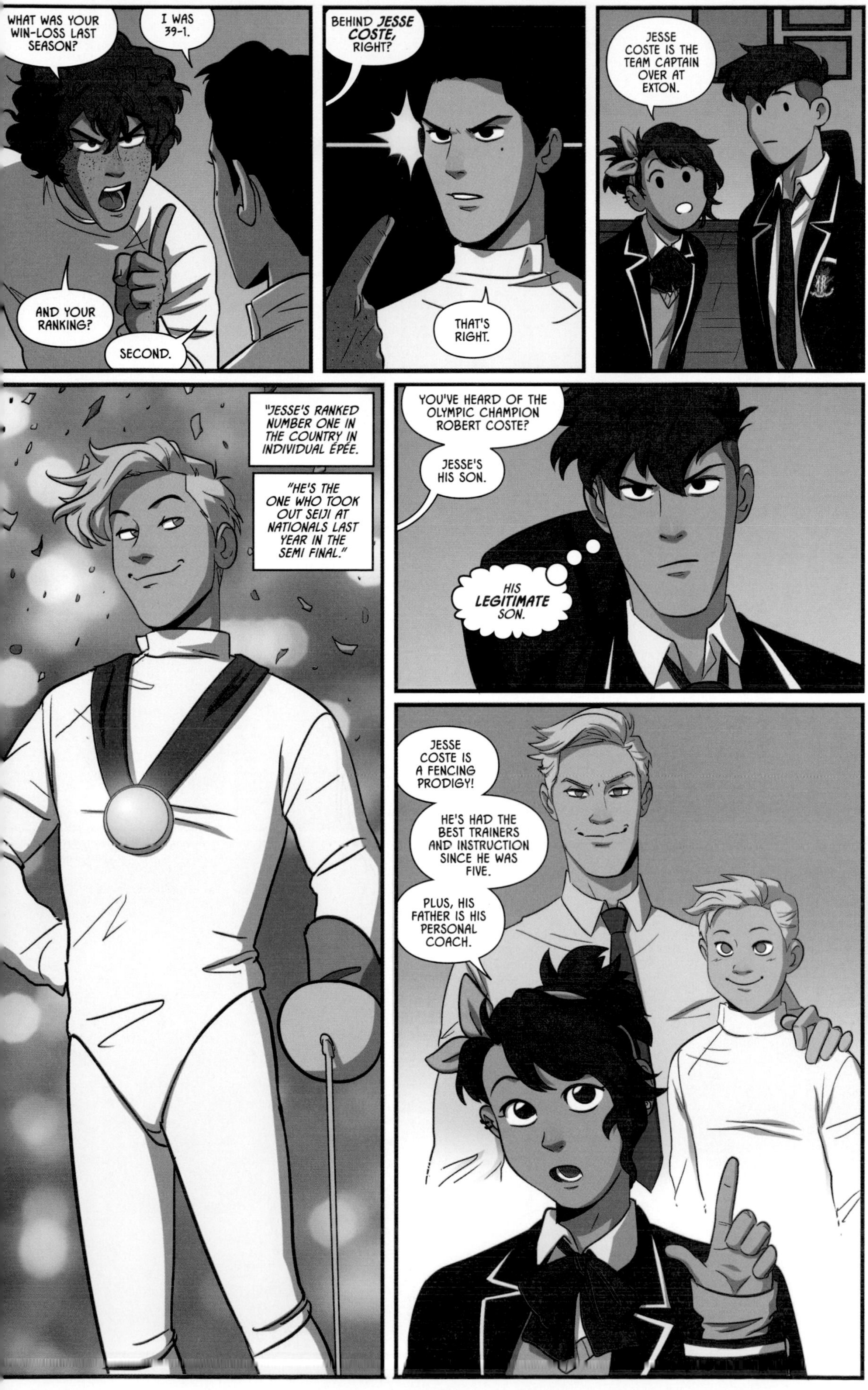
WHAT WAS YOUR WIN-LOSS LAST SEASON?
I WAS 39-1.
AND YOUR RANKING?
SECOND.
BEHIND JESSE COSTE, RIGHT?
THAT'S RIGHT.
JESSE COSTE IS THE TEAM CAPTAIN OVER AT EXTON.
"JESSE'S RANKED NUMBER ONE IN THE COUNTRY IN INDIVIDUAL ÉPÉE.
"HE'S THE ONE WHO TOOK OUT SEIJI AT NATIONALS LAST YEAR IN THE SEMI FINAL."
YOU'VE HEARD OF THE OLYMPIC CHAMPION ROBERT COSTE?
JESSE'S HIS SON.
HIS LEGITIMATE SON.
JESSE COSTE IS A FENCING PRODIGY!
HE'S HAD THE BEST TRAINERS AND INSTRUCTION SINCE HE WAS FIVE.
PLUS, HIS FATHER IS HIS PERSONAL COACH.

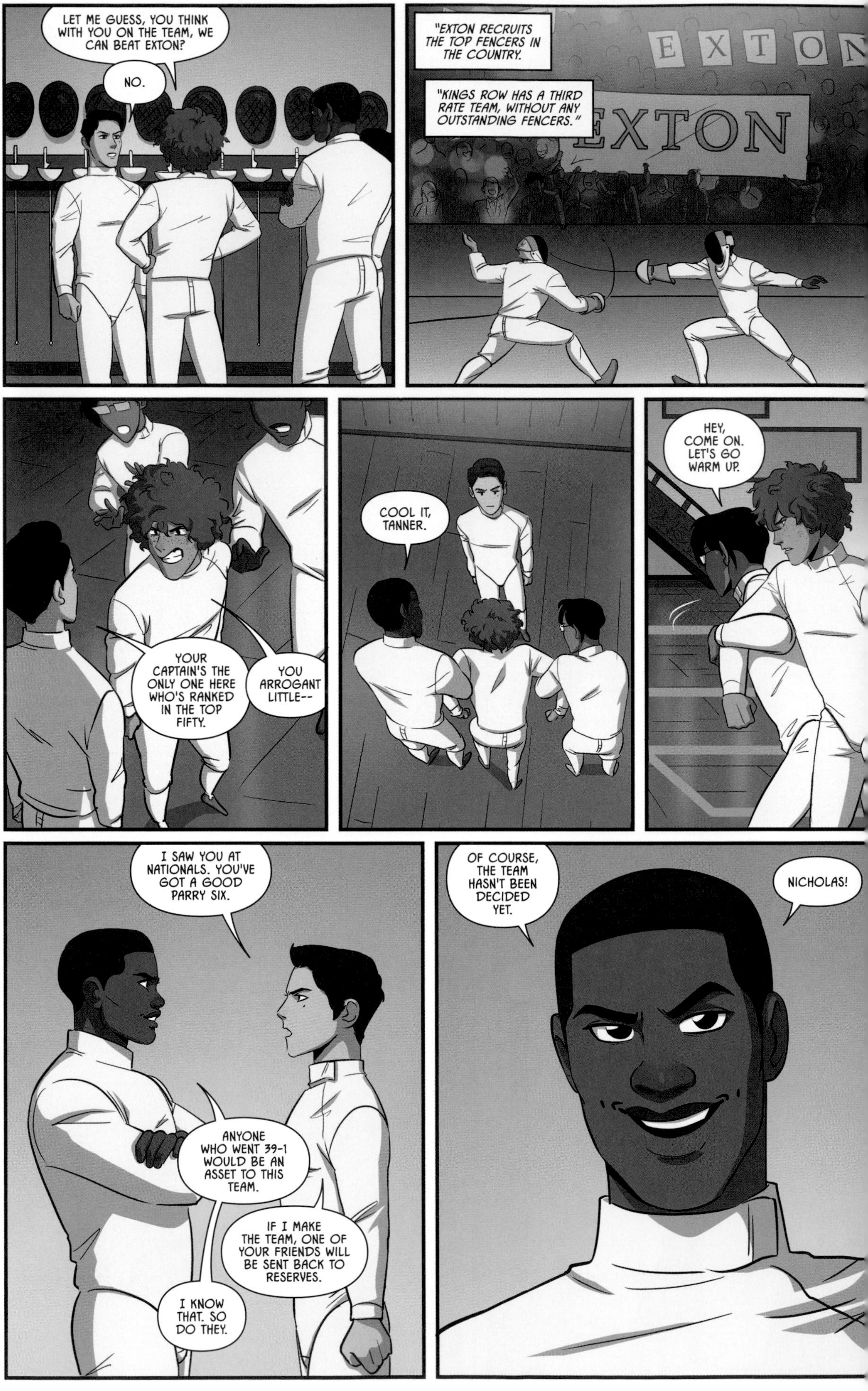
LET ME GUESS, YOU THINK WITH YOU ON THE TEAM, WE CAN BEAT EXTON?
NO.
"EXTON RECRUITS THE TOP FENCERS IN THE COUNTRY.
"KINGS ROW HAS A THIRD RATE TEAM, WITHOUT ANY OUTSTANDING FENCERS."
EXTON
EXTON
YOUR CAPTAIN'S THE ONLY ONE HERE WHO'S RANKED IN THE TOP FIFTY.
YOU ARROGANT LITTLE--
COOL IT, TANNER.
HEY, COME ON. LET'S GO WARM UP.
I SAW YOU AT NATIONALS. YOU'VE GOT A GOOD PARRY SIX.
ANYONE WHO WENT 39-1 WOULD BE AN ASSET TO THIS TEAM.
IF I MAKE THE TEAM, ONE OF YOUR FRIENDS WILL BE SENT BACK TO RESERVES.
I KNOW THAT. SO DO THEY.
OF COURSE, THE TEAM HASN'T BEEN DECIDED YET.
NICHOLAS!

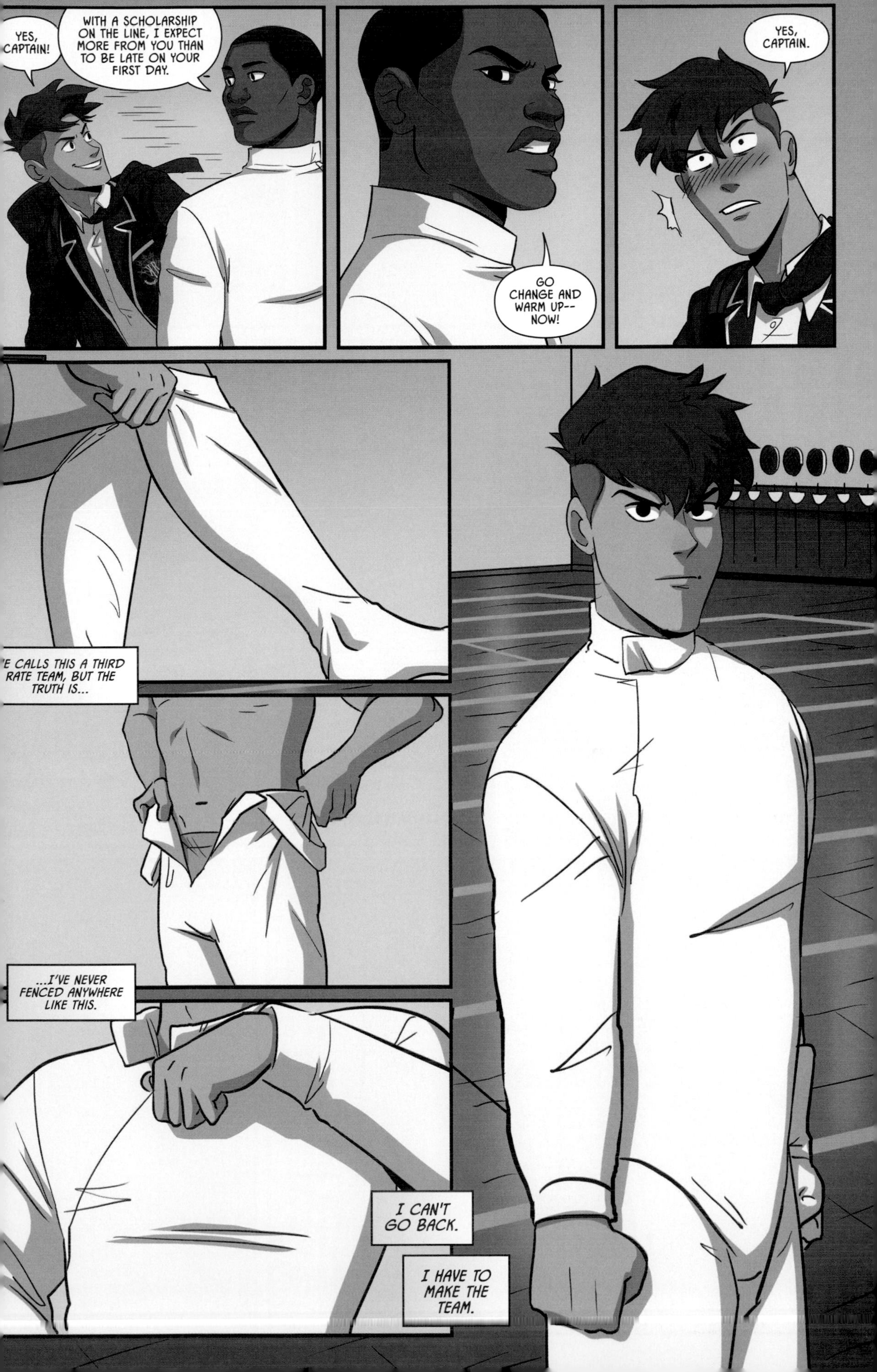
WITH A SCHOLARSHIP ON THE LINE, I EXPECT MORE FROM YOU THAN TO BE LATE ON YOUR FIRST DAY.
YES, CAPTAIN!
GO CHANGE AND WARM UP-- NOW!
YES, CAPTAIN.
'E CALLS THIS A THIRD RATE TEAM, BUT THE TRUTH IS...
...I'VE NEVER FENCED ANYWHERE LIKE THIS.
I CAN'T GO BACK.
I HAVE TO MAKE THE TEAM.

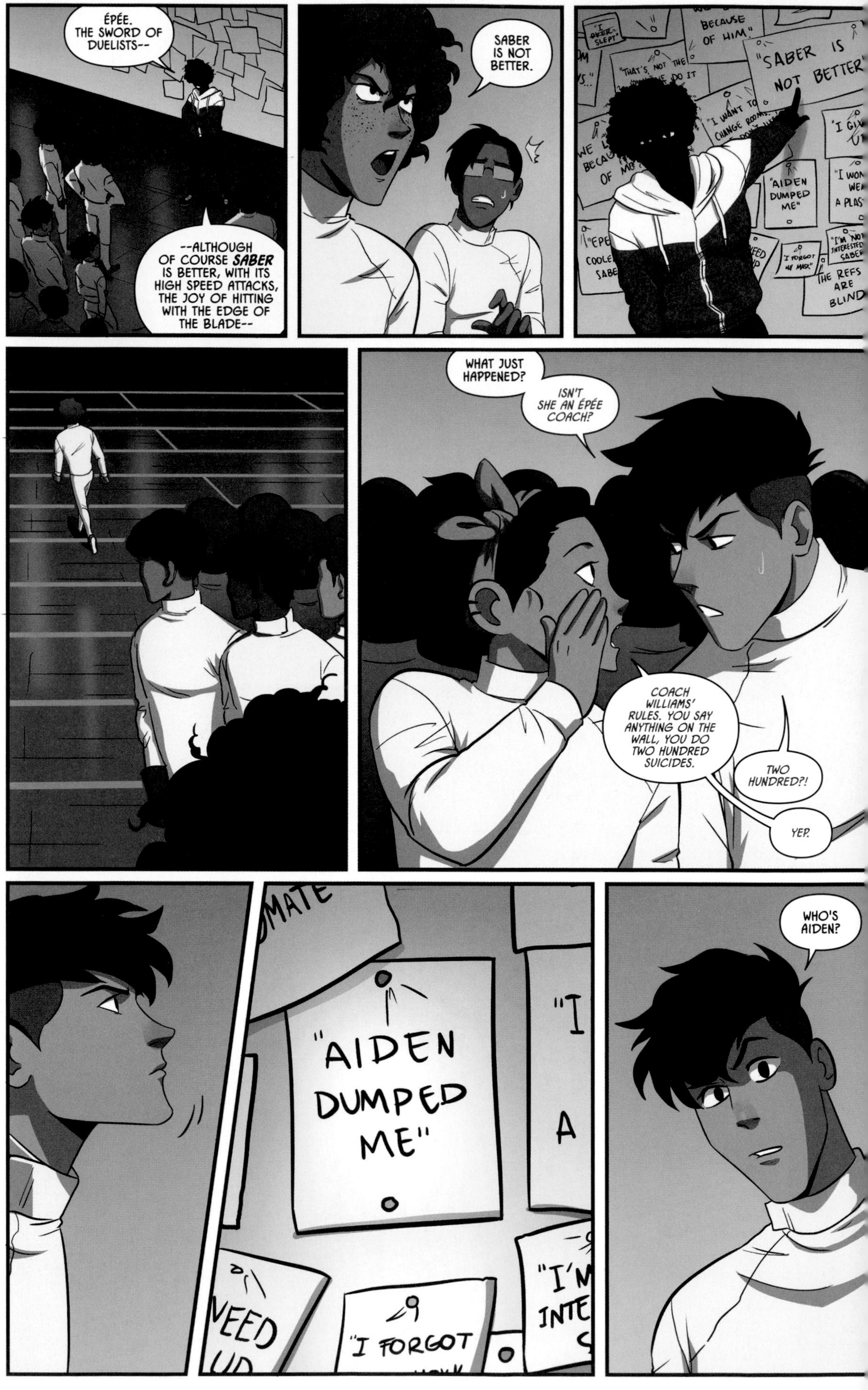
ÉPÉE. THE SWORD OF DUELISTS--
--ALTHOUGH OF COURSE SABER IS BETTER, WITH ITS HIGH SPEED ATTACKS, THE JOY OF HITTING WITH THE EDGE OF THE BLADE--
SABER IS NOT BETTER.
"SABER IS NOT BETTER"
"AIDEN DUMPED ME"
"THE REFS ARE BLIND"
WHAT JUST HAPPENED?
ISN'T SHE AN ÉPÉE COACH?
COACH WILLIAMS' RULES. YOU SAY ANYTHING ON THE WALL, YOU DO TWO HUNDRED SUICIDES.
TWO HUNDRED?!
YEP.
"AIDEN DUMPED ME"
"I FORGOT
WHO'S AIDEN?

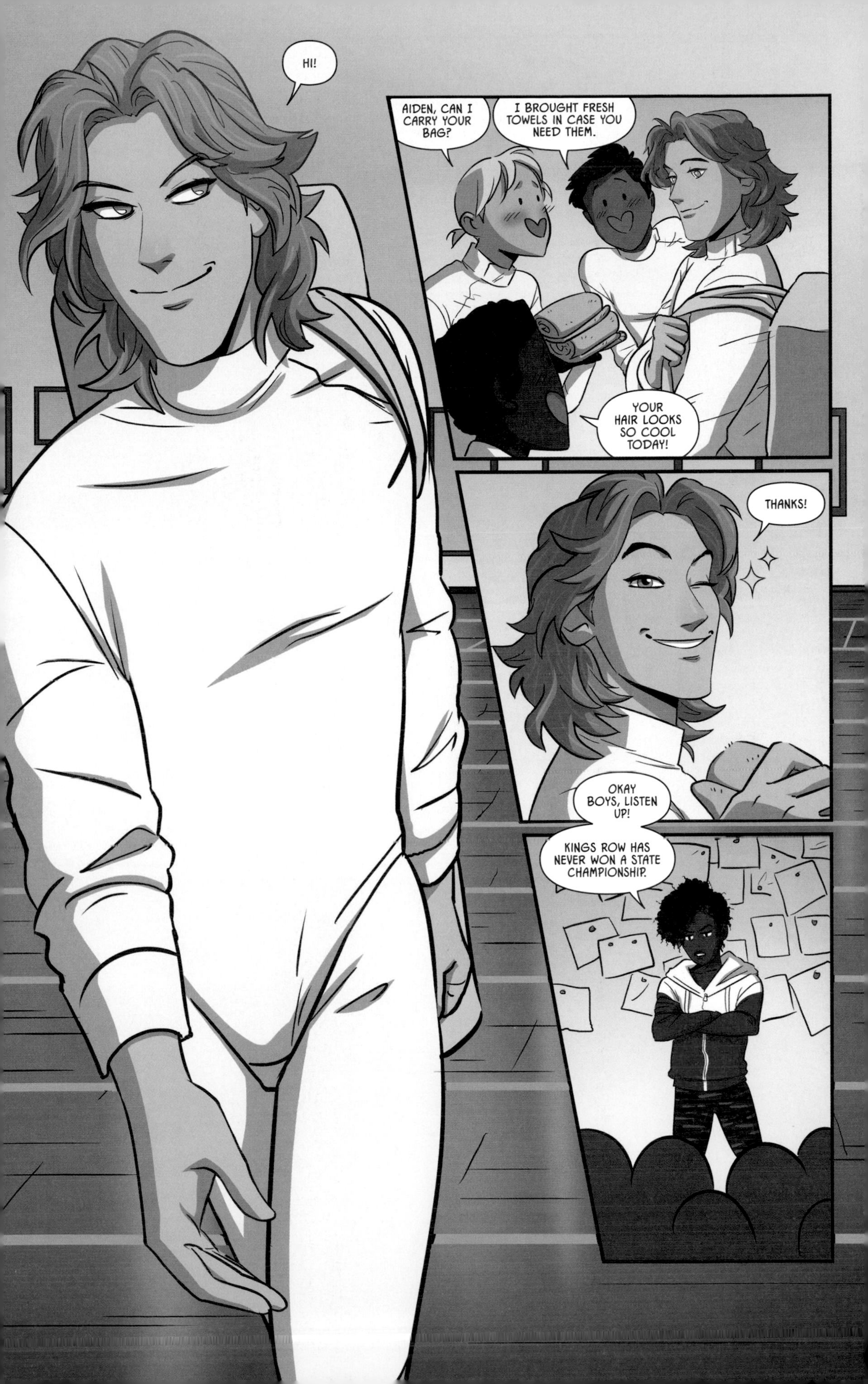
HI!
AIDEN, CAN I CARRY YOUR BAG?
I BROUGHT FRESH TOWELS IN CASE YOU NEED THEM.
YOUR HAIR LOOKS SO COOL TODAY!
THANKS!
OKAY BOYS, LISTEN UP!
KINGS ROW HAS NEVER WON A STATE CHAMPIONSHIP.

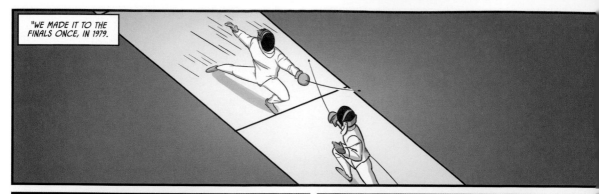

"WE MADE IT TO THE FINALS ONCE, IN 1979.

"THAT YEAR, ROBERT COSTE WAS A STUDENT HERE. HE WENT ON TO WIN OLYMPIC GOLD."

ROBERT COSTE WAS A STUDENT HERE!

BUT EVEN ONE EXTRAORDINARY FENCER IS NOT ENOUGH TO WIN A STATE TITLE.

THAT TAKES A TEAM.

AND FOR THE LAST TEN YEARS, THE STATE FINALS HAVE BEEN DOMINATED BY ONE TEAM ONLY.

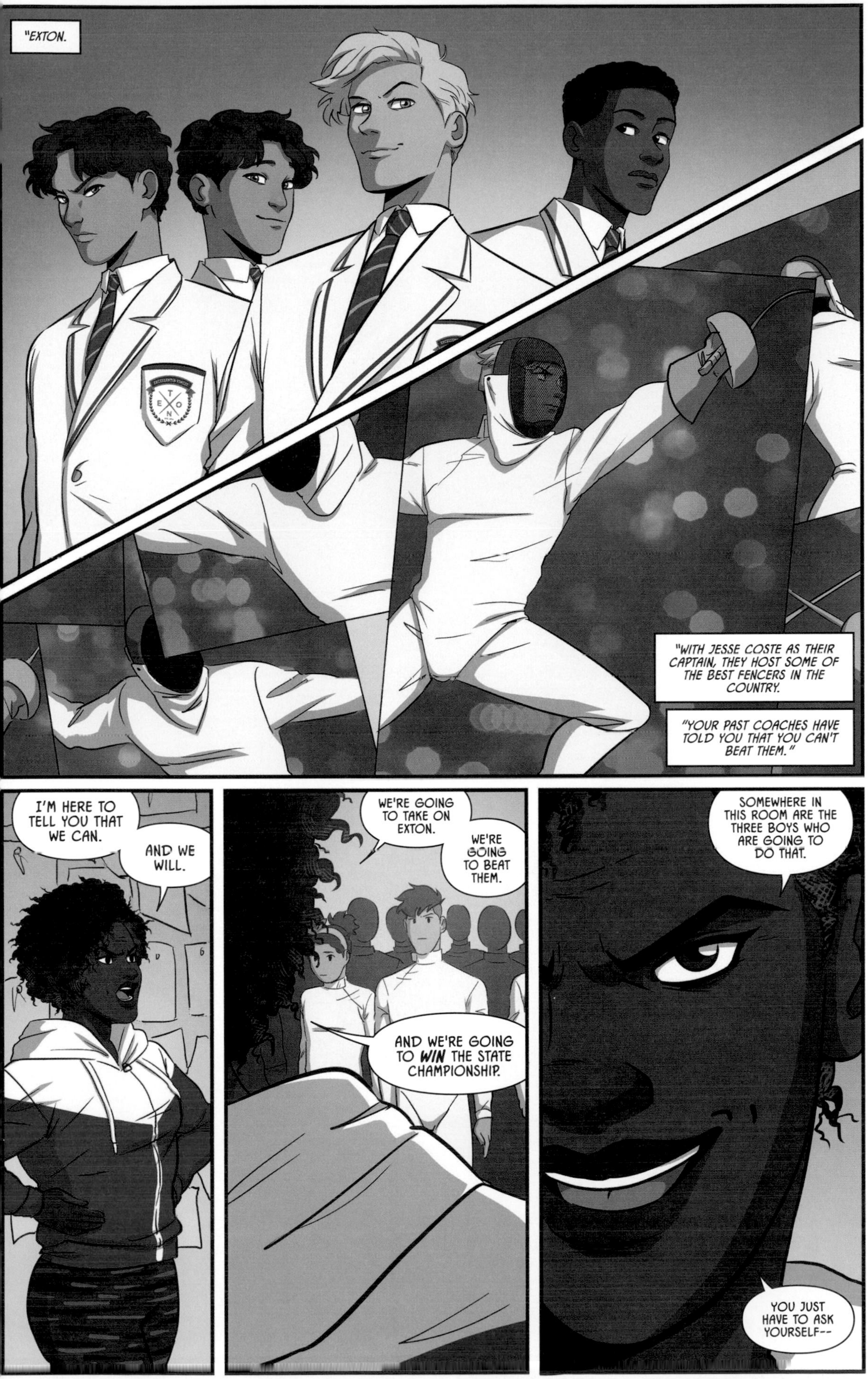
"EXTON.
"WITH JESSE COSTE AS THEIR CAPTAIN, THEY HOST SOME OF THE BEST FENCERS IN THE COUNTRY.
"YOUR PAST COACHES HAVE TOLD YOU THAT YOU CAN'T BEAT THEM."
I'M HERE TO TELL YOU THAT WE CAN.
AND WE WILL.
WE'RE GOING TO TAKE ON EXTON.
WE'RE GOING TO BEAT THEM.
AND WE'RE GOING TO **WIN** THE STATE CHAMPIONSHIP.
SOMEWHERE IN THIS ROOM ARE THE THREE BOYS WHO ARE GOING TO DO THAT.
YOU JUST HAVE TO ASK YOURSELF--

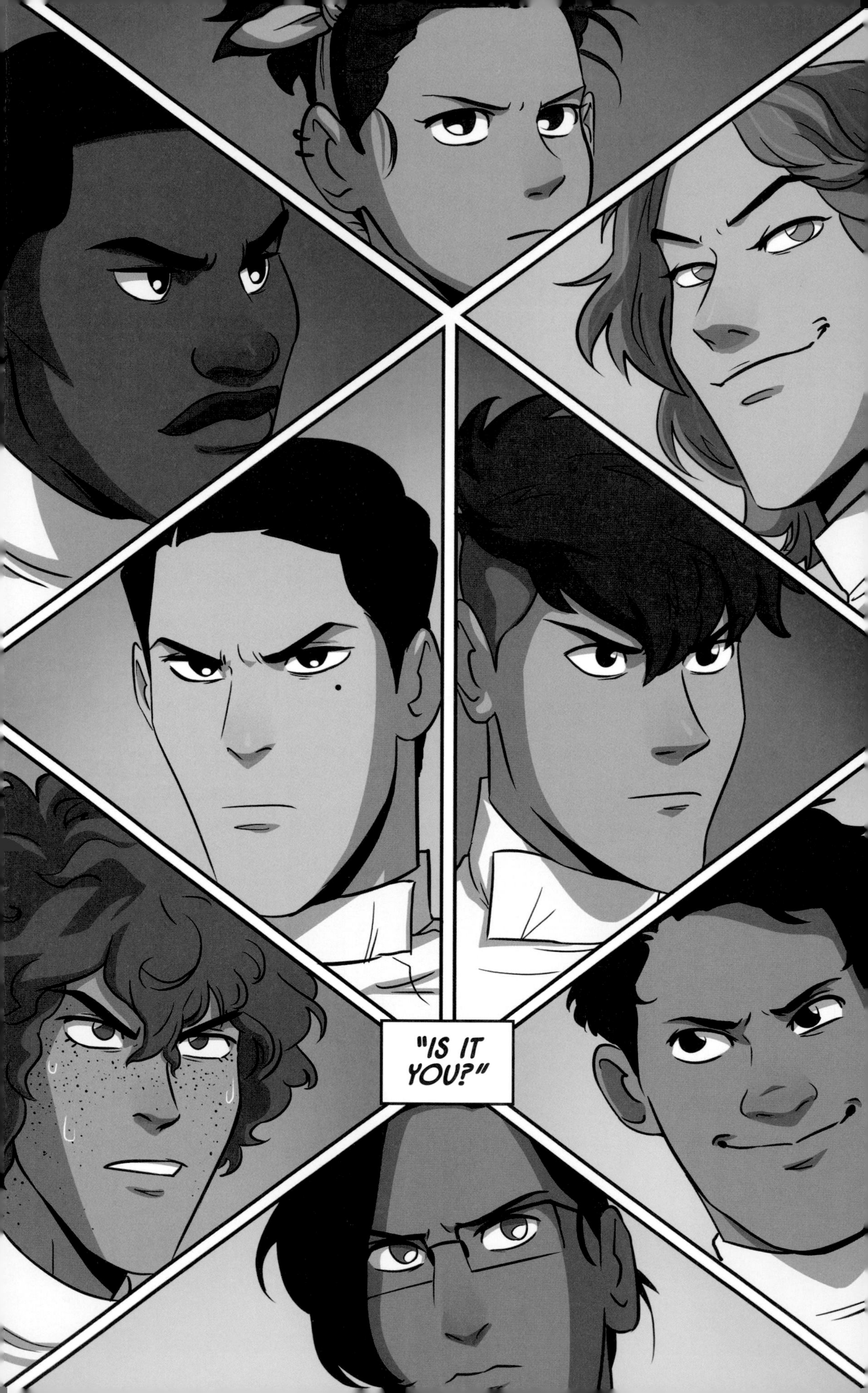
"IS IT YOU?"

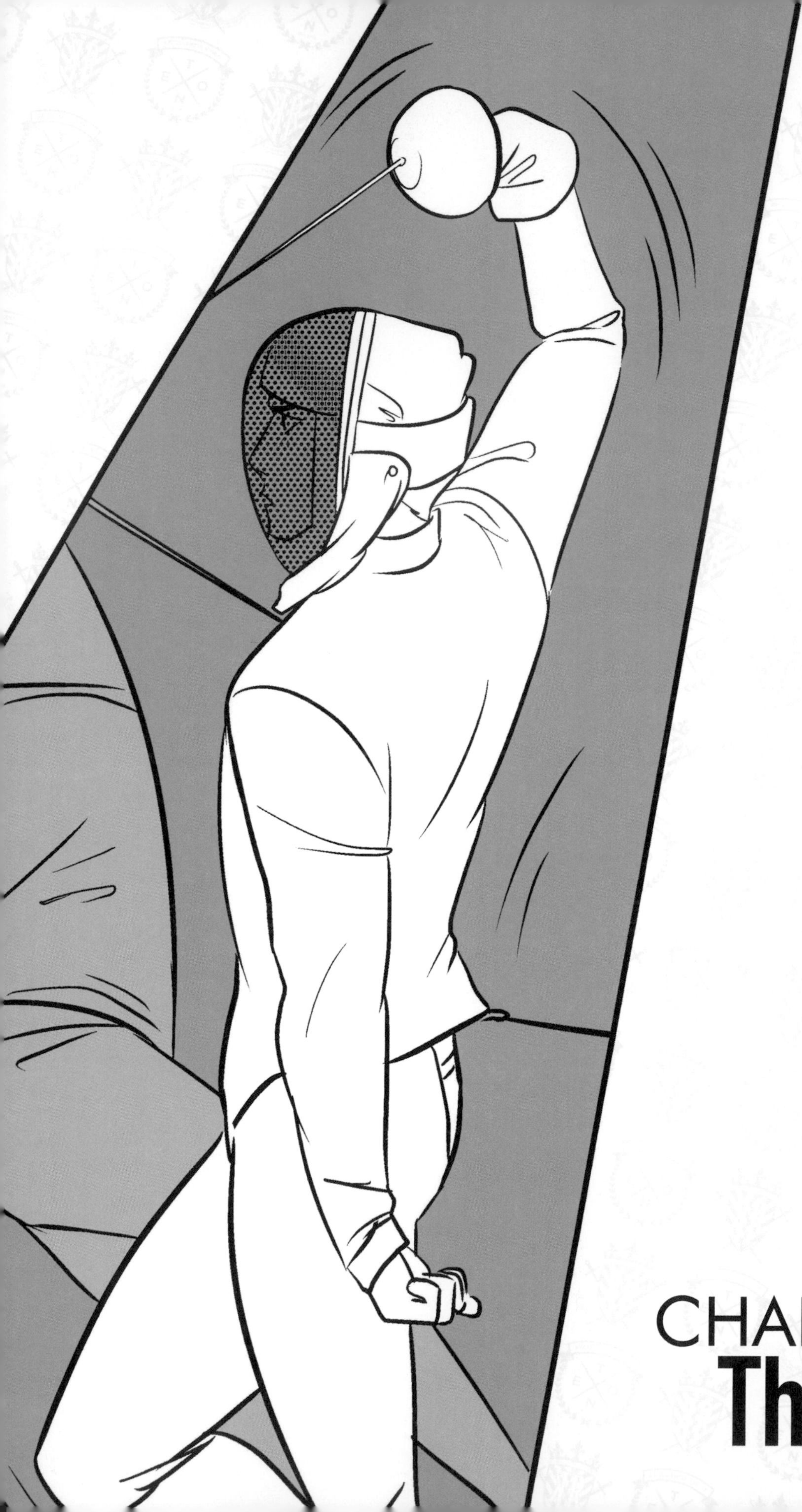

# CHAPTER
# Three

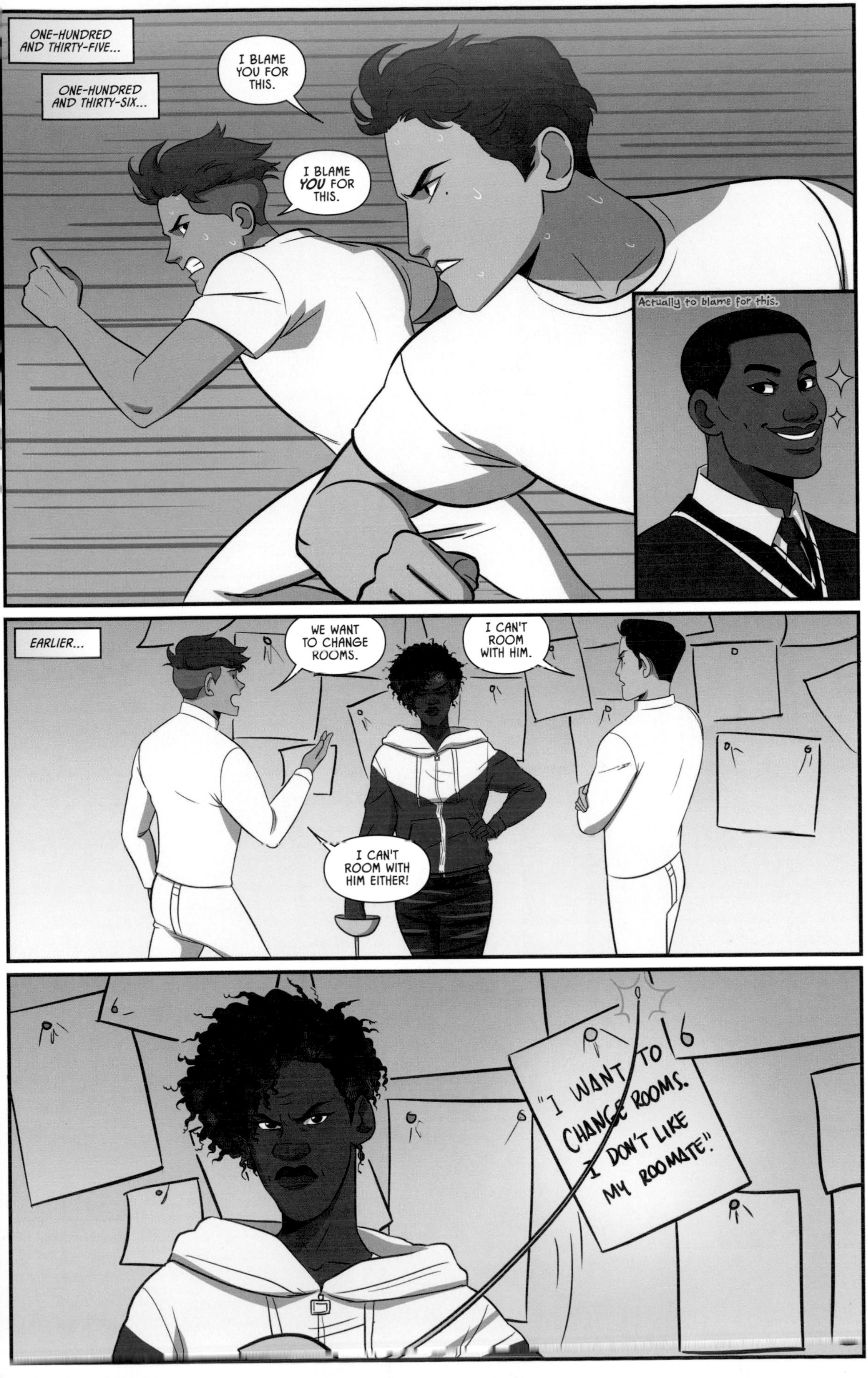
ONE-HUNDRED AND THIRTY-FIVE...
I BLAME YOU FOR THIS.
ONE-HUNDRED AND THIRTY-SIX...
I BLAME YOU FOR THIS.
Actually to blame for this.
EARLIER...
WE WANT TO CHANGE ROOMS.
I CAN'T ROOM WITH HIM.
I CAN'T ROOM WITH HIM EITHER!
"I WANT TO CHANGE ROOMS. I DON'T LIKE MY ROOMATE".
6
6

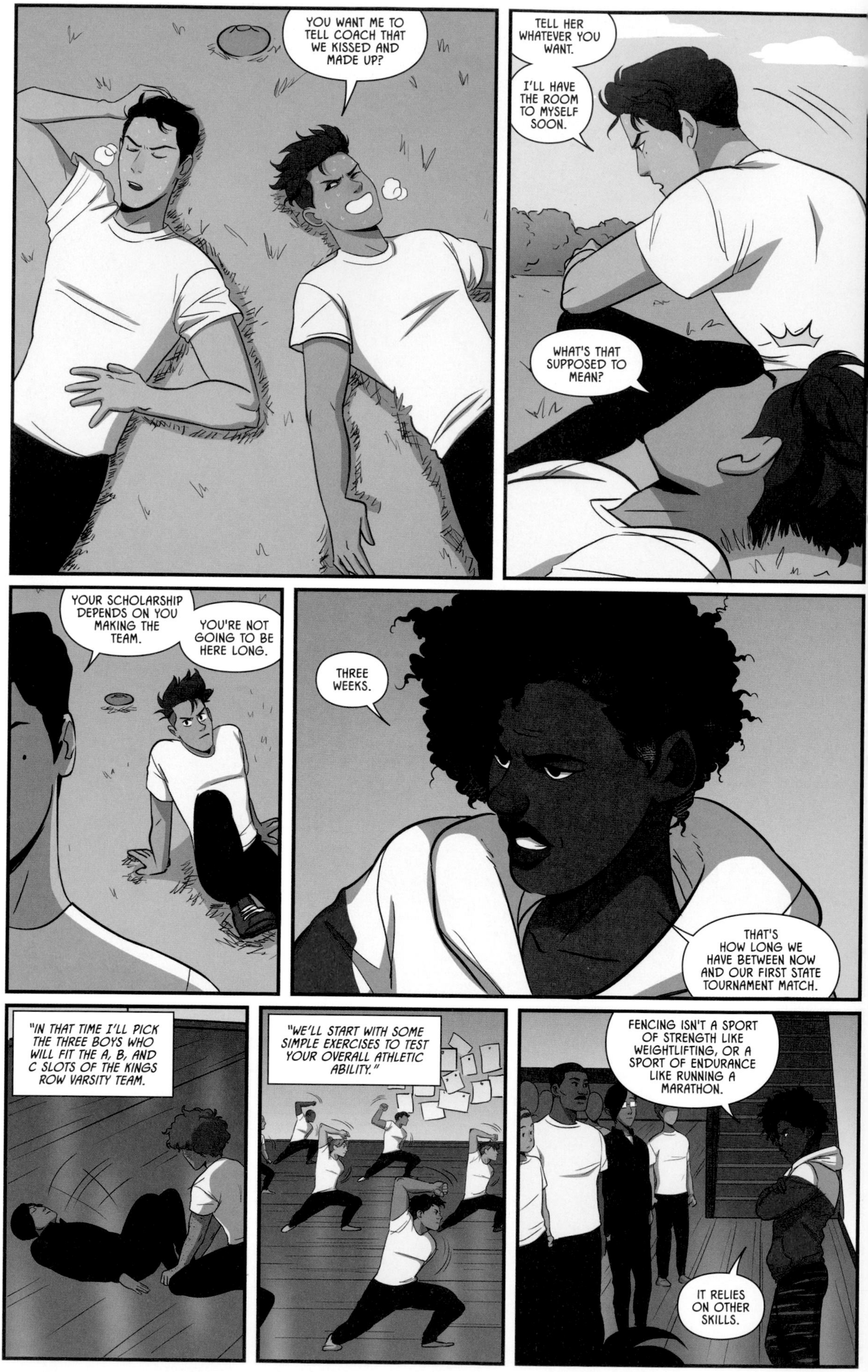
YOU WANT ME TO TELL COACH THAT WE KISSED AND MADE UP?
TELL HER WHATEVER YOU WANT.
I'LL HAVE THE ROOM TO MYSELF SOON.
WHAT'S THAT SUPPOSED TO MEAN?
YOUR SCHOLARSHIP DEPENDS ON YOU MAKING THE TEAM.
YOU'RE NOT GOING TO BE HERE LONG.
THREE WEEKS.
THAT'S HOW LONG WE HAVE BETWEEN NOW AND OUR FIRST STATE TOURNAMENT MATCH.
"IN THAT TIME I'LL PICK THE THREE BOYS WHO WILL FIT THE A, B, AND C SLOTS OF THE KINGS ROW VARSITY TEAM.
"WE'LL START WITH SOME SIMPLE EXERCISES TO TEST YOUR OVERALL ATHLETIC ABILITY."
FENCING ISN'T A SPORT OF STRENGTH LIKE WEIGHTLIFTING, OR A SPORT OF ENDURANCE LIKE RUNNING A MARATHON.
IT RELIES ON OTHER SKILLS.

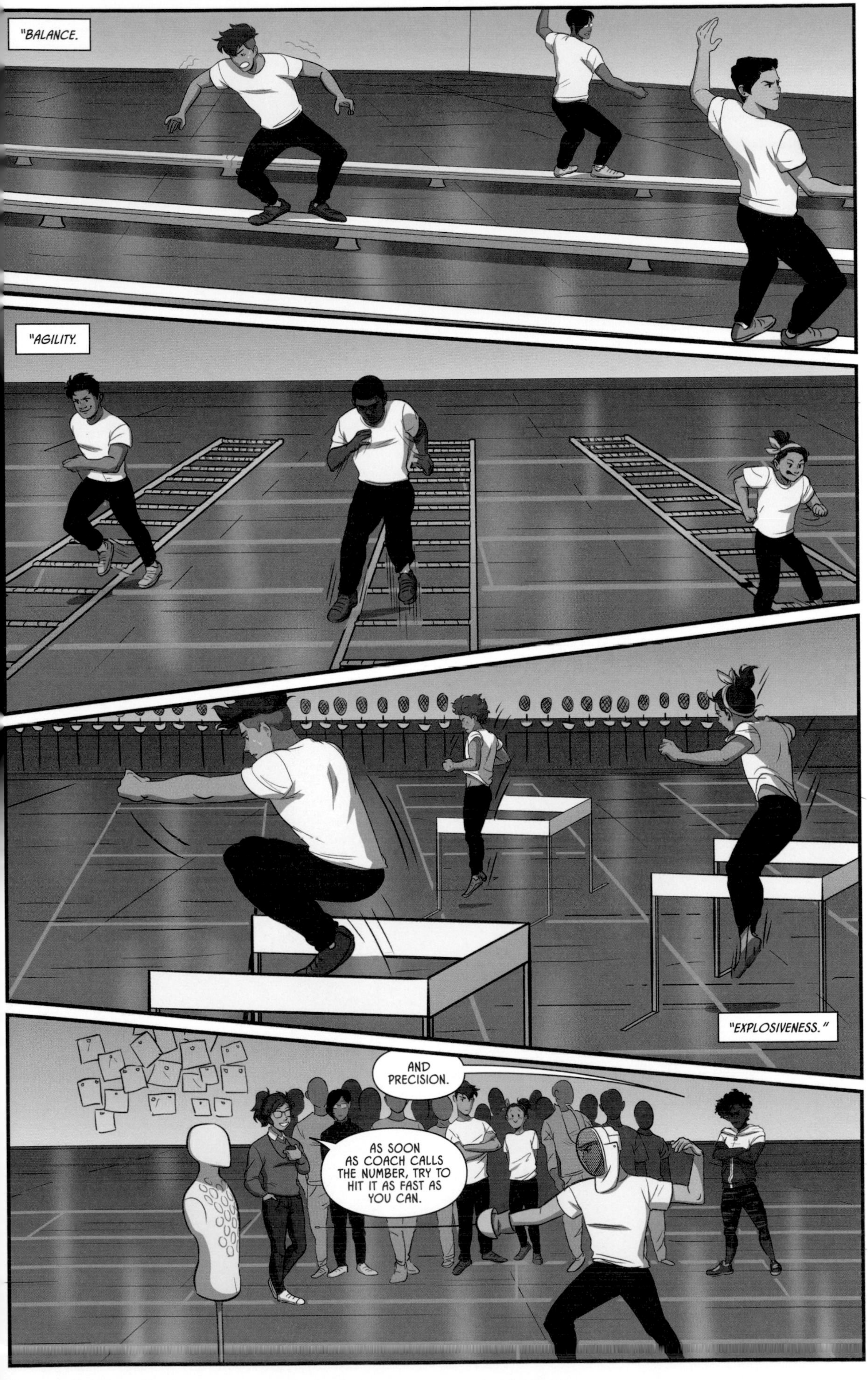
"BALANCE.
"AGILITY.
"EXPLOSIVENESS."
AND PRECISION.
AS SOON AS COACH CALLS THE NUMBER, TRY TO HIT IT AS FAST AS YOU CAN.

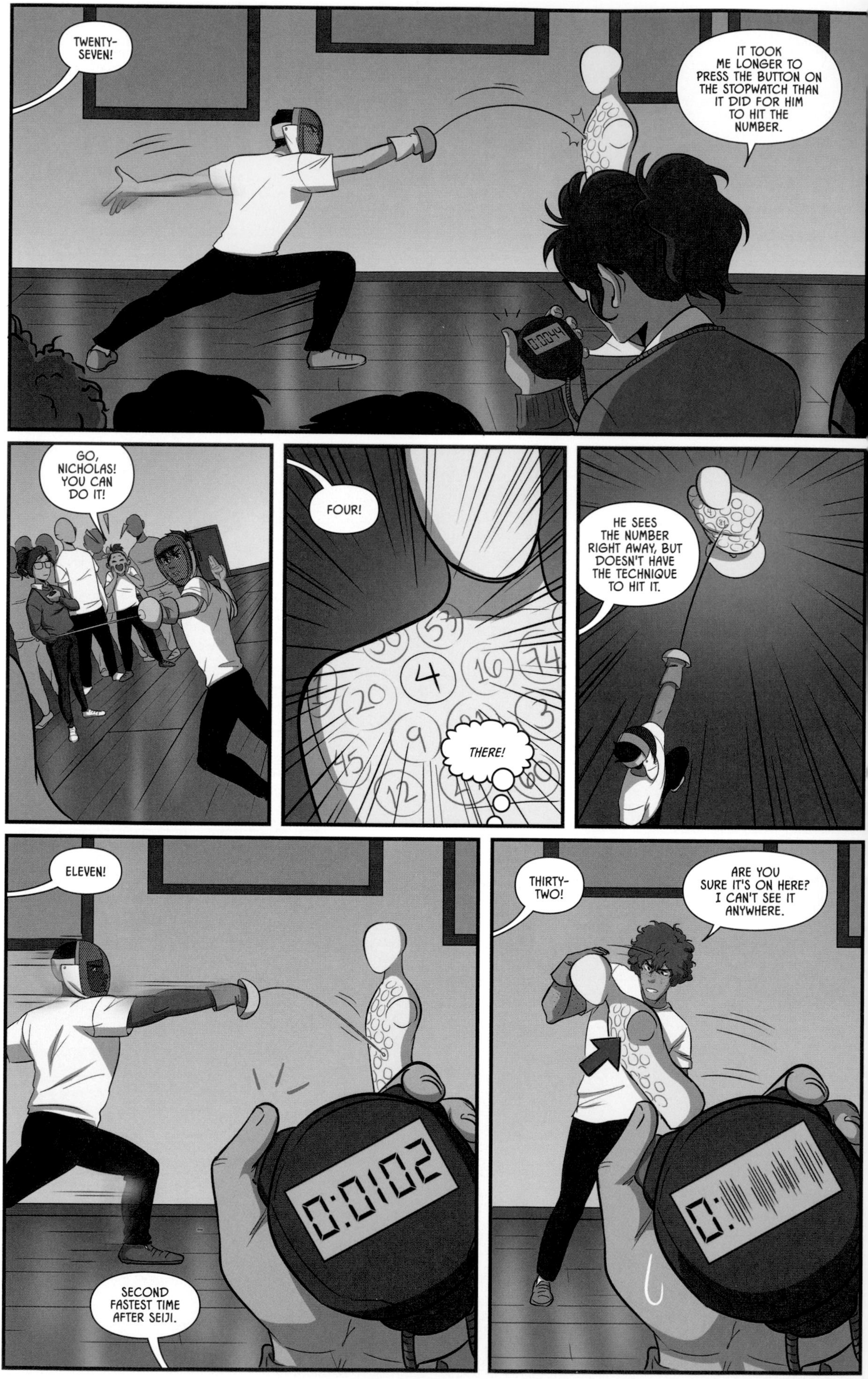
TWENTY-SEVEN!
IT TOOK ME LONGER TO PRESS THE BUTTON ON THE STOPWATCH THAN IT DID FOR HIM TO HIT THE NUMBER.
0:0044
GO, NICHOLAS! YOU CAN DO IT!
FOUR!
THERE!
HE SEES THE NUMBER RIGHT AWAY, BUT DOESN'T HAVE THE TECHNIQUE TO HIT IT.
ELEVEN!
0:0102
SECOND FASTEST TIME AFTER SEIJI.
THIRTY-TWO!
ARE YOU SURE IT'S ON HERE? I CAN'T SEE IT ANYWHERE.

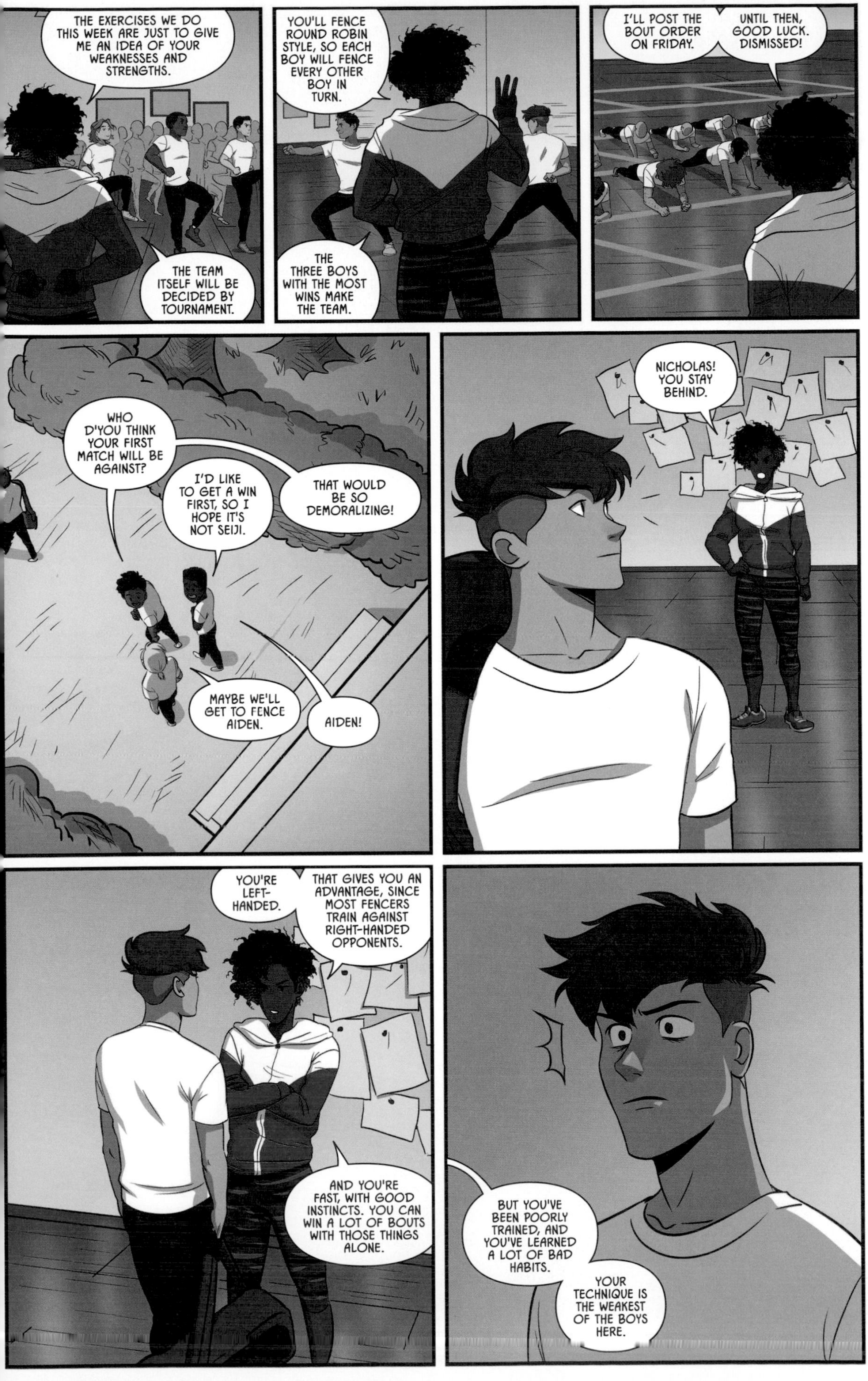
THE EXERCISES WE DO THIS WEEK ARE JUST TO GIVE ME AN IDEA OF YOUR WEAKNESSES AND STRENGTHS.
THE TEAM ITSELF WILL BE DECIDED BY TOURNAMENT.
YOU'LL FENCE ROUND ROBIN STYLE, SO EACH BOY WILL FENCE EVERY OTHER BOY IN TURN.
THE THREE BOYS WITH THE MOST WINS MAKE THE TEAM.
I'LL POST THE BOUT ORDER ON FRIDAY.
UNTIL THEN, GOOD LUCK. DISMISSED!
WHO D'YOU THINK YOUR FIRST MATCH WILL BE AGAINST?
I'D LIKE TO GET A WIN FIRST, SO I HOPE IT'S NOT SEIJI.
THAT WOULD BE SO DEMORALIZING!
MAYBE WE'LL GET TO FENCE AIDEN.
AIDEN!
NICHOLAS! YOU STAY BEHIND.
YOU'RE LEFT-HANDED.
THAT GIVES YOU AN ADVANTAGE, SINCE MOST FENCERS TRAIN AGAINST RIGHT-HANDED OPPONENTS.
AND YOU'RE FAST, WITH GOOD INSTINCTS. YOU CAN WIN A LOT OF BOUTS WITH THOSE THINGS ALONE.
BUT YOU'VE BEEN POORLY TRAINED, AND YOU'VE LEARNED A LOT OF BAD HABITS.
YOUR TECHNIQUE IS THE WEAKEST OF THE BOYS HERE.

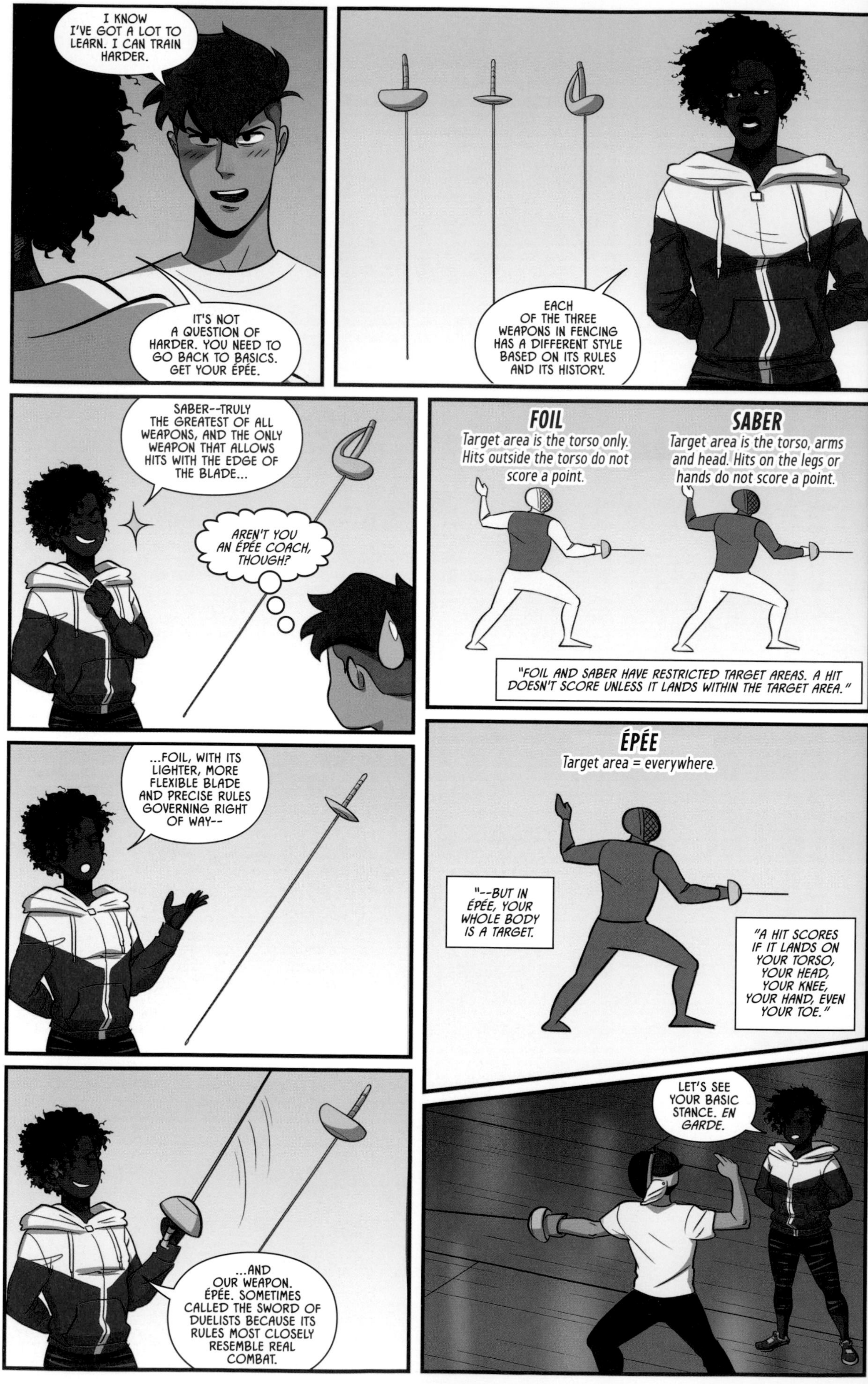
I KNOW I'VE GOT A LOT TO LEARN. I CAN TRAIN HARDER.
IT'S NOT A QUESTION OF HARDER. YOU NEED TO GO BACK TO BASICS. GET YOUR ÉPÉE.
EACH OF THE THREE WEAPONS IN FENCING HAS A DIFFERENT STYLE BASED ON ITS RULES AND ITS HISTORY.
SABER--TRULY THE GREATEST OF ALL WEAPONS, AND THE ONLY WEAPON THAT ALLOWS HITS WITH THE EDGE OF THE BLADE...
AREN'T YOU AN ÉPÉE COACH, THOUGH?
FOIL
Target area is the torso only. Hits outside the torso do not score a point.
SABER
Target area is the torso, arms and head. Hits on the legs or hands do not score a point.
"FOIL AND SABER HAVE RESTRICTED TARGET AREAS. A HIT DOESN'T SCORE UNLESS IT LANDS WITHIN THE TARGET AREA."
...FOIL, WITH ITS LIGHTER, MORE FLEXIBLE BLADE AND PRECISE RULES GOVERNING RIGHT OF WAY--
ÉPÉE
Target area = everywhere.
"--BUT IN ÉPÉE, YOUR WHOLE BODY IS A TARGET.
"A HIT SCORES IF IT LANDS ON YOUR TORSO, YOUR HEAD, YOUR KNEE, YOUR HAND, EVEN YOUR TOE."
...AND OUR WEAPON. ÉPÉE. SOMETIMES CALLED THE SWORD OF DUELISTS BECAUSE ITS RULES MOST CLOSELY RESEMBLE REAL COMBAT.
LET'S SEE YOUR BASIC STANCE. EN GARDE.

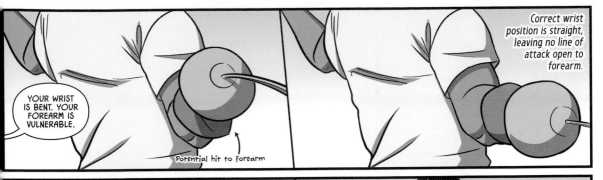

Correct wrist position is straight, leaving no line of attack open to forearm.

YOUR WRIST IS BENT. YOUR FOREARM IS VULNERABLE.

Potential hit to forearm

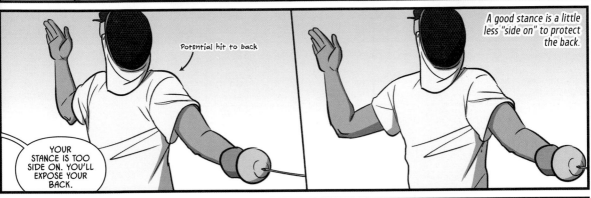

Potential hit to back

A good stance is a little less "side on" to protect the back.

YOUR STANCE IS TOO SIDE ON. YOU'LL EXPOSE YOUR BACK.

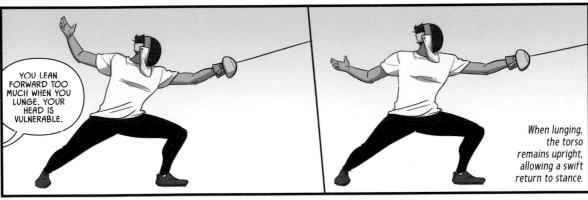

YOU LEAN FORWARD TOO MUCH WHEN YOU LUNGE. YOUR HEAD IS VULNERABLE.

When lunging, the torso remains upright, allowing a swift return to stance.

BUT YOUR WORST HABIT IS THAT YOU STEP BEFORE YOU EXTEND YOUR SWORD ARM TO ATTACK.

THAT'S HOW SEIJI SCORED ALL THOSE POINTS ON YOU AT REGIONALS, DESPITE YOUR AGGRESSIVE INSTINCTS AND NATURAL SPEED.

YES...I SAW THAT MATCH.

HE BEAT YOU UTTERLY.

HE'S HAD YEARS OF TRAINING.

SO THE QUESTION IS, CAN YOU CATCH UP?

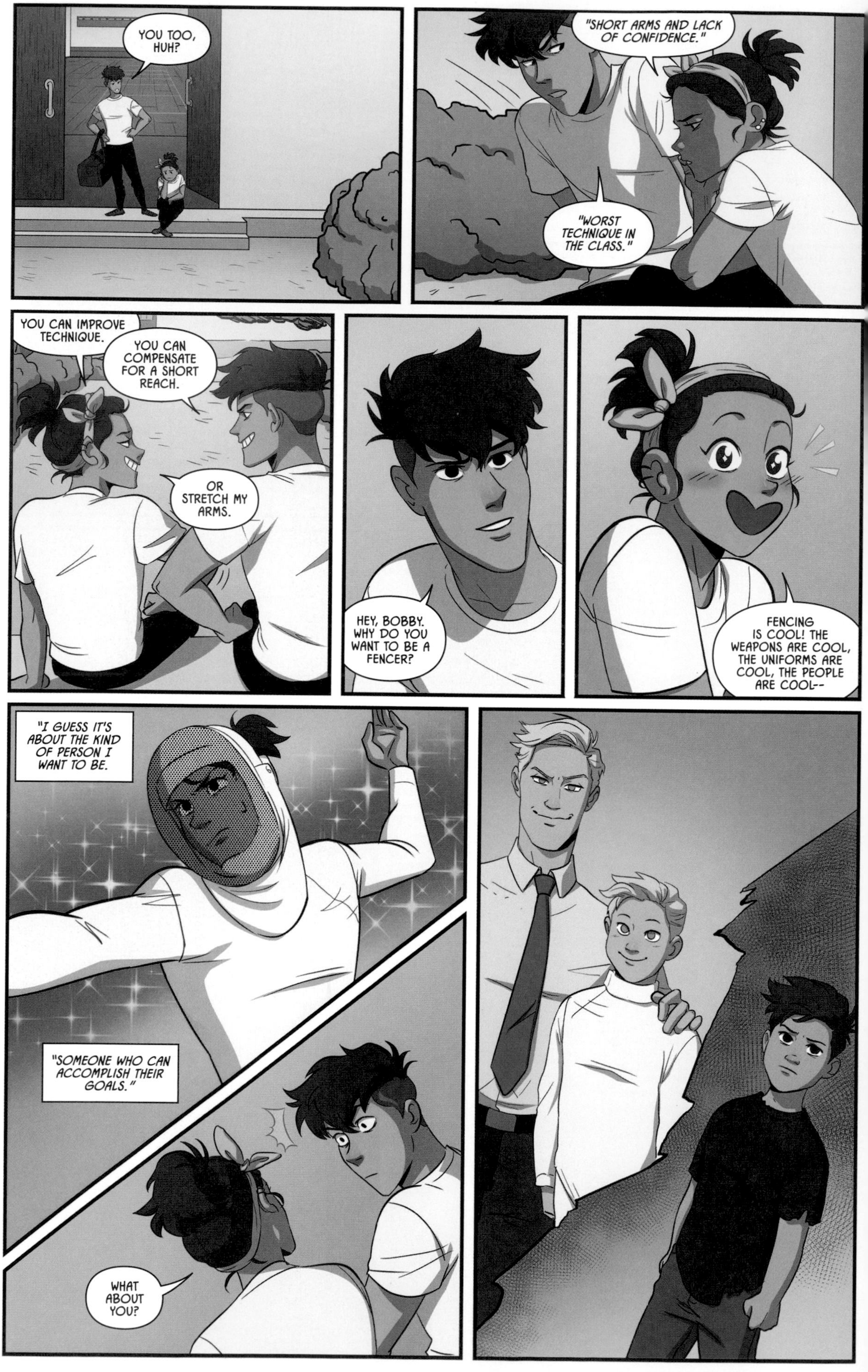
YOU TOO, HUH?
"SHORT ARMS AND LACK OF CONFIDENCE."
"WORST TECHNIQUE IN THE CLASS."
YOU CAN IMPROVE TECHNIQUE.
YOU CAN COMPENSATE FOR A SHORT REACH.
OR STRETCH MY ARMS.
HEY, BOBBY. WHY DO YOU WANT TO BE A FENCER?
FENCING IS COOL! THE WEAPONS ARE COOL, THE UNIFORMS ARE COOL, THE PEOPLE ARE COOL--
"I GUESS IT'S ABOUT THE KIND OF PERSON I WANT TO BE.
"SOMEONE WHO CAN ACCOMPLISH THEIR GOALS."
WHAT ABOUT YOU?

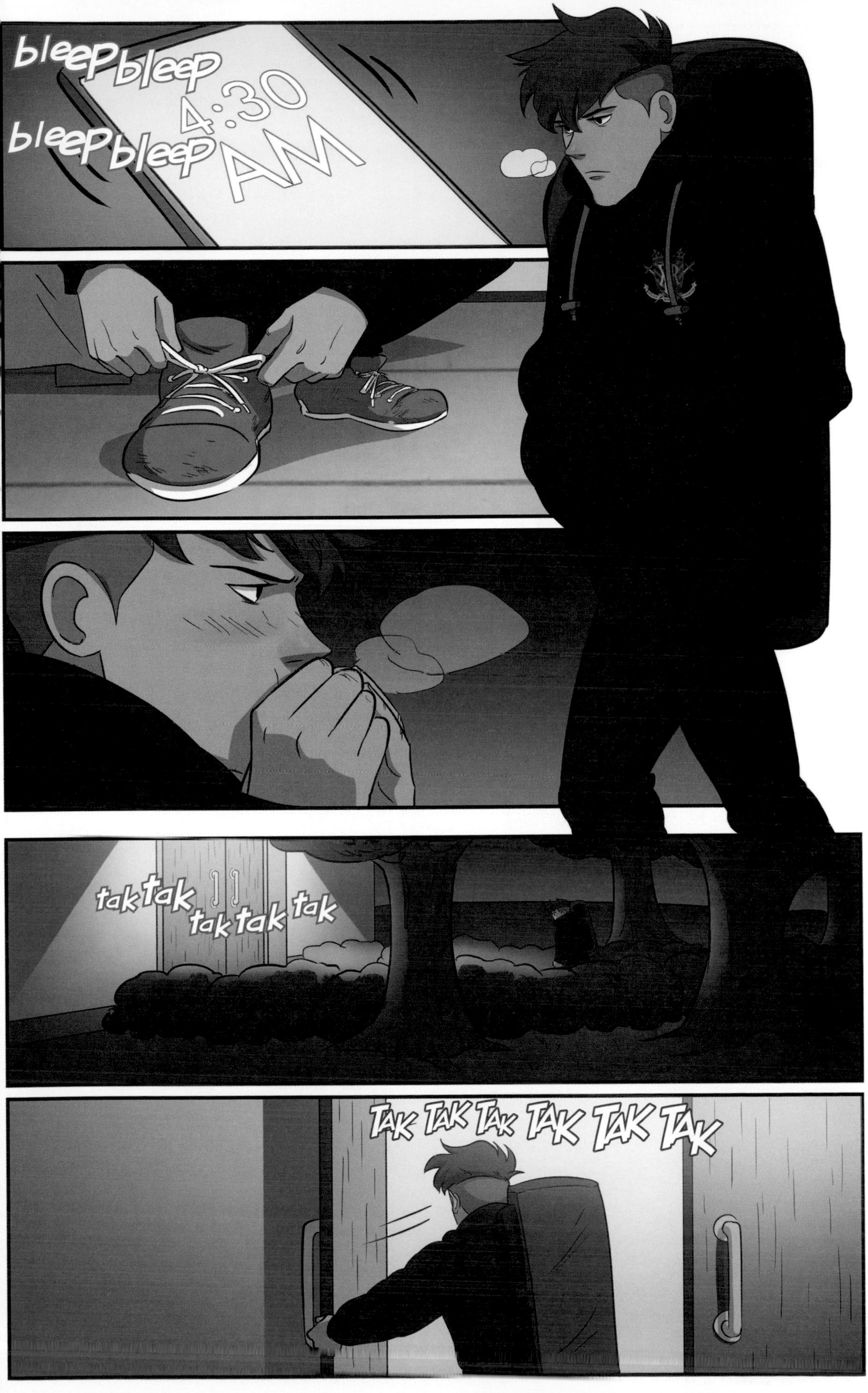
bleep bleep 4:30
bleep bleep AM
tak tak tak tak tak
TAK TAK TAK TAK TAK TAK

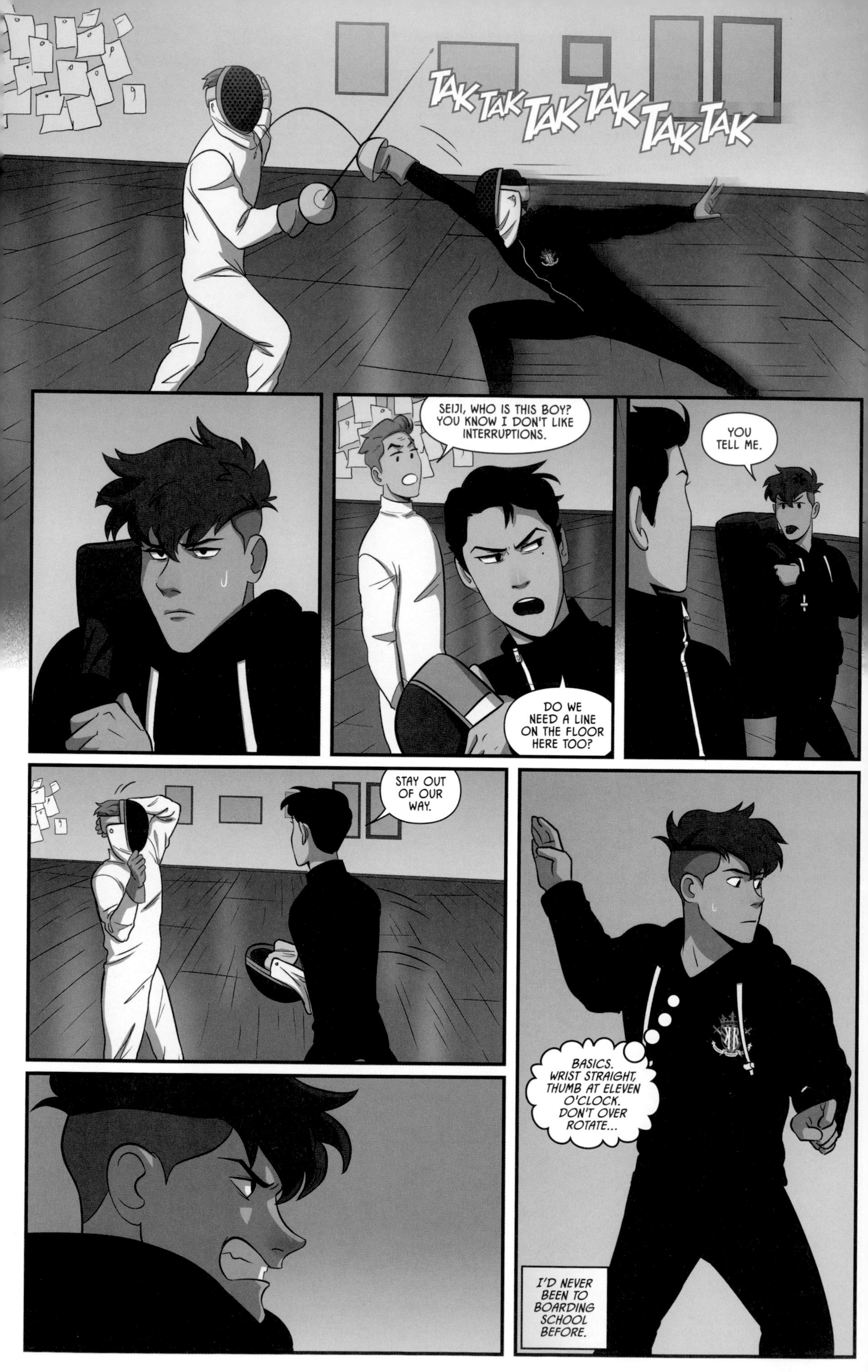
TAK TAK TAK TAK TAK TAK
SEIJI, WHO IS THIS BOY? YOU KNOW I DON'T LIKE INTERRUPTIONS.
DO WE NEED A LINE ON THE FLOOR HERE TOO?
YOU TELL ME.
STAY OUT OF OUR WAY.
BASICS. WRIST STRAIGHT, THUMB AT ELEVEN O'CLOCK. DON'T OVER ROTATE...
I'D NEVER BEEN TO BOARDING SCHOOL BEFORE.

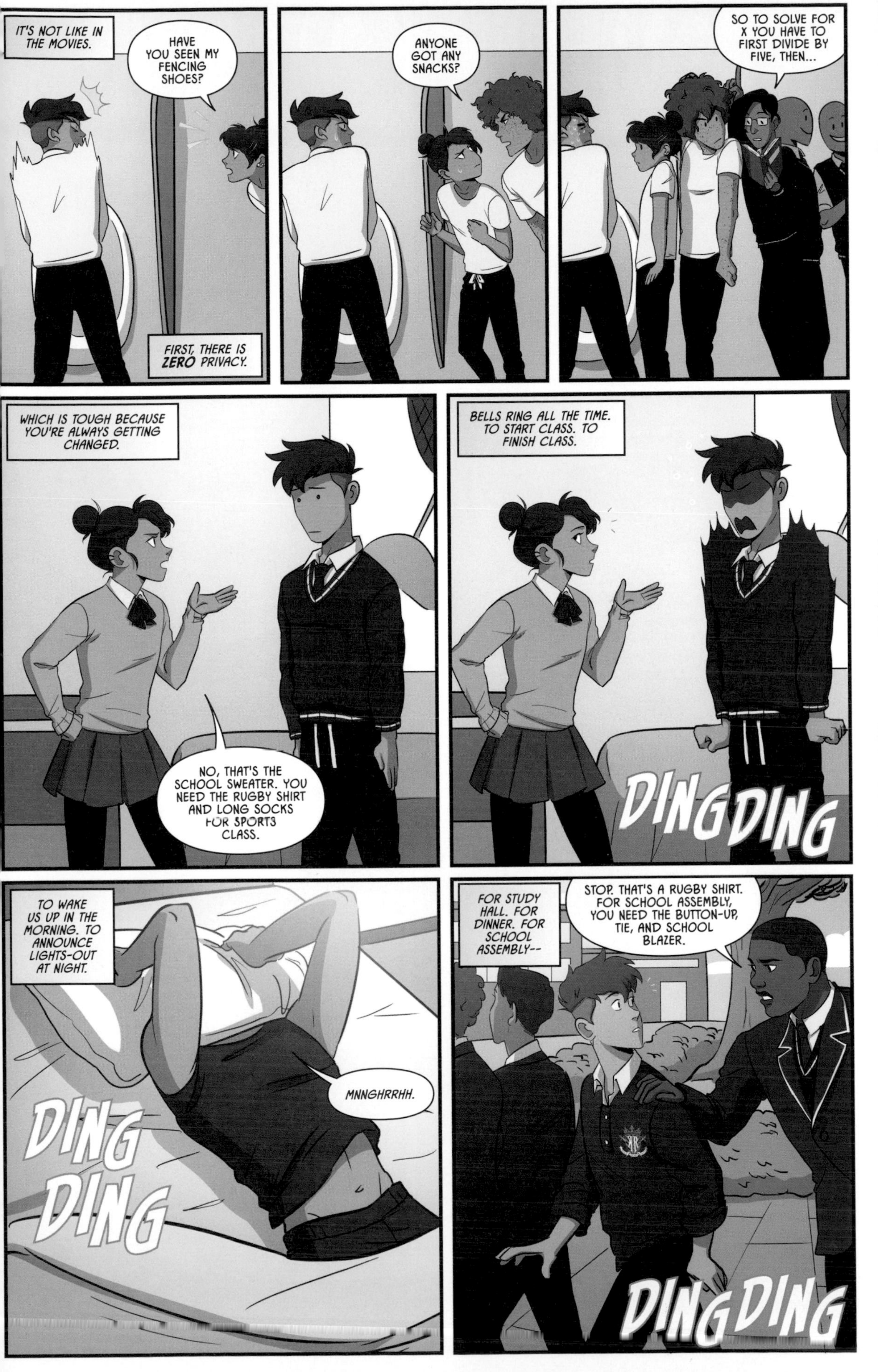
IT'S NOT LIKE IN THE MOVIES.
HAVE YOU SEEN MY FENCING SHOES?
FIRST, THERE IS ZERO PRIVACY.
ANYONE GOT ANY SNACKS?
SO TO SOLVE FOR X YOU HAVE TO FIRST DIVIDE BY FIVE, THEN...
WHICH IS TOUGH BECAUSE YOU'RE ALWAYS GETTING CHANGED.
NO, THAT'S THE SCHOOL SWEATER. YOU NEED THE RUGBY SHIRT AND LONG SOCKS FOR SPORTS CLASS.
BELLS RING ALL THE TIME. TO START CLASS. TO FINISH CLASS.
DING DING
TO WAKE US UP IN THE MORNING. TO ANNOUNCE LIGHTS-OUT AT NIGHT.
DING DING
MNNGHRRHH.
FOR STUDY HALL. FOR DINNER. FOR SCHOOL ASSEMBLY--
STOP. THAT'S A RUGBY SHIRT. FOR SCHOOL ASSEMBLY, YOU NEED THE BUTTON-UP, TIE, AND SCHOOL BLAZER.
DING DING

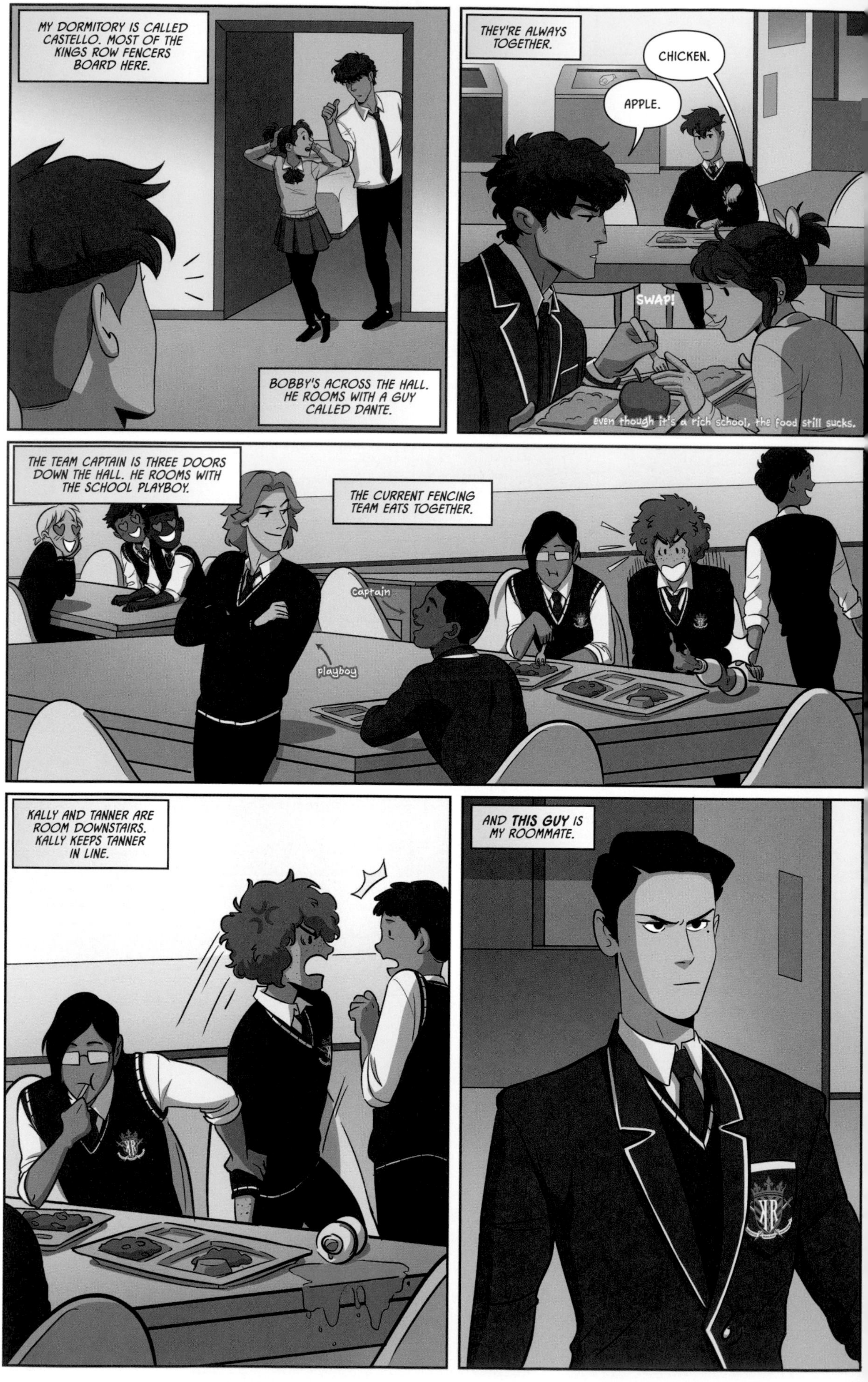
MY DORMITORY IS CALLED CASTELLO. MOST OF THE KINGS ROW FENCERS BOARD HERE.
BOBBY'S ACROSS THE HALL. HE ROOMS WITH A GUY CALLED DANTE.
THEY'RE ALWAYS TOGETHER.
CHICKEN.
APPLE.
SWAP!
even though it's a rich school, the food still sucks.
THE TEAM CAPTAIN IS THREE DOORS DOWN THE HALL. HE ROOMS WITH THE SCHOOL PLAYBOY.
THE CURRENT FENCING TEAM EATS TOGETHER.
captain
playboy
KALLY AND TANNER ARE ROOM DOWNSTAIRS. KALLY KEEPS TANNER IN LINE.
AND THIS GUY IS MY ROOMMATE.

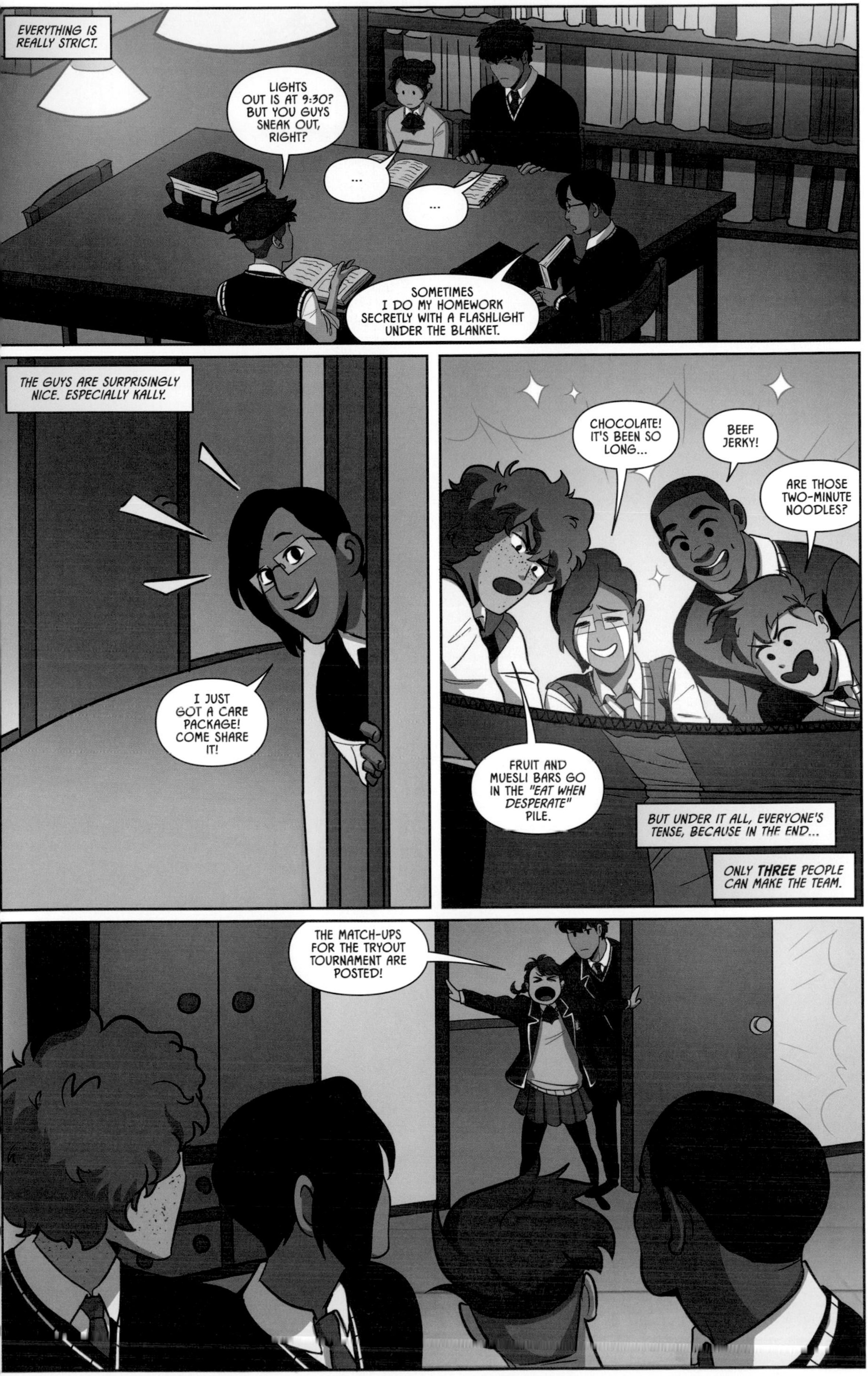
EVERYTHING IS REALLY STRICT.
LIGHTS OUT IS AT 9:30? BUT YOU GUYS SNEAK OUT, RIGHT?
...
...
SOMETIMES I DO MY HOMEWORK SECRETLY WITH A FLASHLIGHT UNDER THE BLANKET.
THE GUYS ARE SURPRISINGLY NICE. ESPECIALLY KALLY.
I JUST GOT A CARE PACKAGE! COME SHARE IT!
CHOCOLATE! IT'S BEEN SO LONG...
BEEF JERKY!
ARE THOSE TWO-MINUTE NOODLES?
FRUIT AND MUESLI BARS GO IN THE "EAT WHEN DESPERATE" PILE.
BUT UNDER IT ALL, EVERYONE'S TENSE, BECAUSE IN THE END...
ONLY THREE PEOPLE CAN MAKE THE TEAM.
THE MATCH-UPS FOR THE TRYOUT TOURNAMENT ARE POSTED!

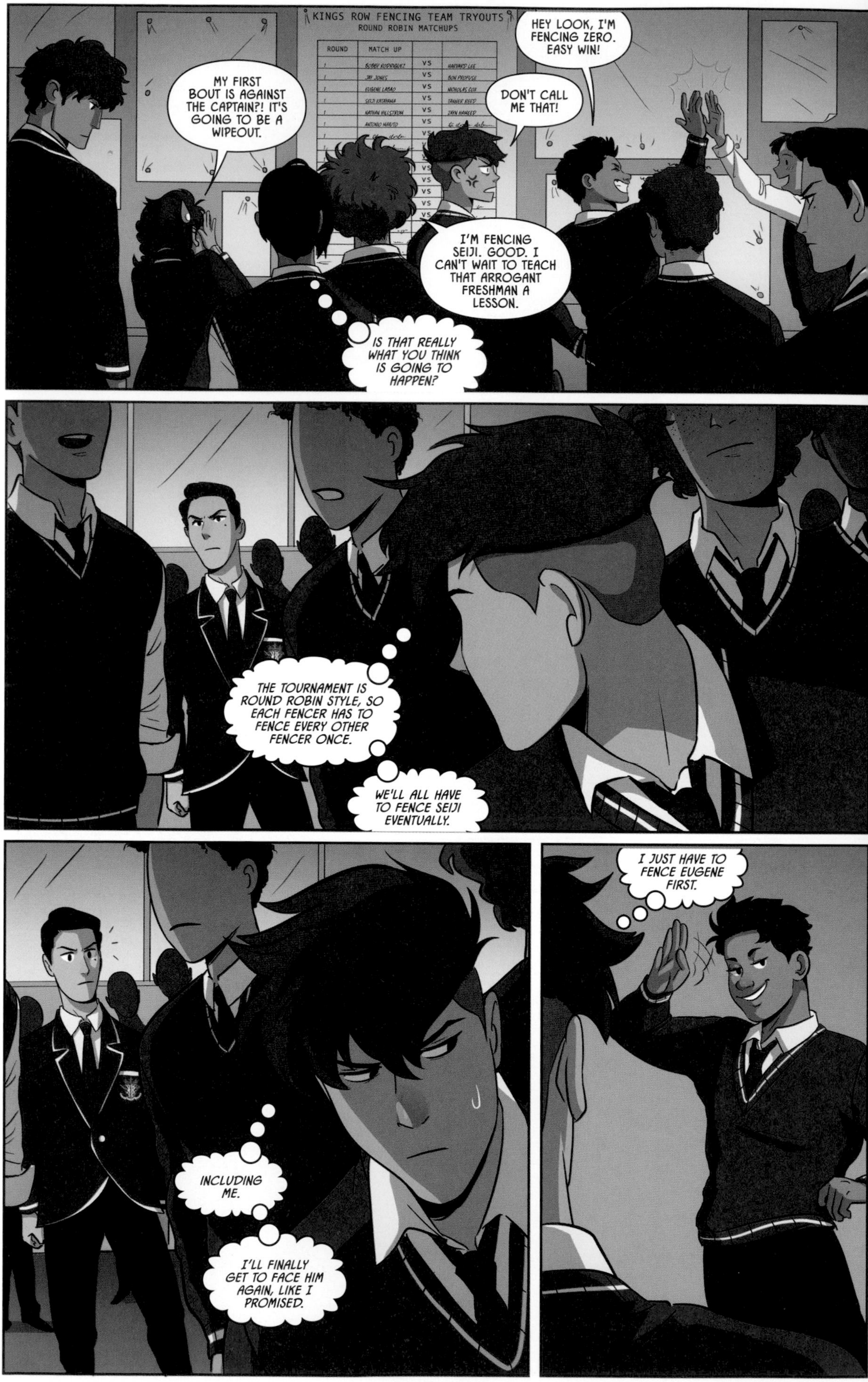
KINGS ROW FENCING TEAM TRYOUTS
ROUND ROBIN MATCHUPS
ROUND | MATCH UP
1 BOBBY RODRIGUEZ VS HARVARD LEE
1 JAY JONES VS BON PROFUSE
1 EUGENE LABAO VS NICHOLAS COX
1 SEIJI KATAYAMA VS TANNER REED
1 NATHAN HILLSTROM VS ZAYN HAMEED
1 ANTONIO MARUTO VS
MY FIRST BOUT IS AGAINST THE CAPTAIN?! IT'S GOING TO BE A WIPEOUT.
HEY LOOK, I'M FENCING ZERO. EASY WIN!
DON'T CALL ME THAT!
I'M FENCING SEIJI. GOOD. I CAN'T WAIT TO TEACH THAT ARROGANT FRESHMAN A LESSON.
IS THAT REALLY WHAT YOU THINK IS GOING TO HAPPEN?
THE TOURNAMENT IS ROUND ROBIN STYLE, SO EACH FENCER HAS TO FENCE EVERY OTHER FENCER ONCE.
WE'LL ALL HAVE TO FENCE SEIJI EVENTUALLY.
INCLUDING ME.
I'LL FINALLY GET TO FACE HIM AGAIN, LIKE I PROMISED.
I JUST HAVE TO FENCE EUGENE FIRST.

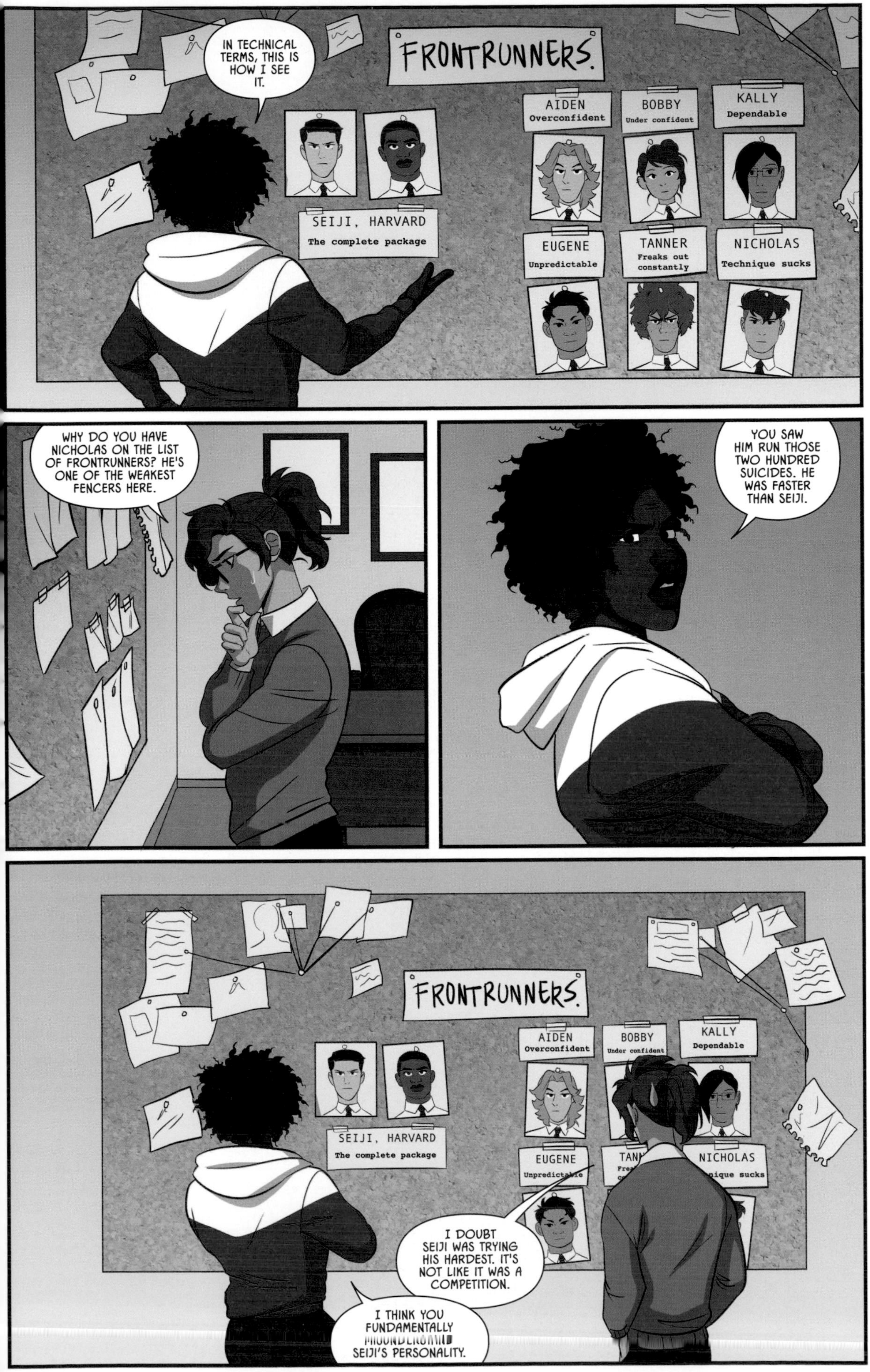

IN TECHNICAL TERMS, THIS IS HOW I SEE IT.
FRONTRUNNERS.
SEIJI, HARVARD
The complete package
AIDEN
Overconfident
BOBBY
Under confident
KALLY
Dependable
EUGENE
Unpredictable
TANNER
Freaks out constantly
NICHOLAS
Technique sucks
WHY DO YOU HAVE NICHOLAS ON THE LIST OF FRONTRUNNERS? HE'S ONE OF THE WEAKEST FENCERS HERE.
YOU SAW HIM RUN THOSE TWO HUNDRED SUICIDES. HE WAS FASTER THAN SEIJI.
I DOUBT SEIJI WAS TRYING HIS HARDEST. IT'S NOT LIKE IT WAS A COMPETITION.
I THINK YOU FUNDAMENTALLY
SEIJI'S PERSONALITY.

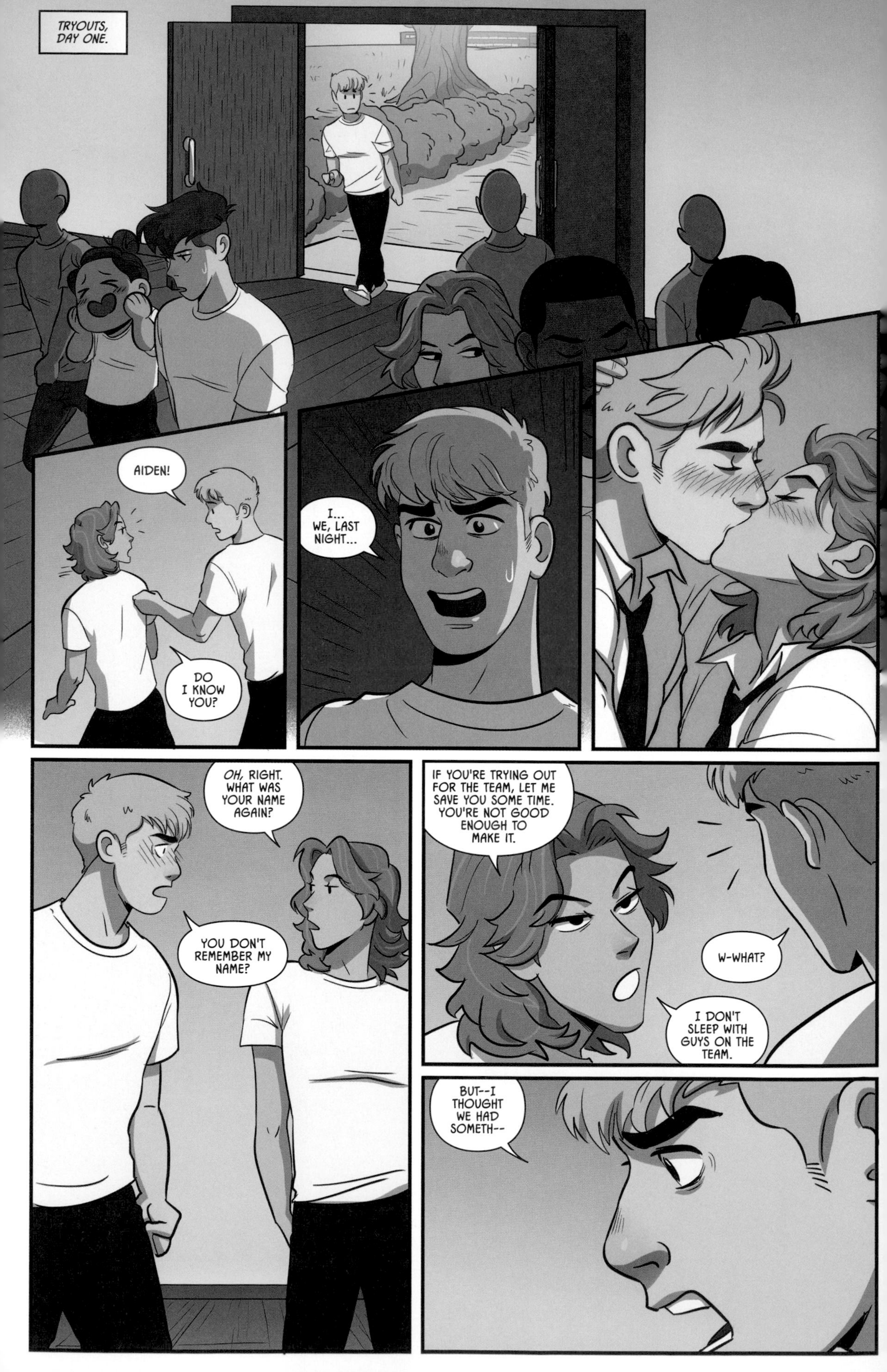
TRYOUTS, DAY ONE.
AIDEN!
DO I KNOW YOU?
I... WE, LAST NIGHT...
OH, RIGHT. WHAT WAS YOUR NAME AGAIN?
YOU DON'T REMEMBER MY NAME?
IF YOU'RE TRYING OUT FOR THE TEAM, LET ME SAVE YOU SOME TIME. YOU'RE NOT GOOD ENOUGH TO MAKE IT.
W-WHAT?
I DON'T SLEEP WITH GUYS ON THE TEAM.
BUT--I THOUGHT WE HAD SOMETH--

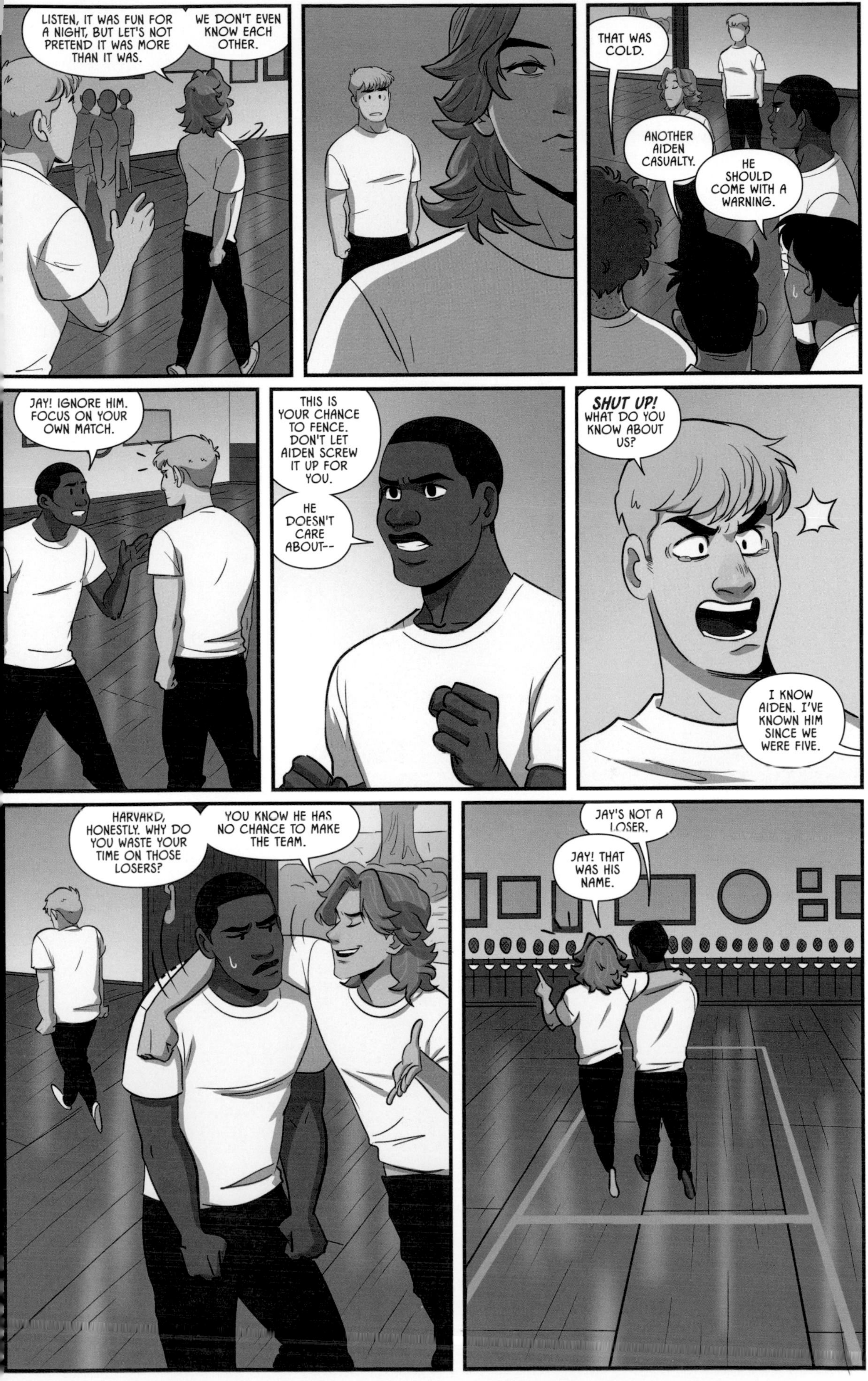
LISTEN, IT WAS FUN FOR A NIGHT, BUT LET'S NOT PRETEND IT WAS MORE THAN IT WAS.
WE DON'T EVEN KNOW EACH OTHER.
THAT WAS COLD.
ANOTHER AIDEN CASUALTY.
HE SHOULD COME WITH A WARNING.
JAY! IGNORE HIM. FOCUS ON YOUR OWN MATCH.
THIS IS YOUR CHANCE TO FENCE. DON'T LET AIDEN SCREW IT UP FOR YOU.
HE DOESN'T CARE ABOUT--
SHUT UP! WHAT DO YOU KNOW ABOUT US?
I KNOW AIDEN. I'VE KNOWN HIM SINCE WE WERE FIVE.
HARVARD, HONESTLY. WHY DO YOU WASTE YOUR TIME ON THOSE LOSERS?
YOU KNOW HE HAS NO CHANCE TO MAKE THE TEAM.
JAY'S NOT A LOSER.
JAY! THAT WAS HIS NAME.

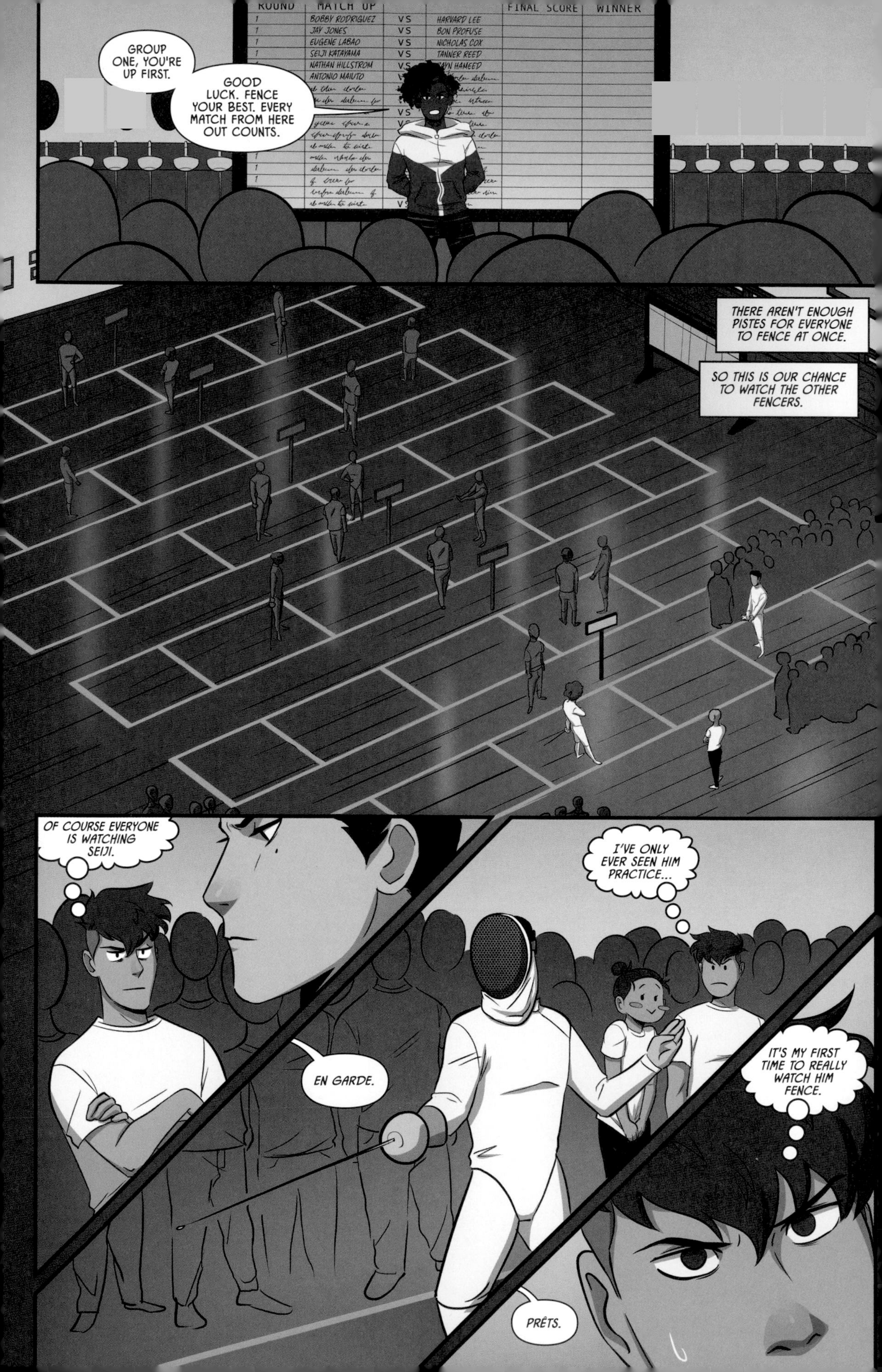

ROUND
MATCH UP
FINAL SCORE
WINNER
1 BOBBY RODRIGUEZ VS HARVARD LEE
1 JAY JONES VS BON PROFUSE
1 EUGENE LABAO VS NICHOLAS COX
1 SEIJI KATAYAMA VS TANNER REED
1 NATHAN HILLSTROM
ANTONIO MAIUTO
GROUP ONE, YOU'RE UP FIRST.
GOOD LUCK. FENCE YOUR BEST. EVERY MATCH FROM HERE OUT COUNTS.
THERE AREN'T ENOUGH PISTES FOR EVERYONE TO FENCE AT ONCE.
SO THIS IS OUR CHANCE TO WATCH THE OTHER FENCERS.
OF COURSE EVERYONE IS WATCHING SEIJI.
EN GARDE.
I'VE ONLY EVER SEEN HIM PRACTICE...
IT'S MY FIRST TIME TO REALLY WATCH HIM FENCE.
PRÊTS.

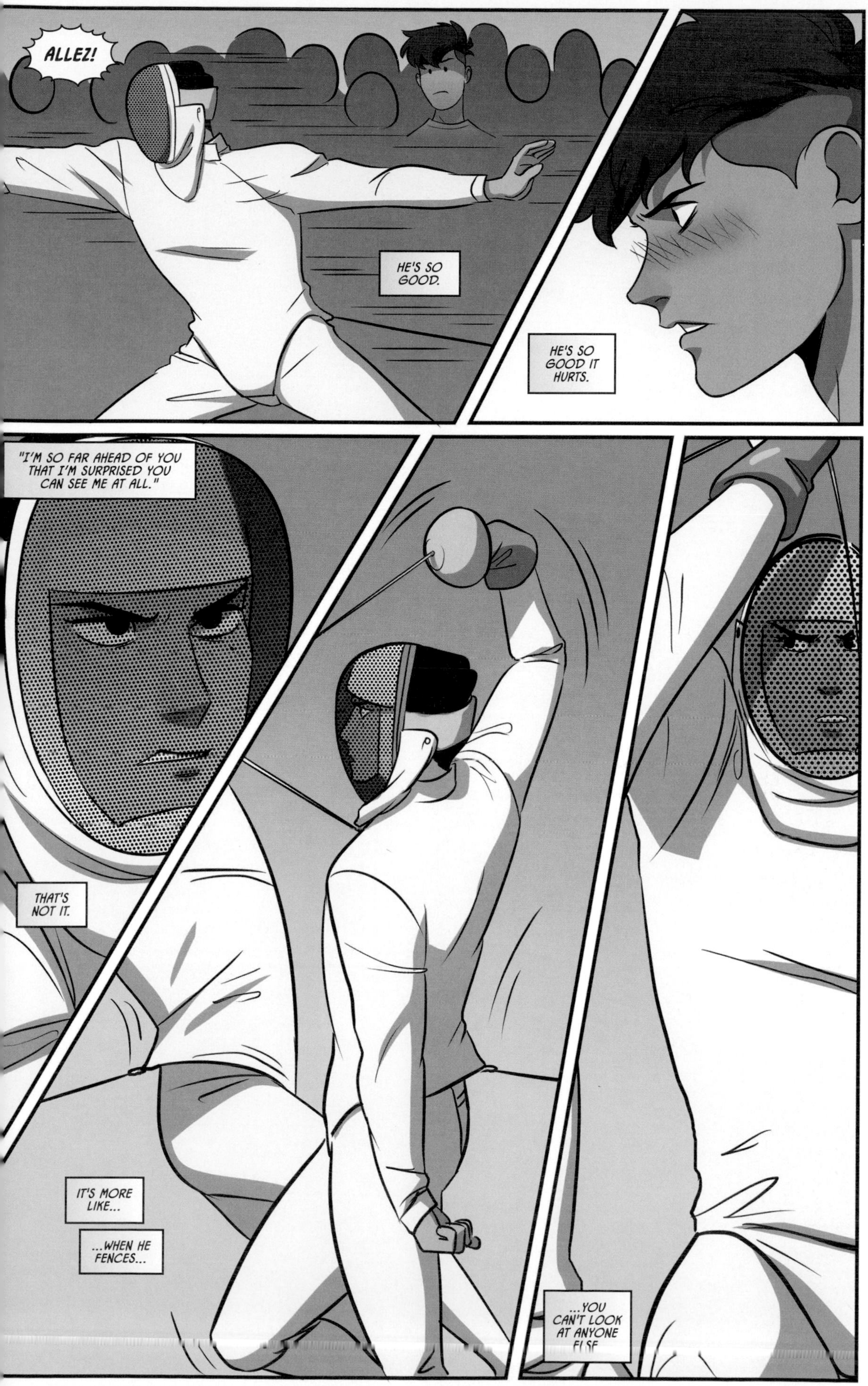
ALLEZ!
HE'S SO GOOD.
HE'S SO GOOD IT HURTS.
"I'M SO FAR AHEAD OF YOU THAT I'M SURPRISED YOU CAN SEE ME AT ALL."
THAT'S NOT IT.
IT'S MORE LIKE...
...WHEN HE FENCES...
...YOU CAN'T LOOK AT ANYONE ELSE

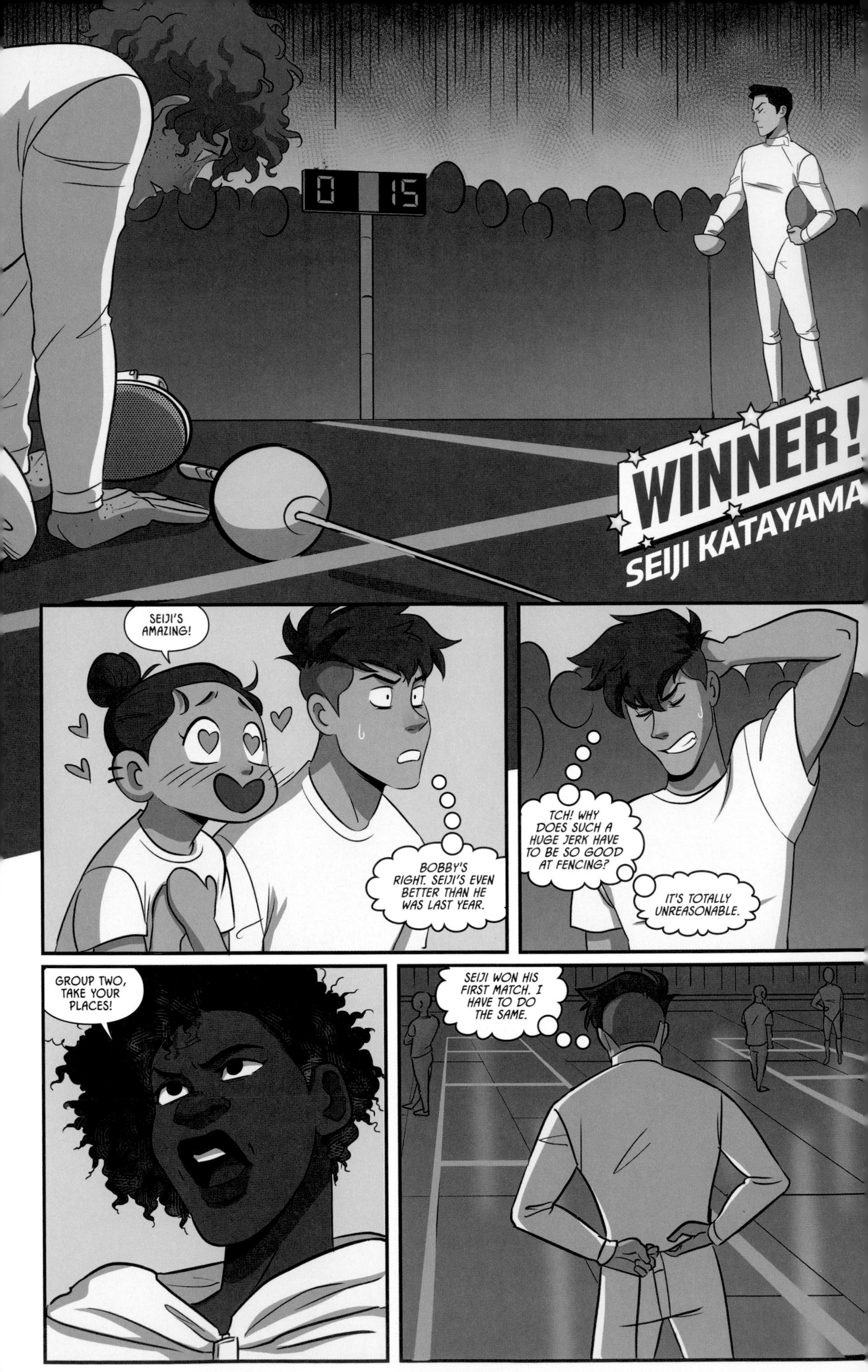
0 15
WINNER!
SEIJI KATAYAMA
SEIJI'S AMAZING!
BOBBY'S RIGHT. SEIJI'S EVEN BETTER THAN HE WAS LAST YEAR.
TCH! WHY DOES SUCH A HUGE JERK HAVE TO BE SO GOOD AT FENCING?
IT'S TOTALLY UNREASONABLE.
GROUP TWO, TAKE YOUR PLACES!
SEIJI WON HIS FIRST MATCH. I HAVE TO DO THE SAME.

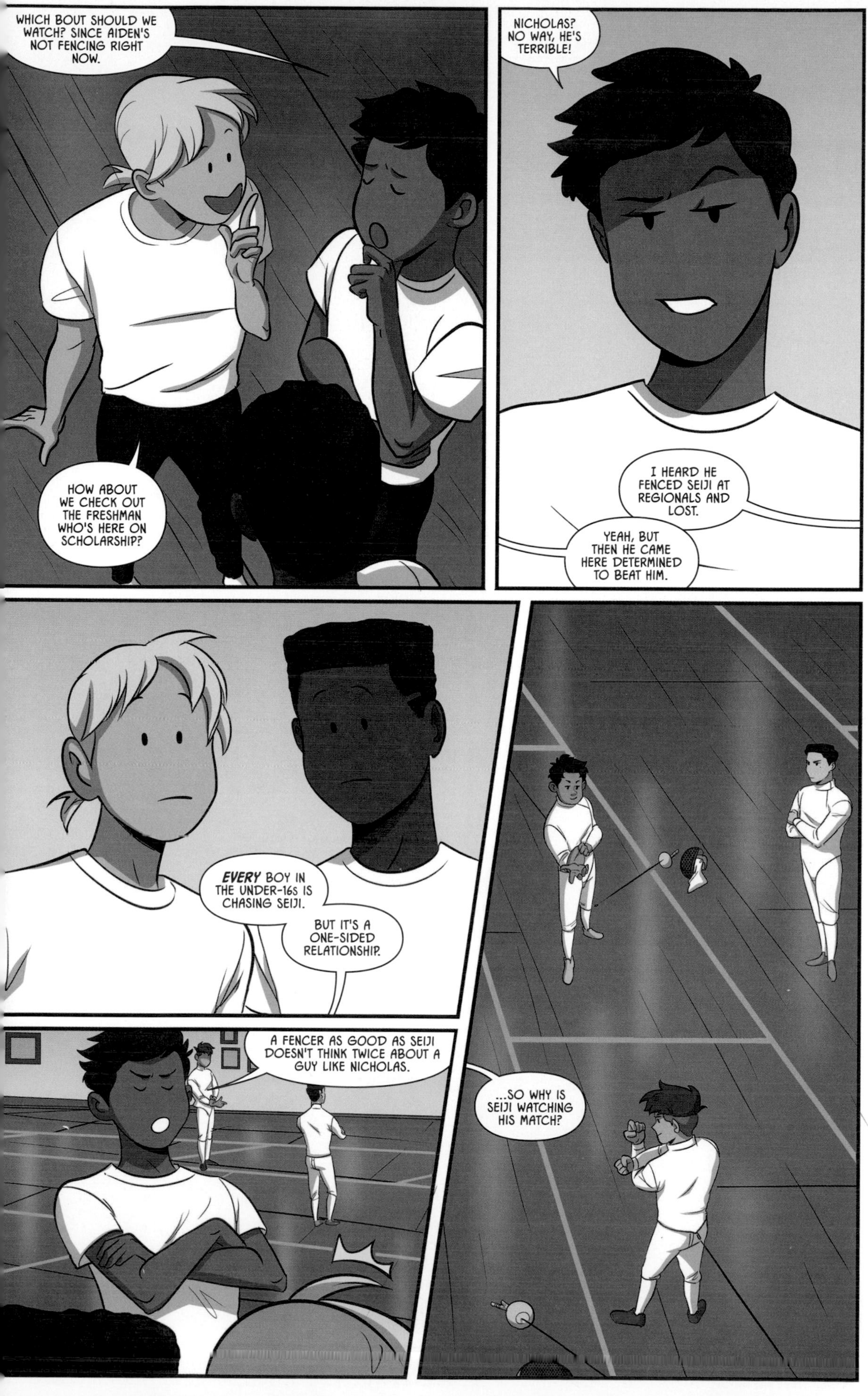
WHICH BOUT SHOULD WE WATCH? SINCE AIDEN'S NOT FENCING RIGHT NOW.
HOW ABOUT WE CHECK OUT THE FRESHMAN WHO'S HERE ON SCHOLARSHIP?
NICHOLAS? NO WAY, HE'S TERRIBLE!
I HEARD HE FENCED SEIJI AT REGIONALS AND LOST.
YEAH, BUT THEN HE CAME HERE DETERMINED TO BEAT HIM.
*EVERY* BOY IN THE UNDER-16s IS CHASING SEIJI.
BUT IT'S A ONE-SIDED RELATIONSHIP.
A FENCER AS GOOD AS SEIJI DOESN'T THINK TWICE ABOUT A GUY LIKE NICHOLAS.
...SO WHY IS SEIJI WATCHING HIS MATCH?

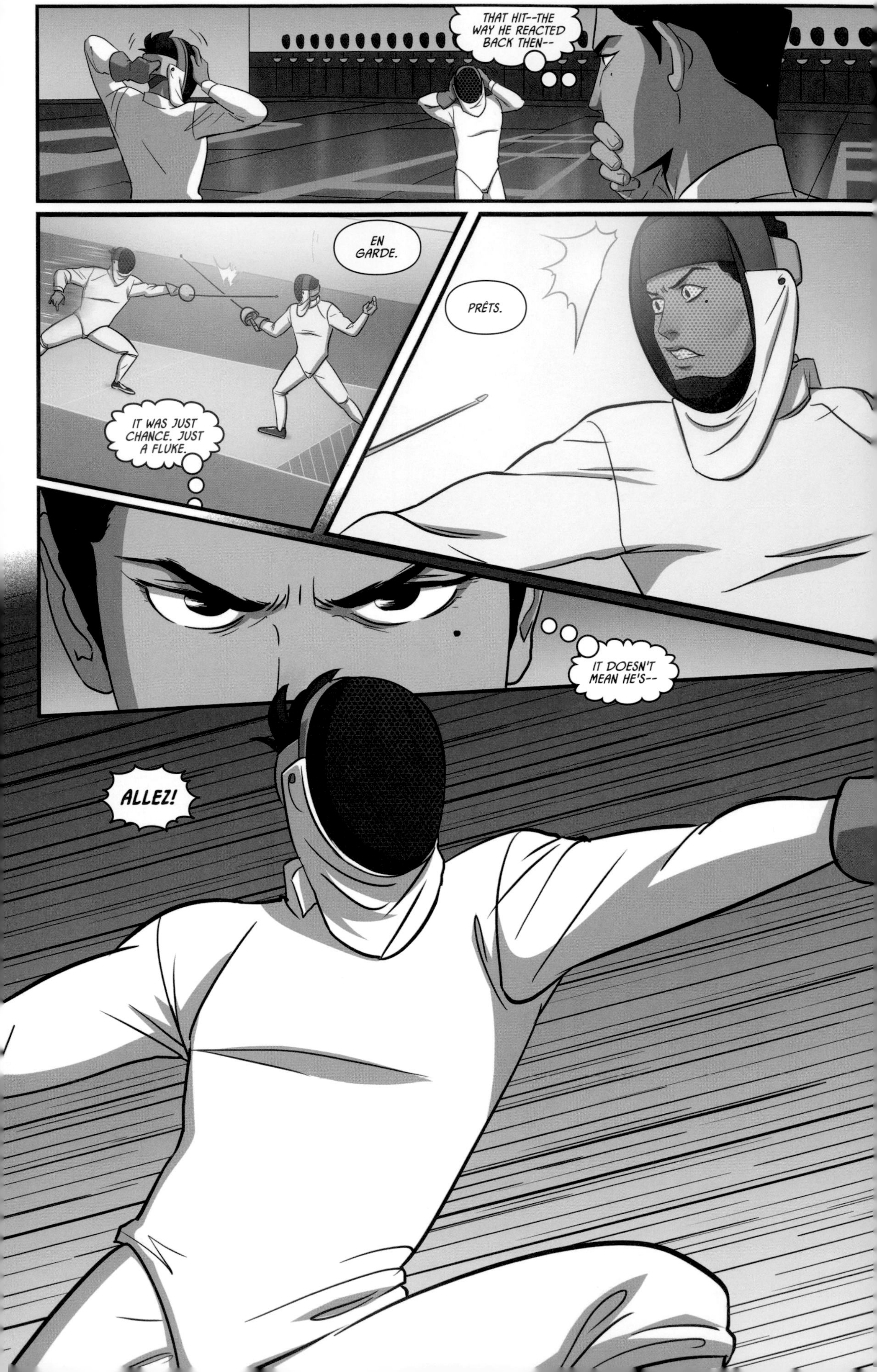
THAT HIT--THE WAY HE REACTED BACK THEN--
EN GARDE.
IT WAS JUST CHANCE. JUST A FLUKE.
PRÊTS.
IT DOESN'T MEAN HE'S--
ALLEZ!

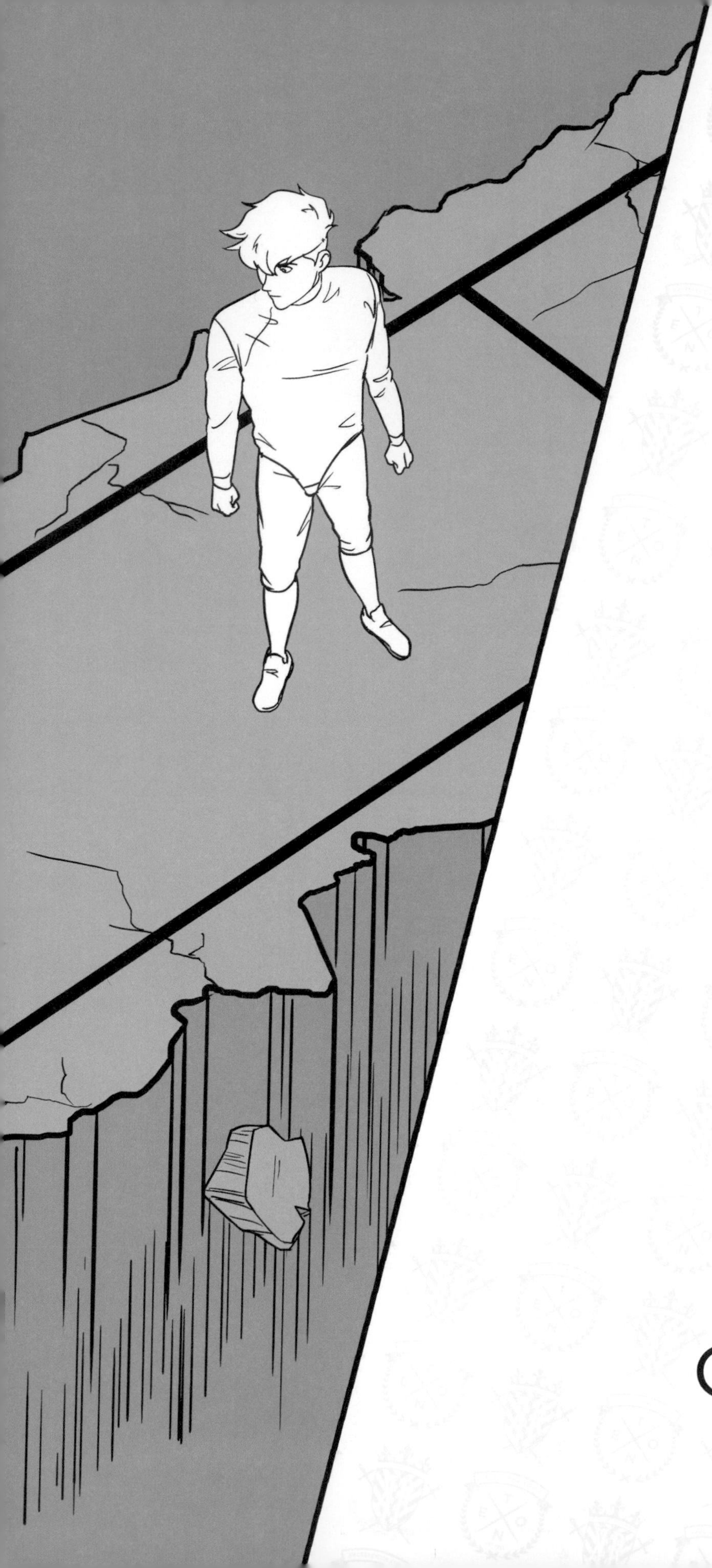

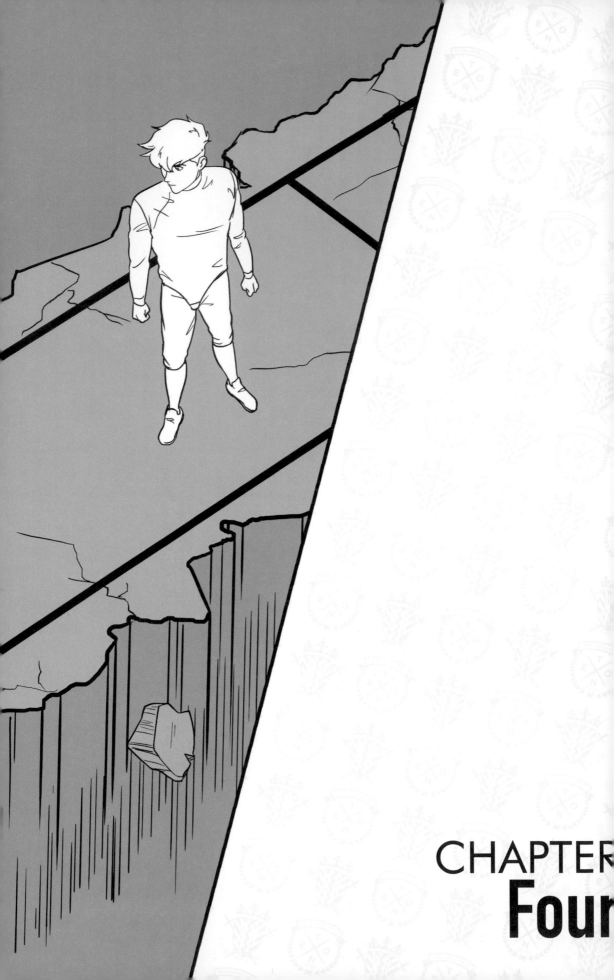

# CHAPTER
# Four

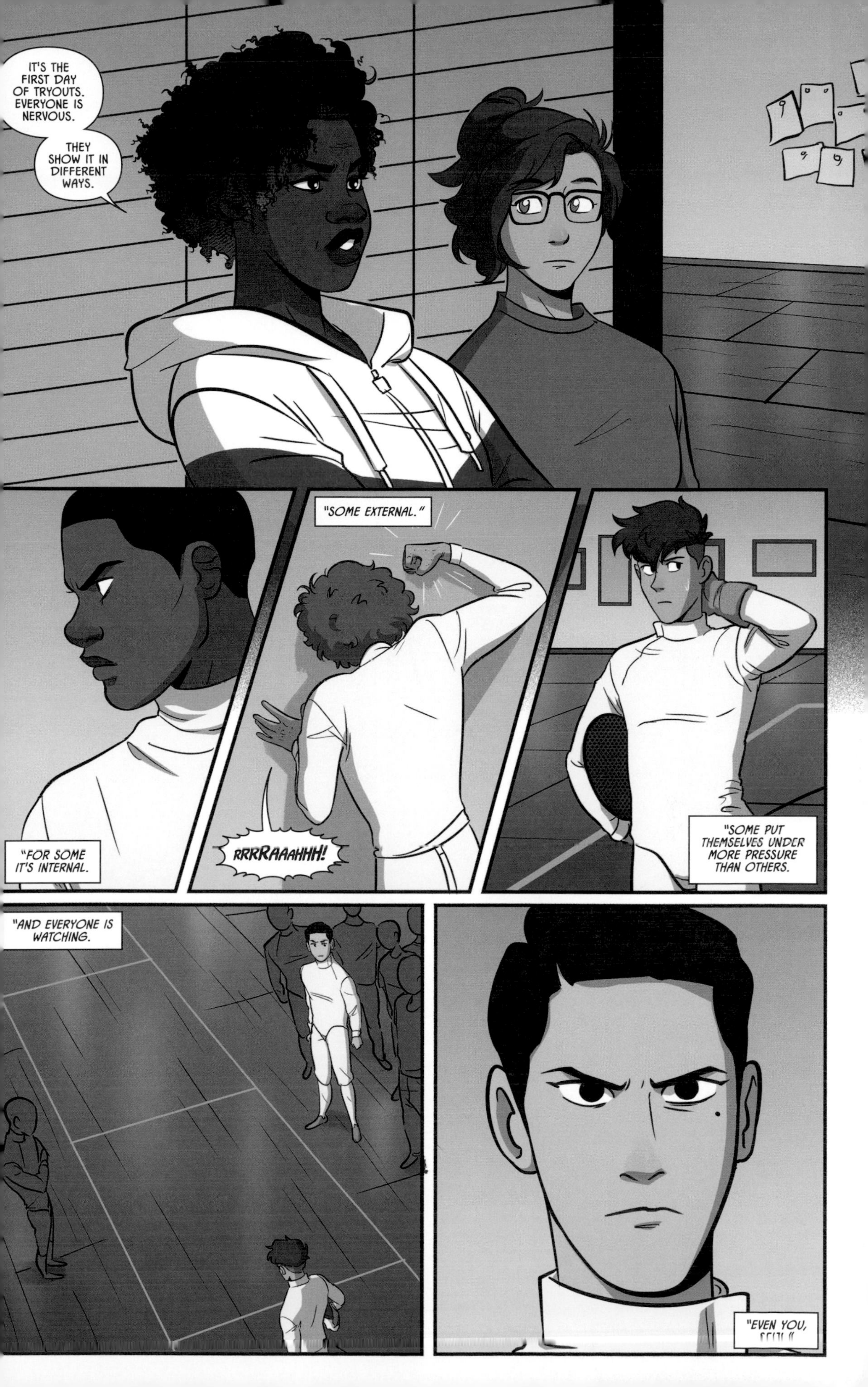
IT'S THE FIRST DAY OF TRYOUTS. EVERYONE IS NERVOUS.
THEY SHOW IT IN DIFFERENT WAYS.
"FOR SOME IT'S INTERNAL.
"SOME EXTERNAL."
RRRRAAAHHH!
"SOME PUT THEMSELVES UNDER MORE PRESSURE THAN OTHERS.
"AND EVERYONE IS WATCHING.
"EVEN YOU,

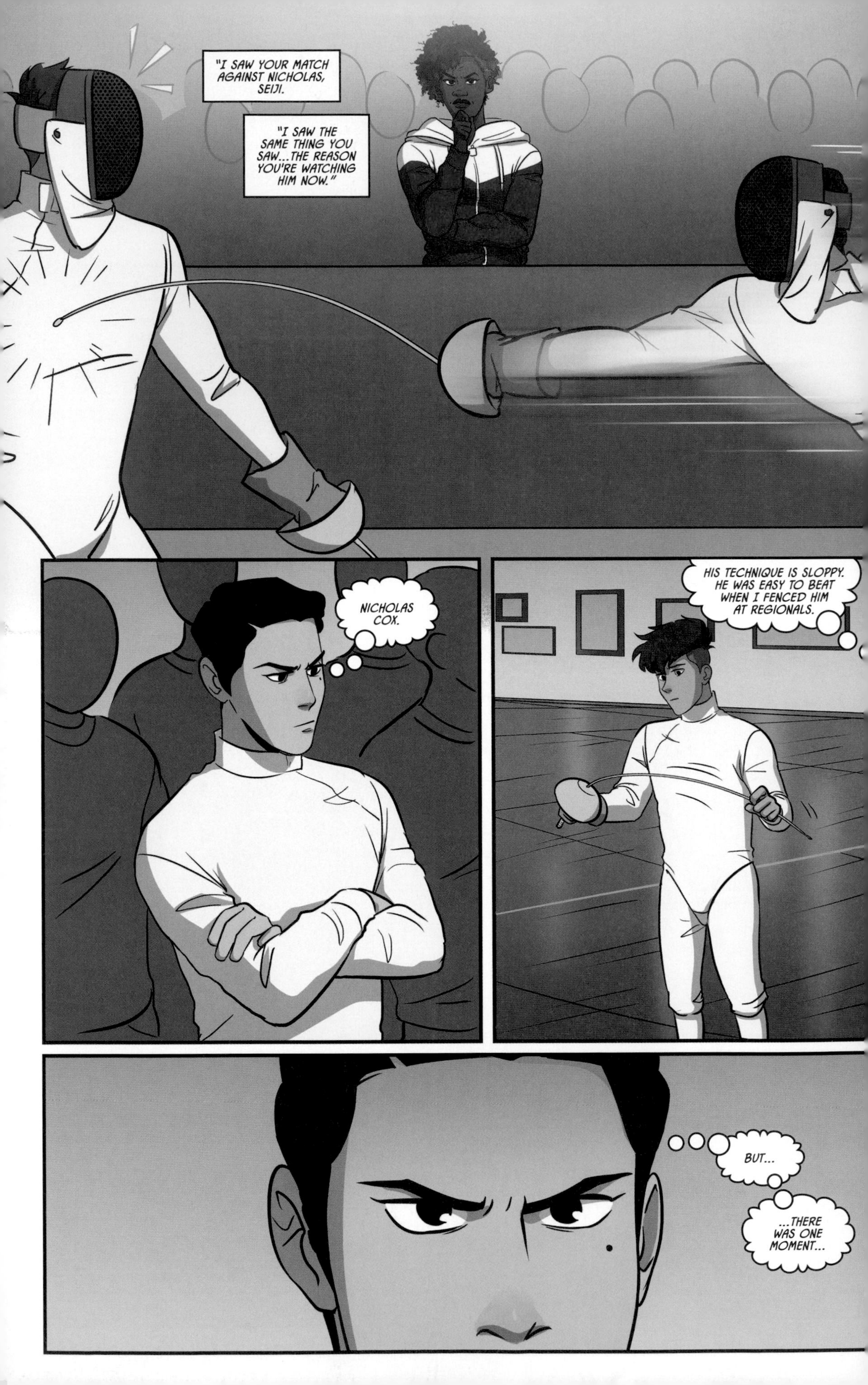
"I SAW YOUR MATCH AGAINST NICHOLAS, SEIJI.
"I SAW THE SAME THING YOU SAW...THE REASON YOU'RE WATCHING HIM NOW."
NICHOLAS COX.
HIS TECHNIQUE IS SLOPPY. HE WAS EASY TO BEAT WHEN I FENCED HIM AT REGIONALS.
BUT...
...THERE WAS ONE MOMENT...

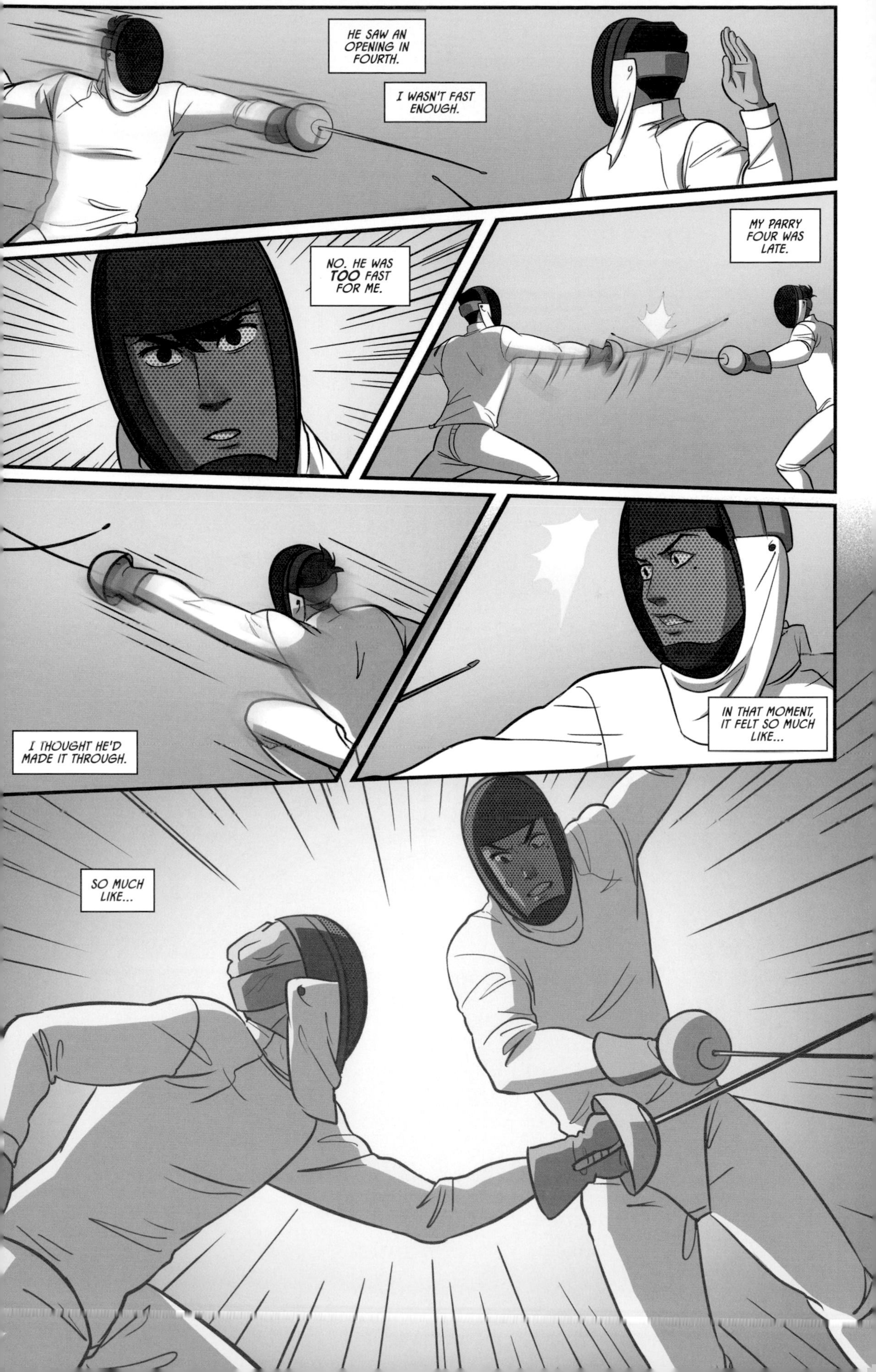
HE SAW AN OPENING IN FOURTH.
I WASN'T FAST ENOUGH.
NO. HE WAS TOO FAST FOR ME.
MY PARRY FOUR WAS LATE.
I THOUGHT HE'D MADE IT THROUGH.
IN THAT MOMENT, IT FELT SO MUCH LIKE...
SO MUCH LIKE...

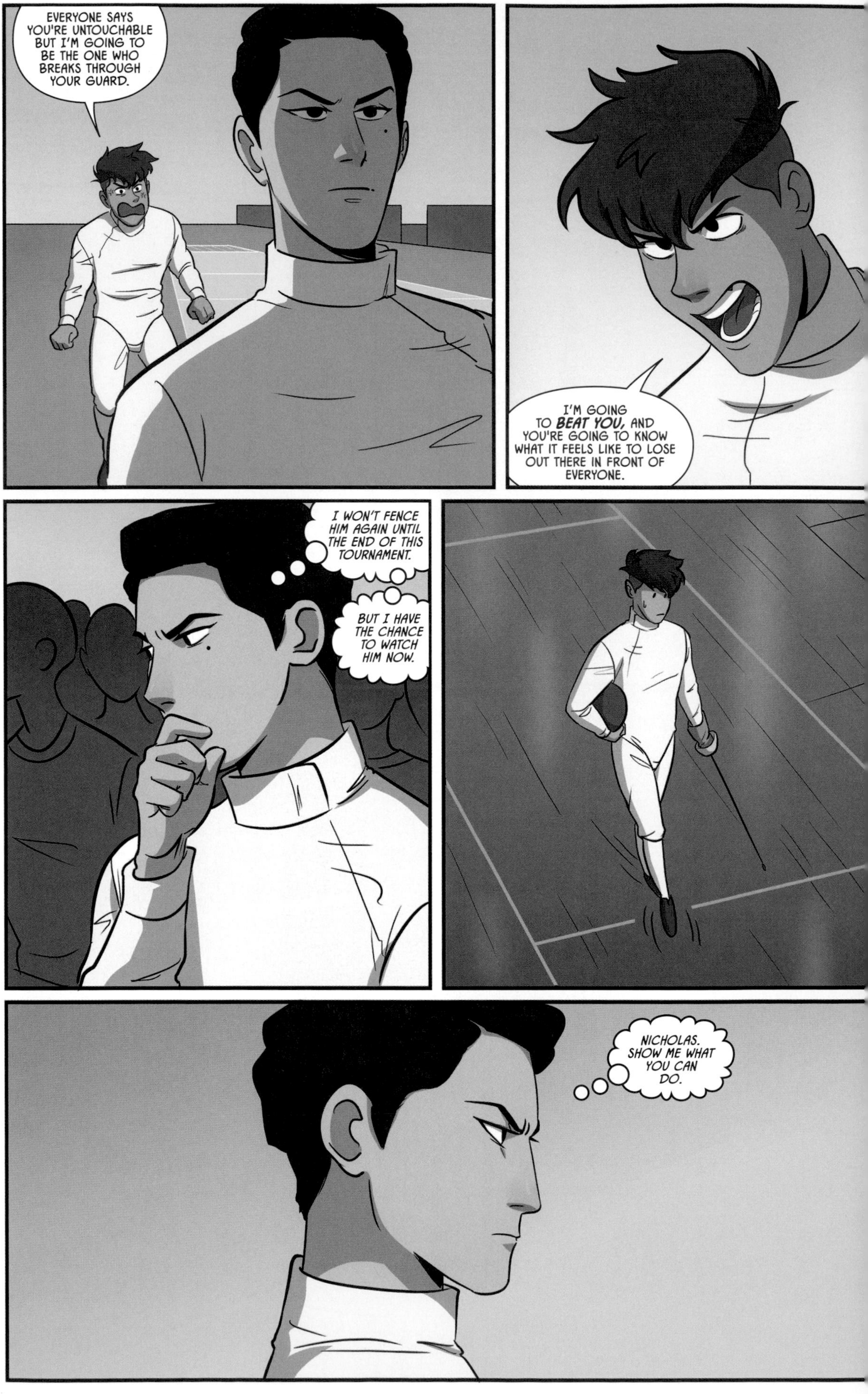
EVERYONE SAYS YOU'RE UNTOUCHABLE BUT I'M GOING TO BE THE ONE WHO BREAKS THROUGH YOUR GUARD.
I'M GOING TO BEAT YOU, AND YOU'RE GOING TO KNOW WHAT IT FEELS LIKE TO LOSE OUT THERE IN FRONT OF EVERYONE.
I WON'T FENCE HIM AGAIN UNTIL THE END OF THIS TOURNAMENT.
BUT I HAVE THE CHANCE TO WATCH HIM NOW.
NICHOLAS. SHOW ME WHAT YOU CAN DO.

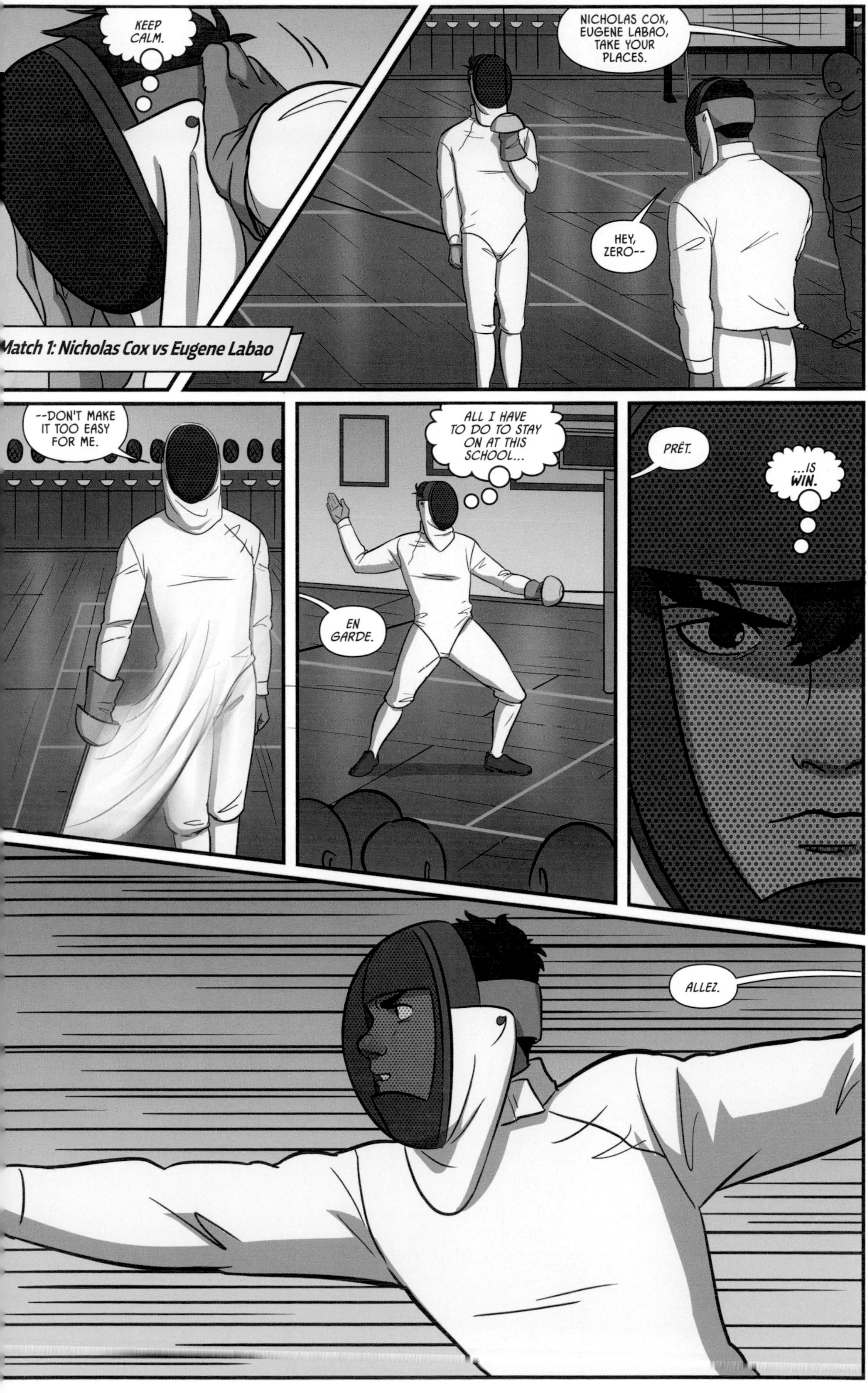
KEEP CALM.
NICHOLAS COX, EUGENE LABAO, TAKE YOUR PLACES.
HEY, ZERO--
Match 1: Nicholas Cox vs Eugene Labao
--DON'T MAKE IT TOO EASY FOR ME.
ALL I HAVE TO DO TO STAY ON AT THIS SCHOOL...
EN GARDE.
PRÊT.
...IS WIN.
ALLEZ.

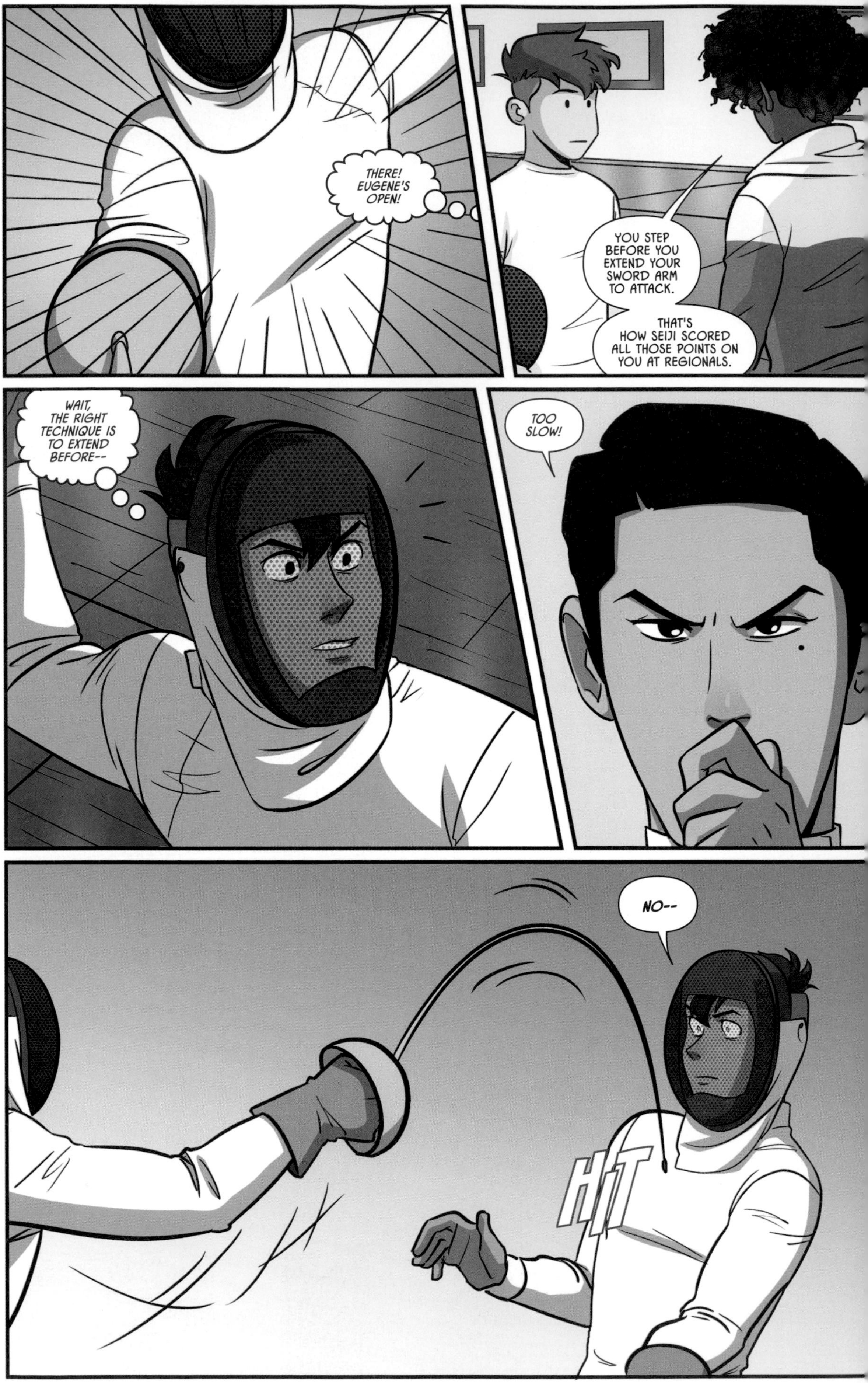
THERE! EUGENE'S OPEN!
YOU STEP BEFORE YOU EXTEND YOUR SWORD ARM TO ATTACK.
THAT'S HOW SEIJI SCORED ALL THOSE POINTS ON YOU AT REGIONALS.
WAIT, THE RIGHT TECHNIQUE IS TO EXTEND BEFORE--
TOO SLOW!
NO--
HIT

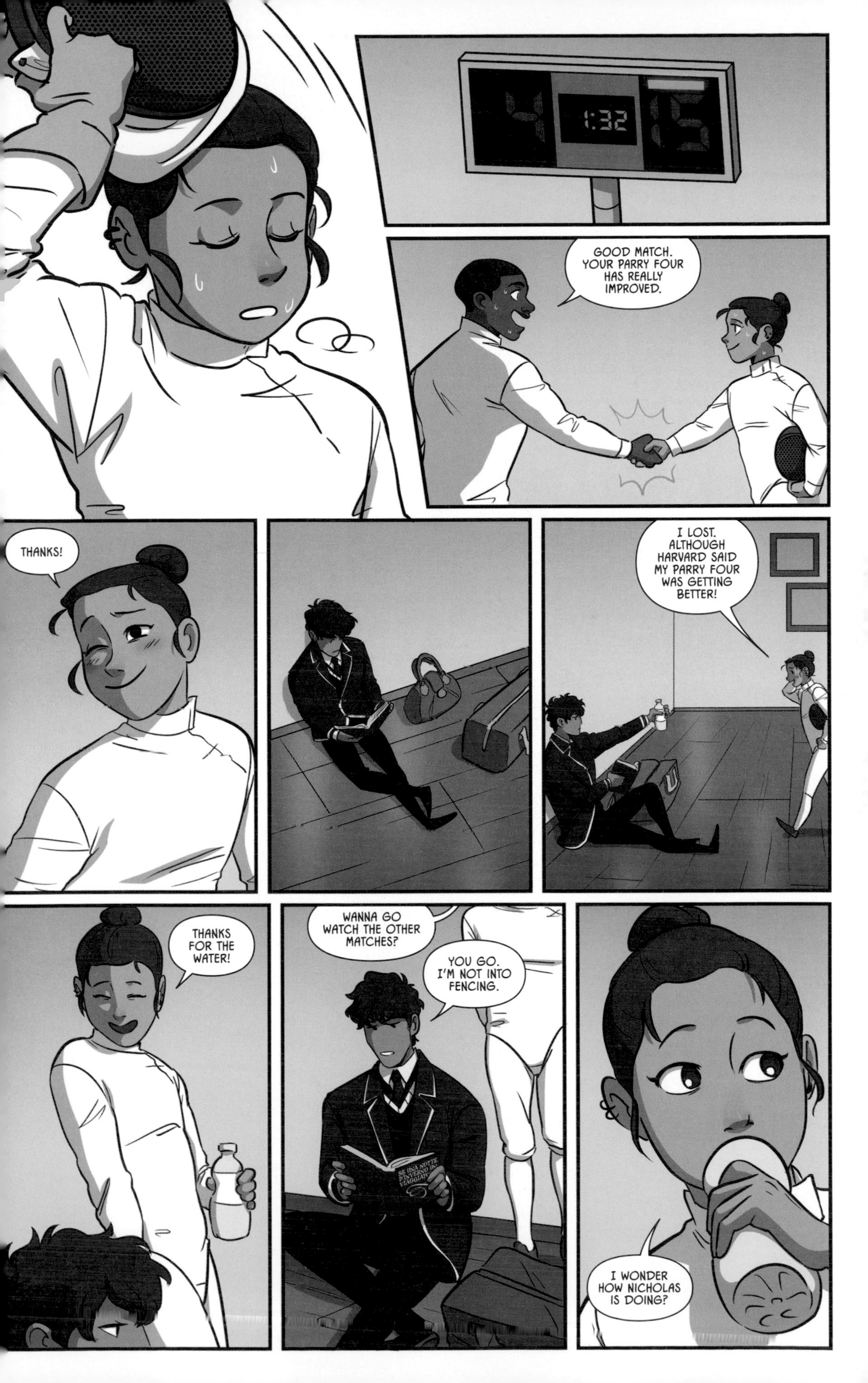
4
1:32
15
GOOD MATCH. YOUR PARRY FOUR HAS REALLY IMPROVED.
THANKS!
I LOST. ALTHOUGH HARVARD SAID MY PARRY FOUR WAS GETTING BETTER!
THANKS FOR THE WATER!
WANNA GO WATCH THE OTHER MATCHES?
YOU GO. I'M NOT INTO FENCING.
I WONDER HOW NICHOLAS IS DOING?

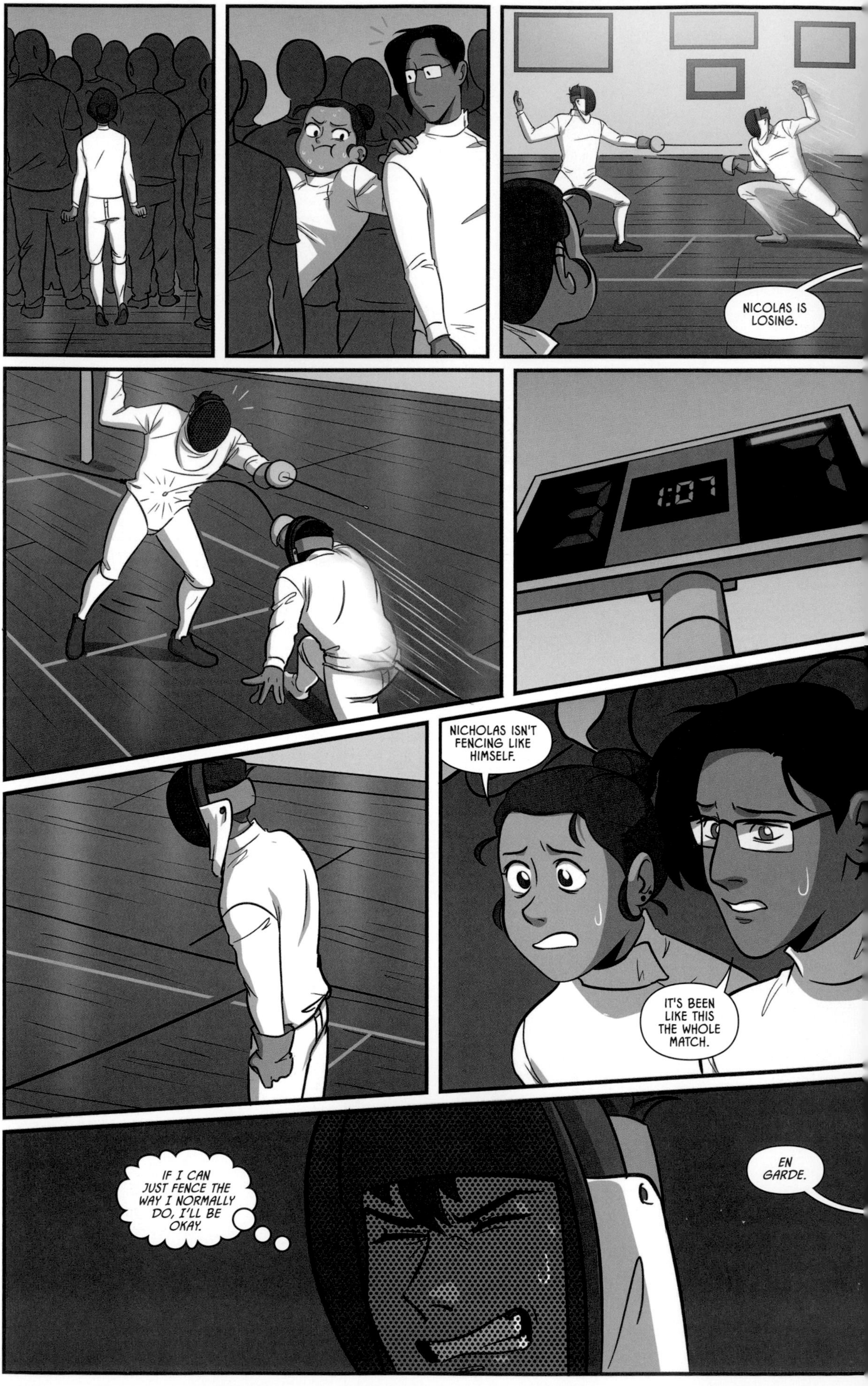
NICOLAS IS LOSING.
NICHOLAS ISN'T FENCING LIKE HIMSELF.
IT'S BEEN LIKE THIS THE WHOLE MATCH.
IF I CAN JUST FENCE THE WAY I NORMALLY DO, I'LL BE OKAY.
EN GARDE.

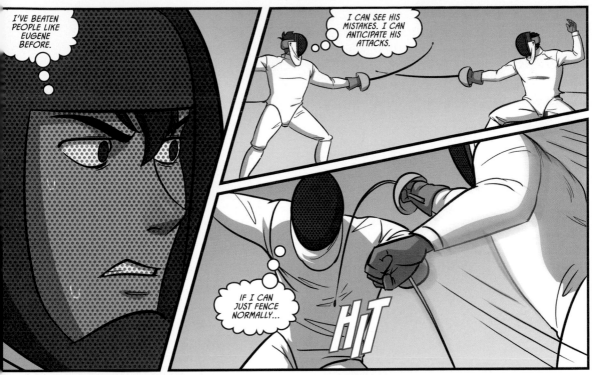

I'VE BEATEN PEOPLE LIKE EUGENE BEFORE.

I CAN SEE HIS MISTAKES. I CAN ANTICIPATE HIS ATTACKS.

IF I CAN JUST FENCE NORMALLY...

HIT

YOU'VE BEEN POORLY TRAINED, AND YOU'VE LEARNED A LOT OF BAD HABITS.

YOUR TECHNIQUE IS THE WEAKEST OF THE BOYS HERE.

HE'S OVERTHINKING.

MAYBE IT'S THE PRESSURE. SOMETHING'S GOT IN HIS HEAD.

HE NEEDS TO JUST RELAX AND FENCE THE WAY HE USUALLY DOES.

BUT FENCING THE WAY YOU USUALLY DO...

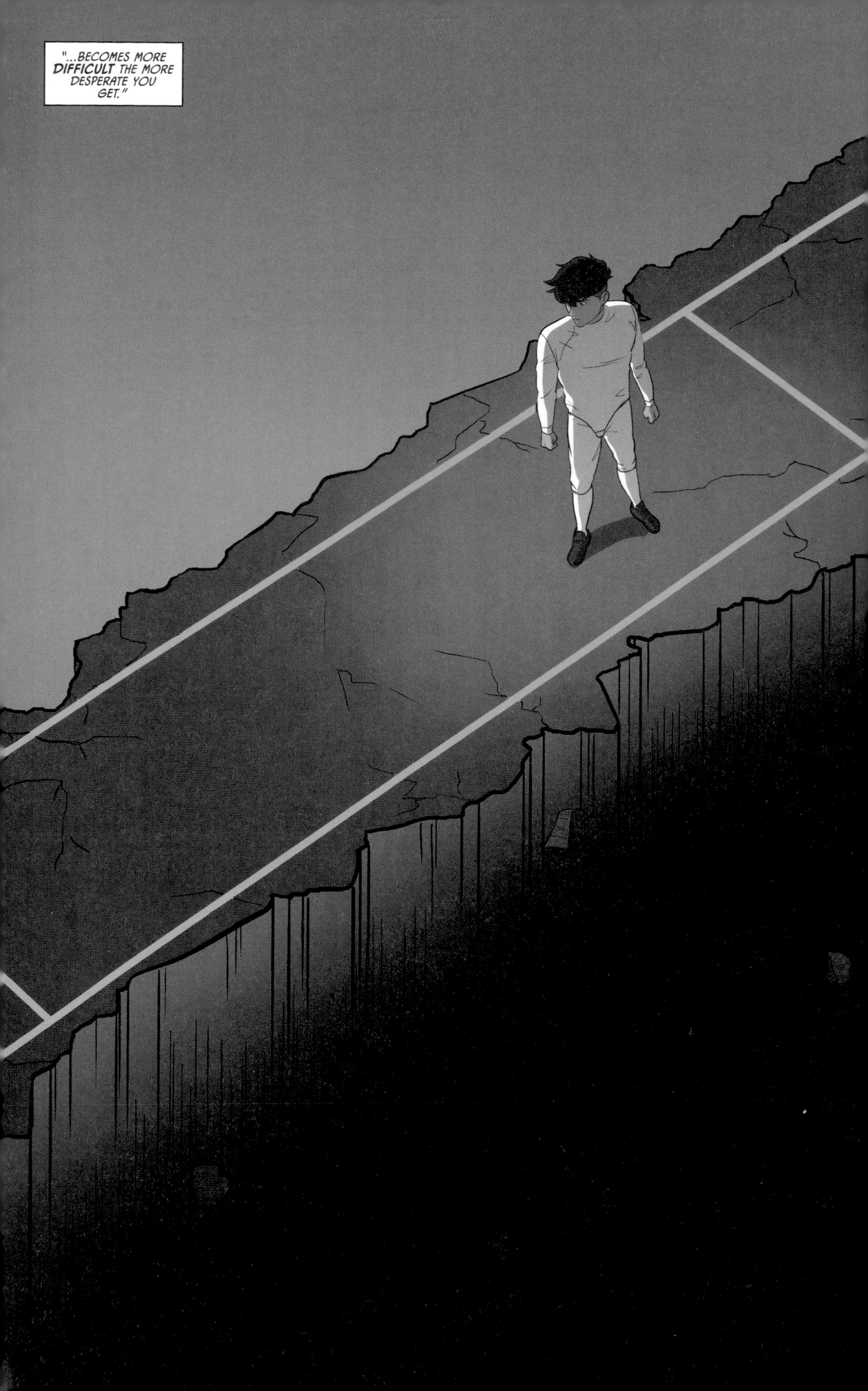
"...BECOMES MORE DIFFICULT THE MORE DESPERATE YOU GET."

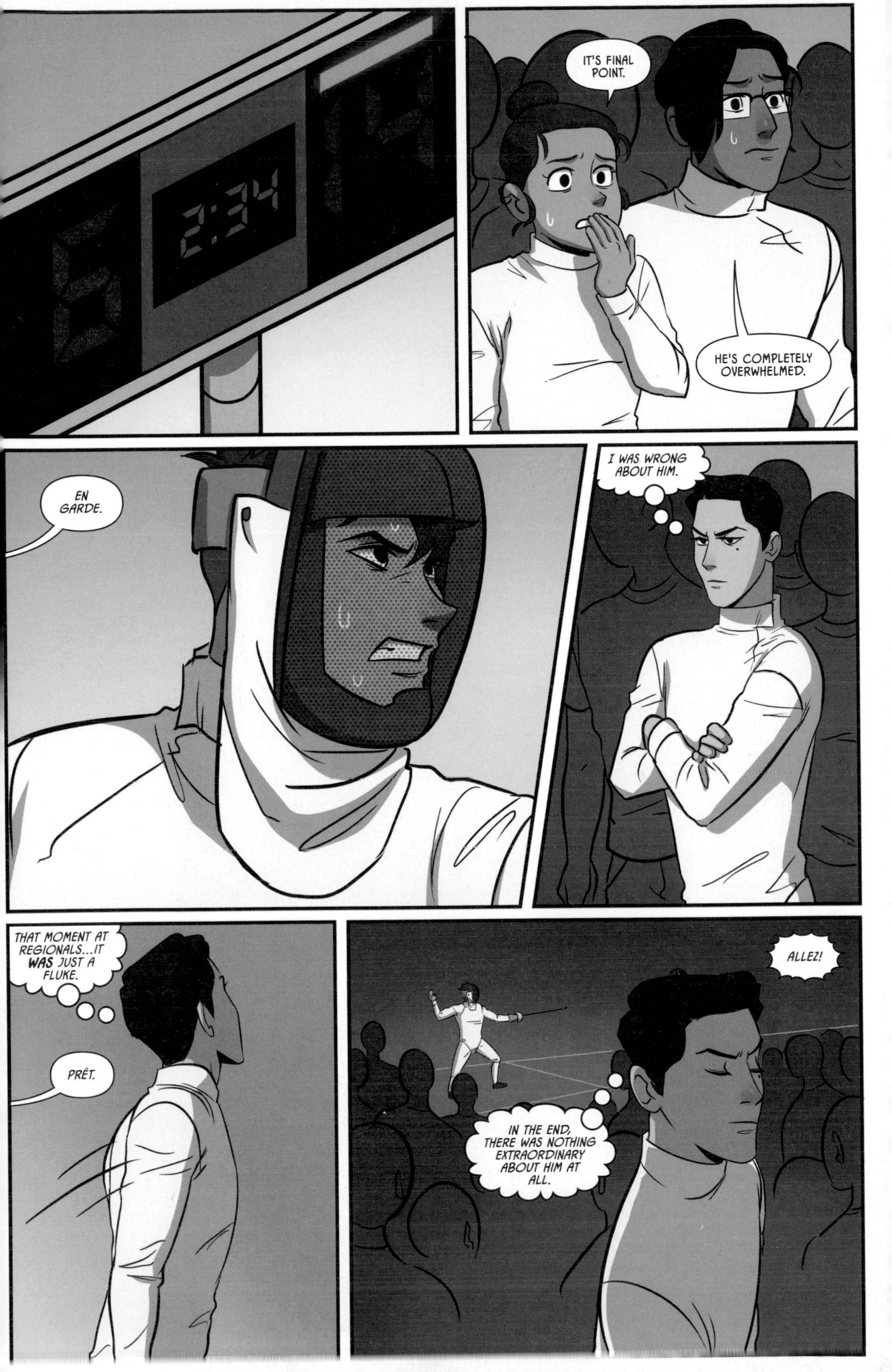
2:34
IT'S FINAL POINT.
HE'S COMPLETELY OVERWHELMED.
EN GARDE.
I WAS WRONG ABOUT HIM.
THAT MOMENT AT REGIONALS...IT **WAS** JUST A FLUKE.
PRÊT.
ALLEZ!
IN THE END, THERE WAS NOTHING EXTRAORDINARY ABOUT HIM AT ALL.

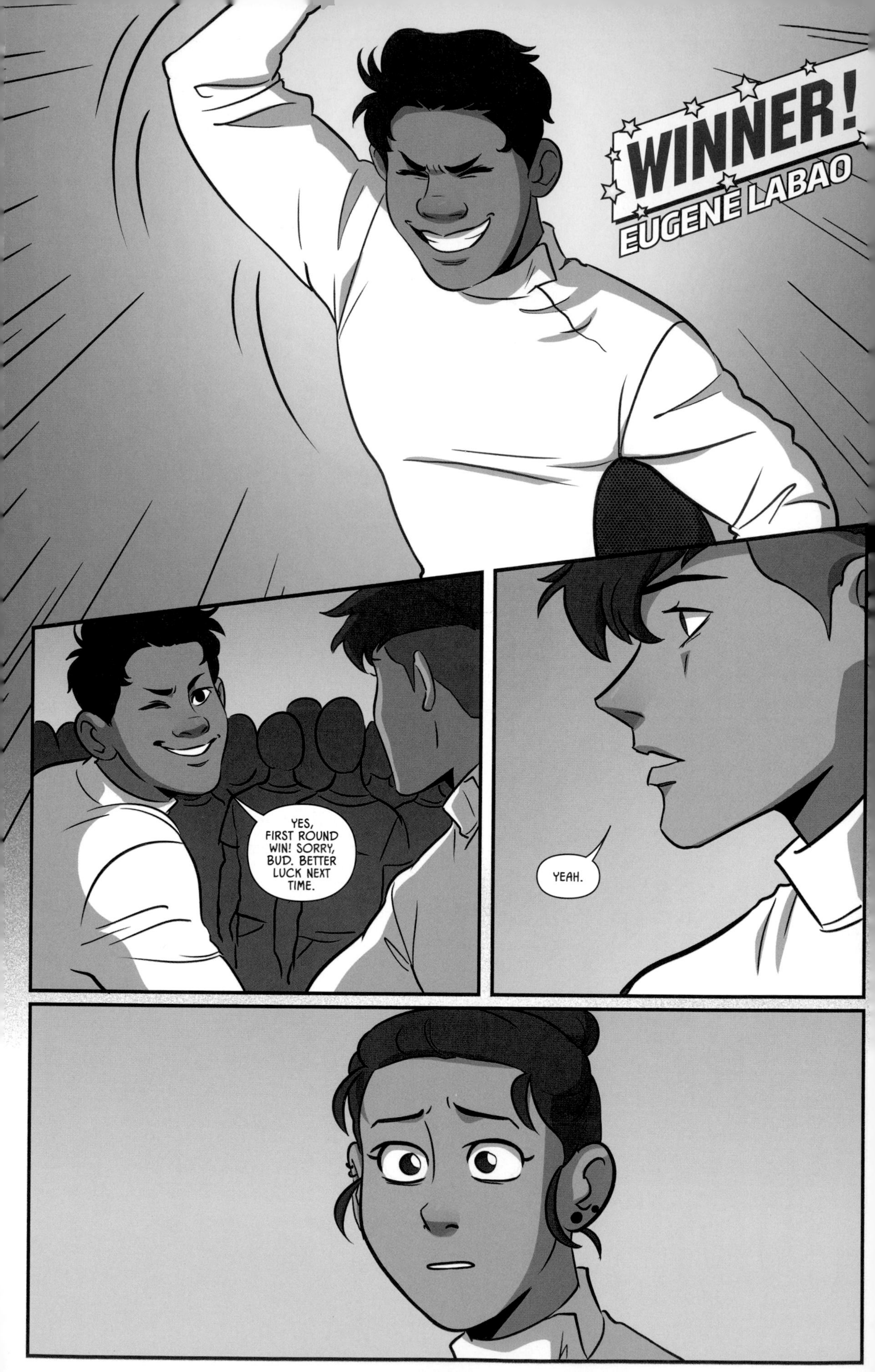
WINNER!
EUGENE LABAO
YES, FIRST ROUND WIN! SORRY, BUD. BETTER LUCK NEXT TIME.
YEAH.

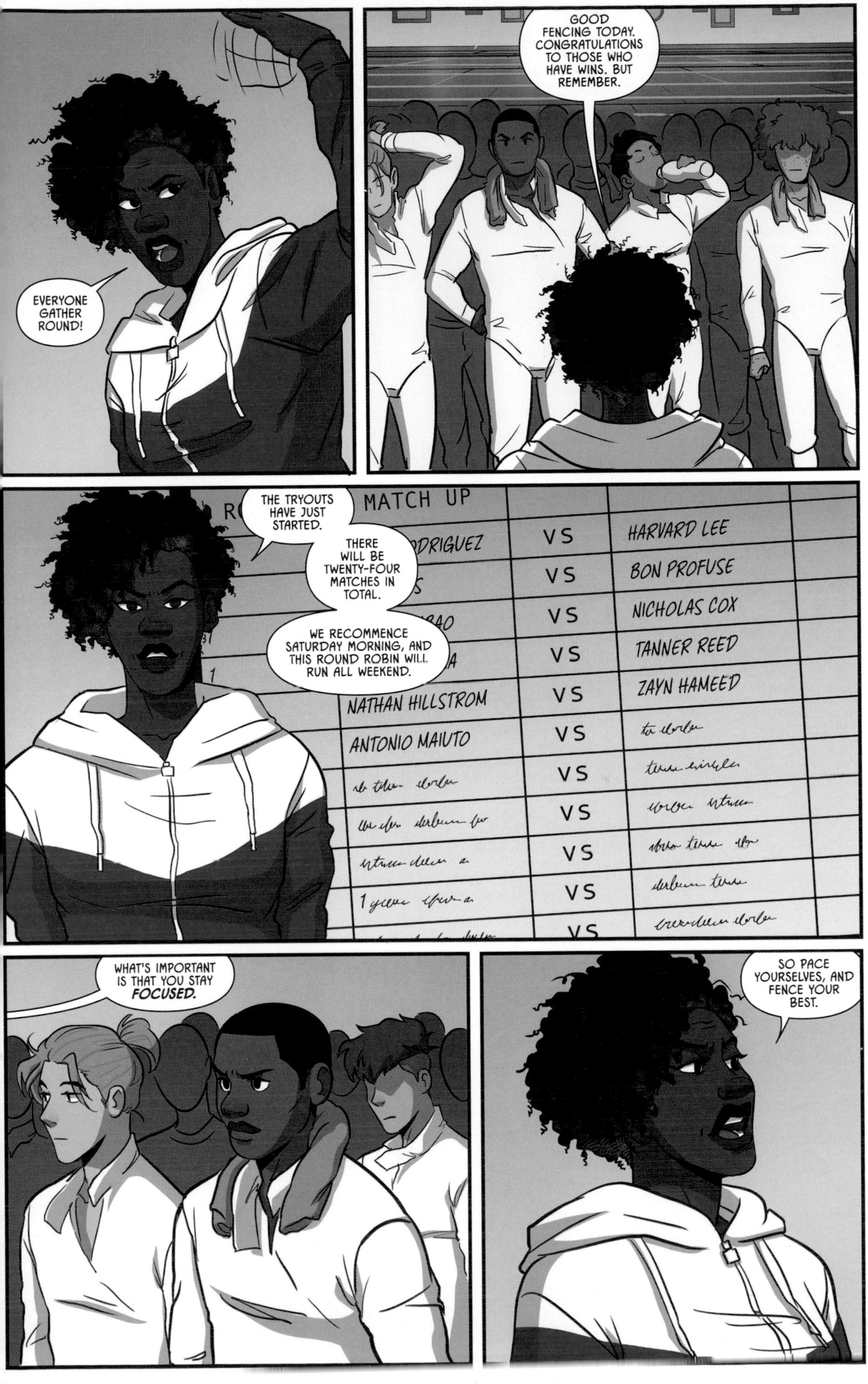
EVERYONE GATHER ROUND!
GOOD FENCING TODAY. CONGRATULATIONS TO THOSE WHO HAVE WINS. BUT REMEMBER.
THE TRYOUTS HAVE JUST STARTED.
THERE WILL BE TWENTY-FOUR MATCHES IN TOTAL.
WE RECOMMENCE SATURDAY MORNING, AND THIS ROUND ROBIN WILL RUN ALL WEEKEND.
MATCH UP
VS HARVARD LEE
VS BON PROFUSE
VS NICHOLAS COX
VS TANNER REED
NATHAN HILLSTROM VS ZAYN HAMEED
ANTONIO MAIUTO VS
WHAT'S IMPORTANT IS THAT YOU STAY *FOCUSED.*
SO PACE YOURSELVES, AND FENCE YOUR BEST.

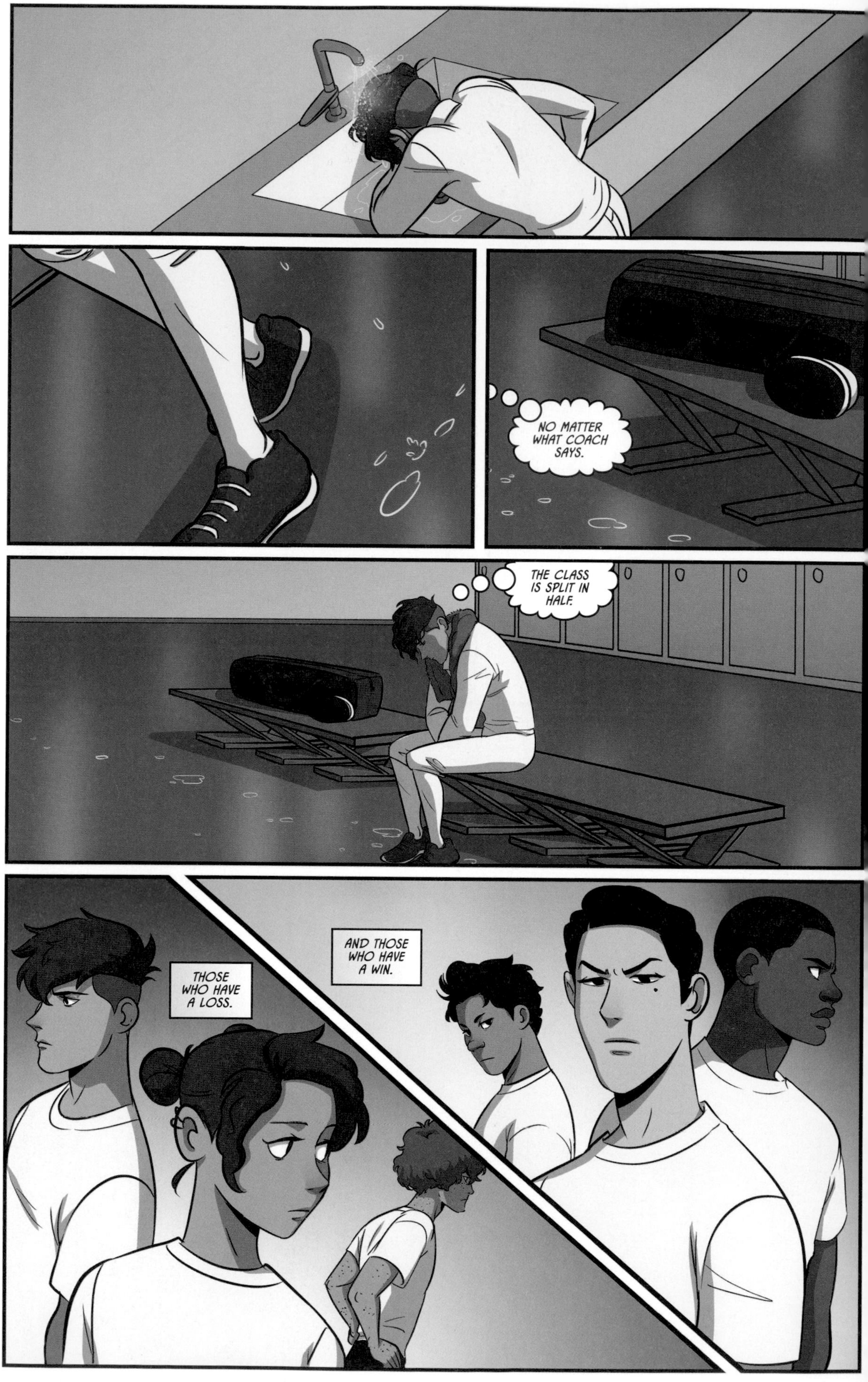

NO MATTER WHAT COACH SAYS.
THE CLASS IS SPLIT IN HALF.
THOSE WHO HAVE A LOSS.
AND THOSE WHO HAVE A WIN.

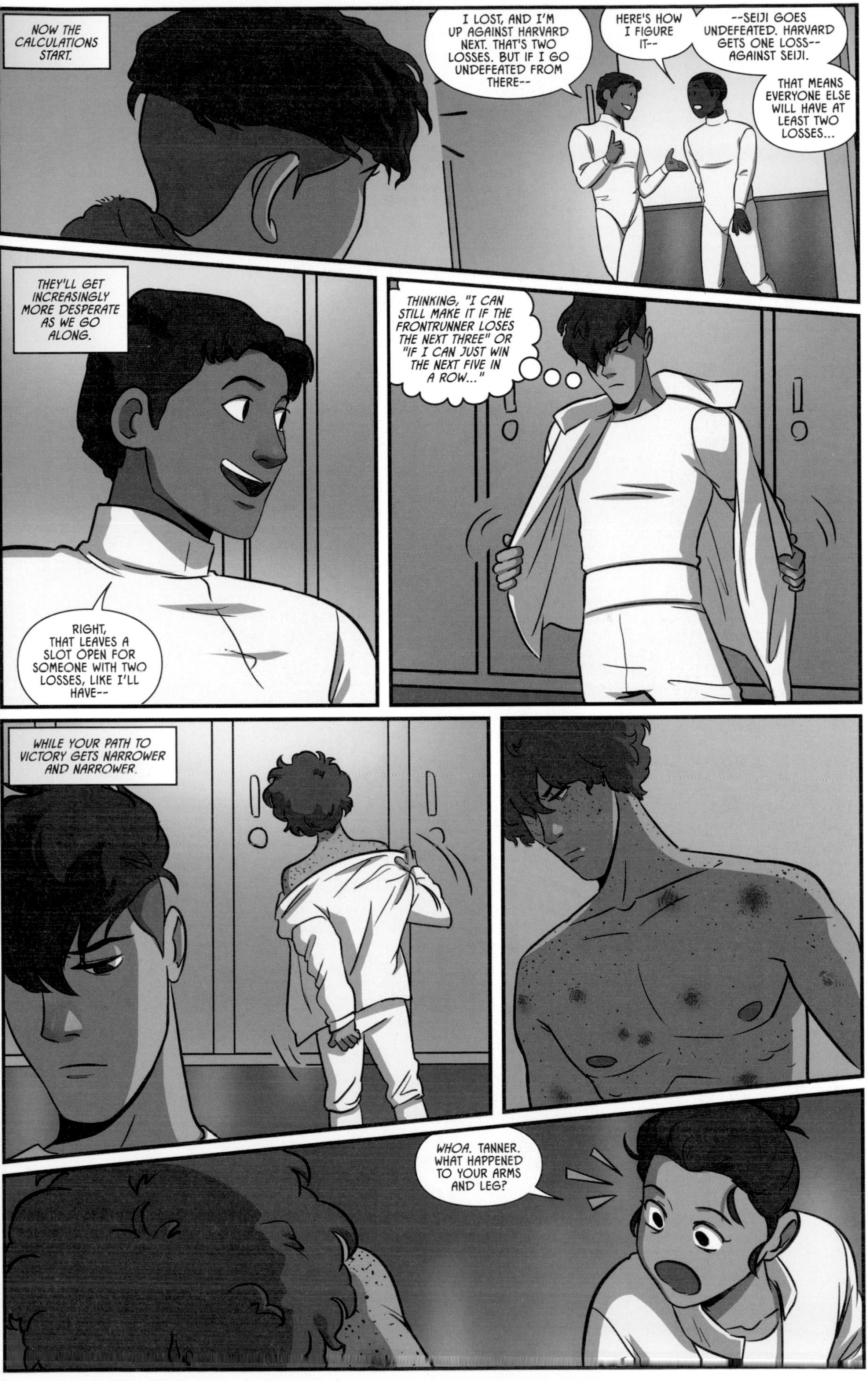
NOW THE CALCULATIONS START.
I LOST, AND I'M UP AGAINST HARVARD NEXT. THAT'S TWO LOSSES. BUT IF I GO UNDEFEATED FROM THERE--
HERE'S HOW I FIGURE IT--
--SEIJI GOES UNDEFEATED. HARVARD GETS ONE LOSS-- AGAINST SEIJI.
THAT MEANS EVERYONE ELSE WILL HAVE AT LEAST TWO LOSSES...
THEY'LL GET INCREASINGLY MORE DESPERATE AS WE GO ALONG.
RIGHT, THAT LEAVES A SLOT OPEN FOR SOMEONE WITH TWO LOSSES, LIKE I'LL HAVE--
THINKING, "I CAN STILL MAKE IT IF THE FRONTRUNNER LOSES THE NEXT THREE" OR "IF I CAN JUST WIN THE NEXT FIVE IN A ROW..."
WHILE YOUR PATH TO VICTORY GETS NARROWER AND NARROWER.
WHOA. TANNER. WHAT HAPPENED TO YOUR ARMS AND LEG?

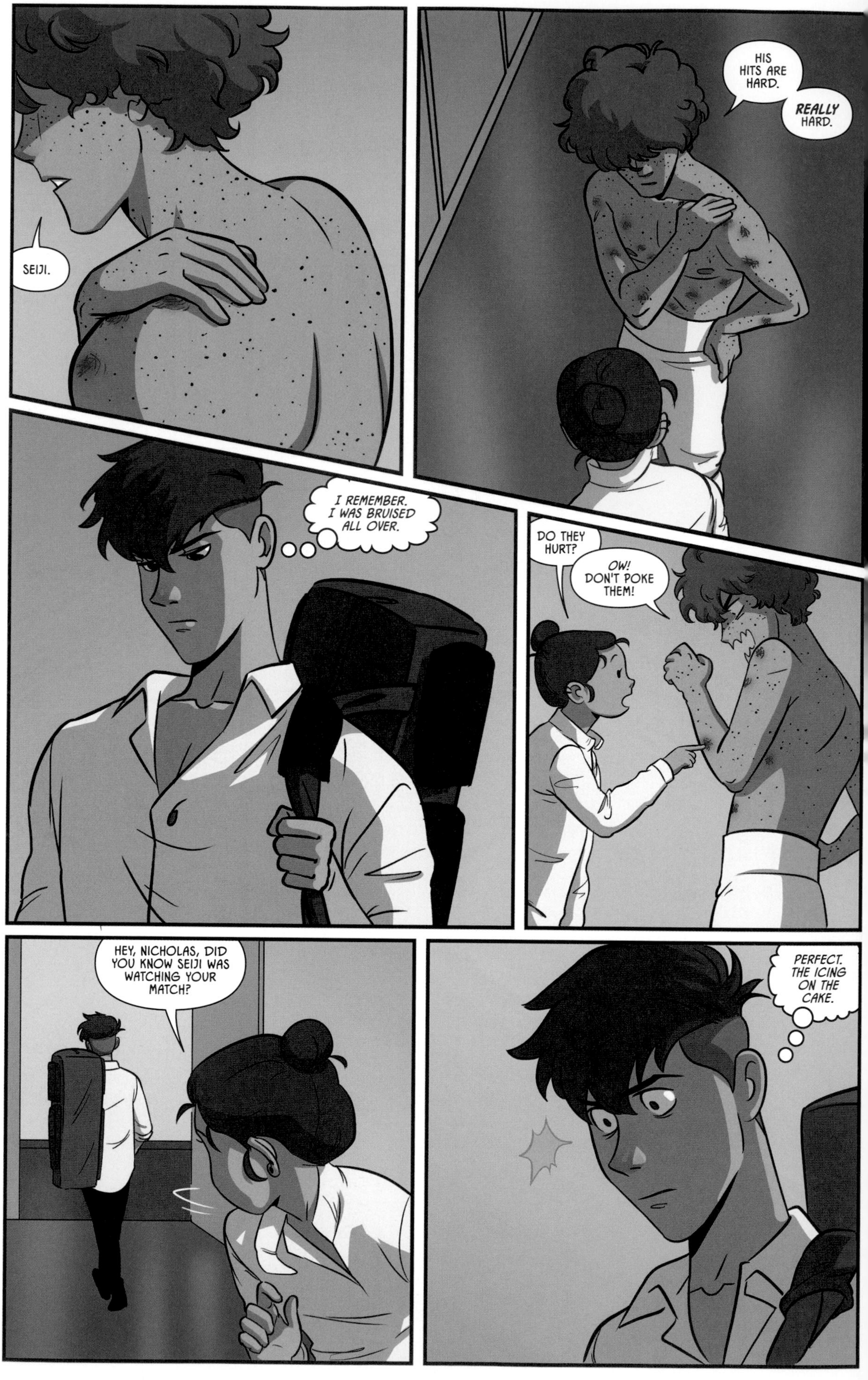
SEIJI.
HIS HITS ARE HARD.
REALLY HARD.
I REMEMBER. I WAS BRUISED ALL OVER.
DO THEY HURT?
OW! DON'T POKE THEM!
HEY, NICHOLAS, DID YOU KNOW SEIJI WAS WATCHING YOUR MATCH?
PERFECT. THE ICING ON THE CAKE.

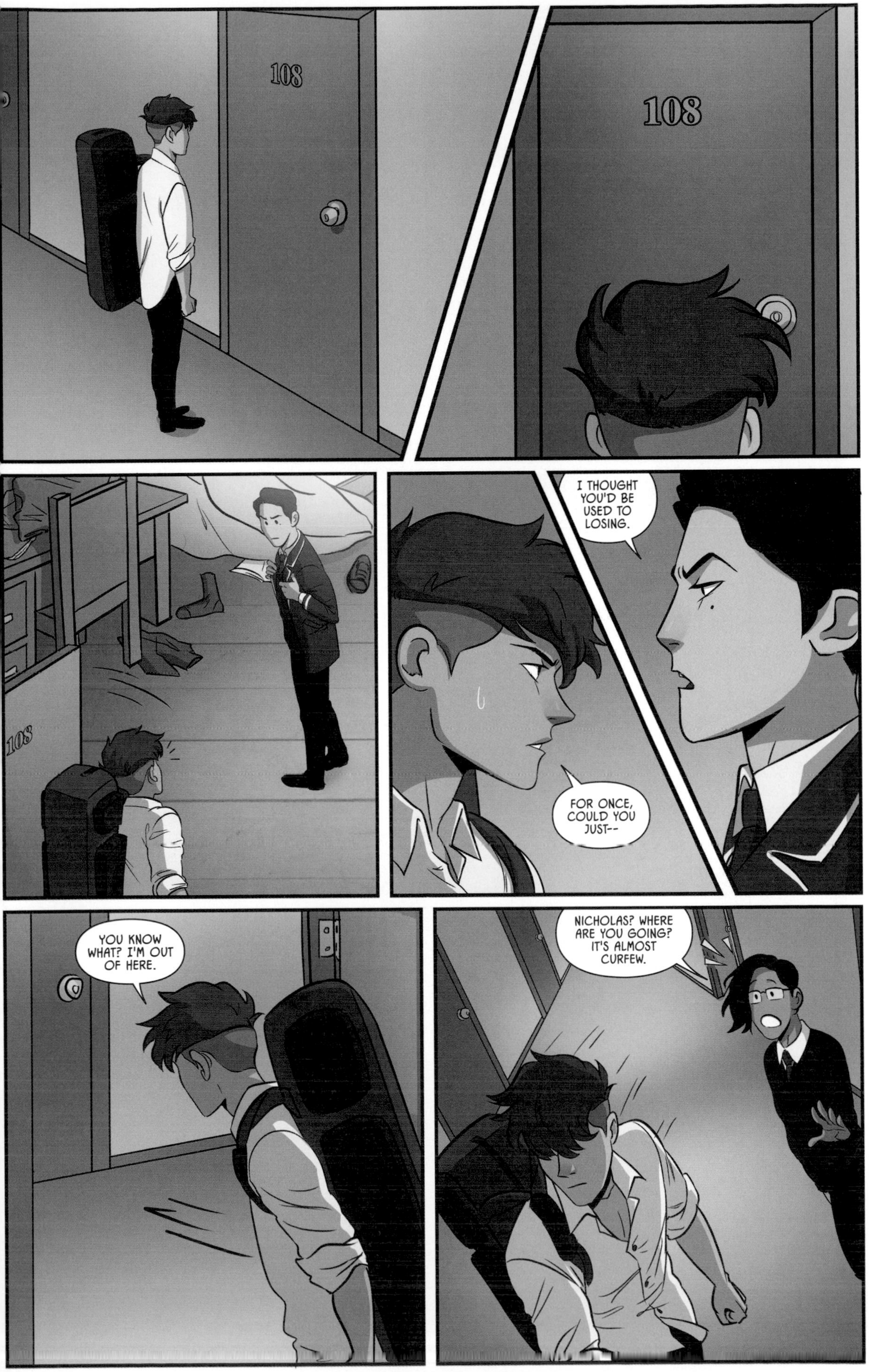
108
108
I THOUGHT YOU'D BE USED TO LOSING.
FOR ONCE, COULD YOU JUST--
YOU KNOW WHAT? I'M OUT OF HERE.
NICHOLAS? WHERE ARE YOU GOING? IT'S ALMOST CURFEW.

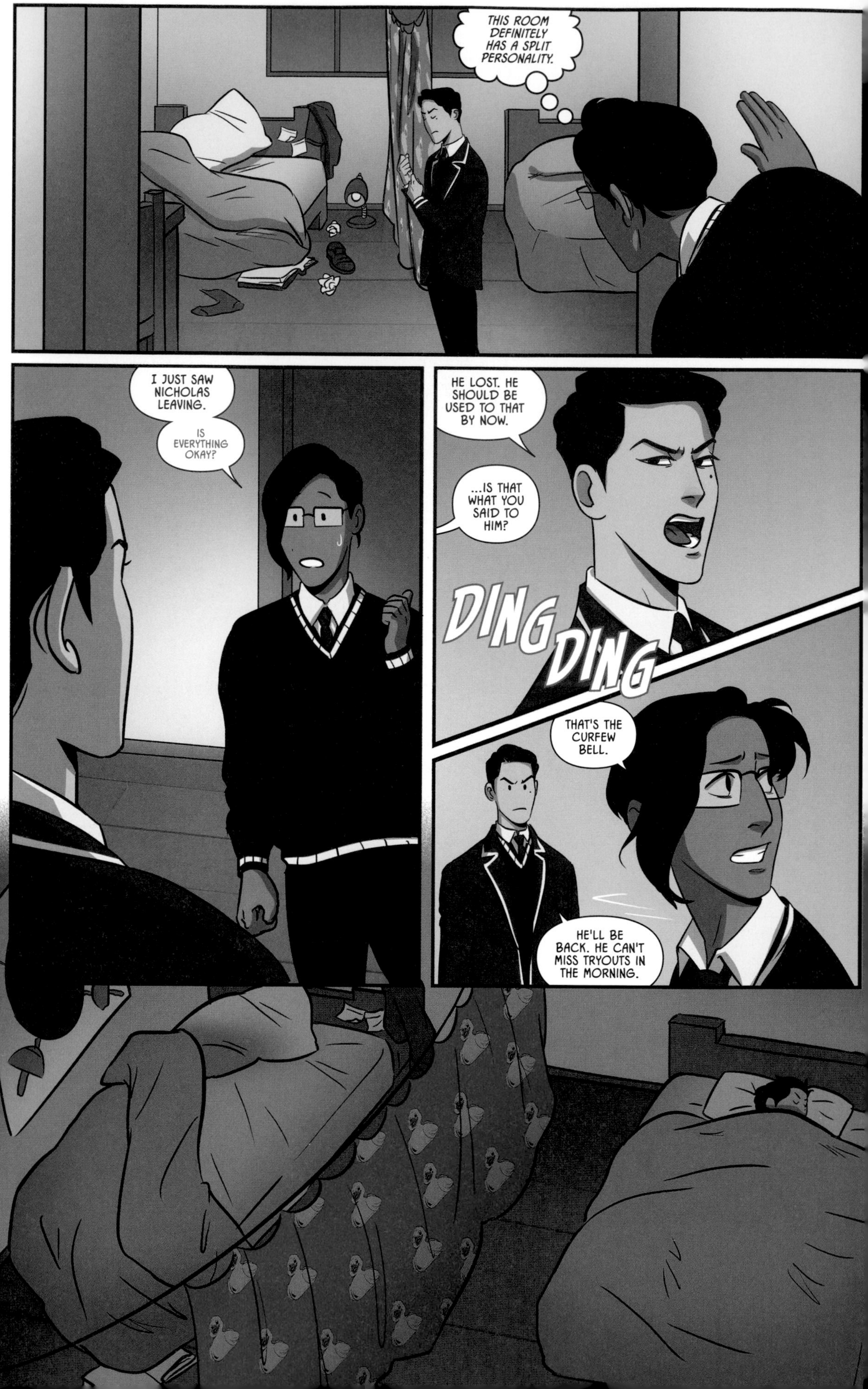

THIS ROOM DEFINITELY HAS A SPLIT PERSONALITY.
I JUST SAW NICHOLAS LEAVING.
IS EVERYTHING OKAY?
HE LOST. HE SHOULD BE USED TO THAT BY NOW.
...IS THAT WHAT YOU SAID TO HIM?
DING DING
THAT'S THE CURFEW BELL.
HE'LL BE BACK. HE CAN'T MISS TRYOUTS IN THE MORNING.

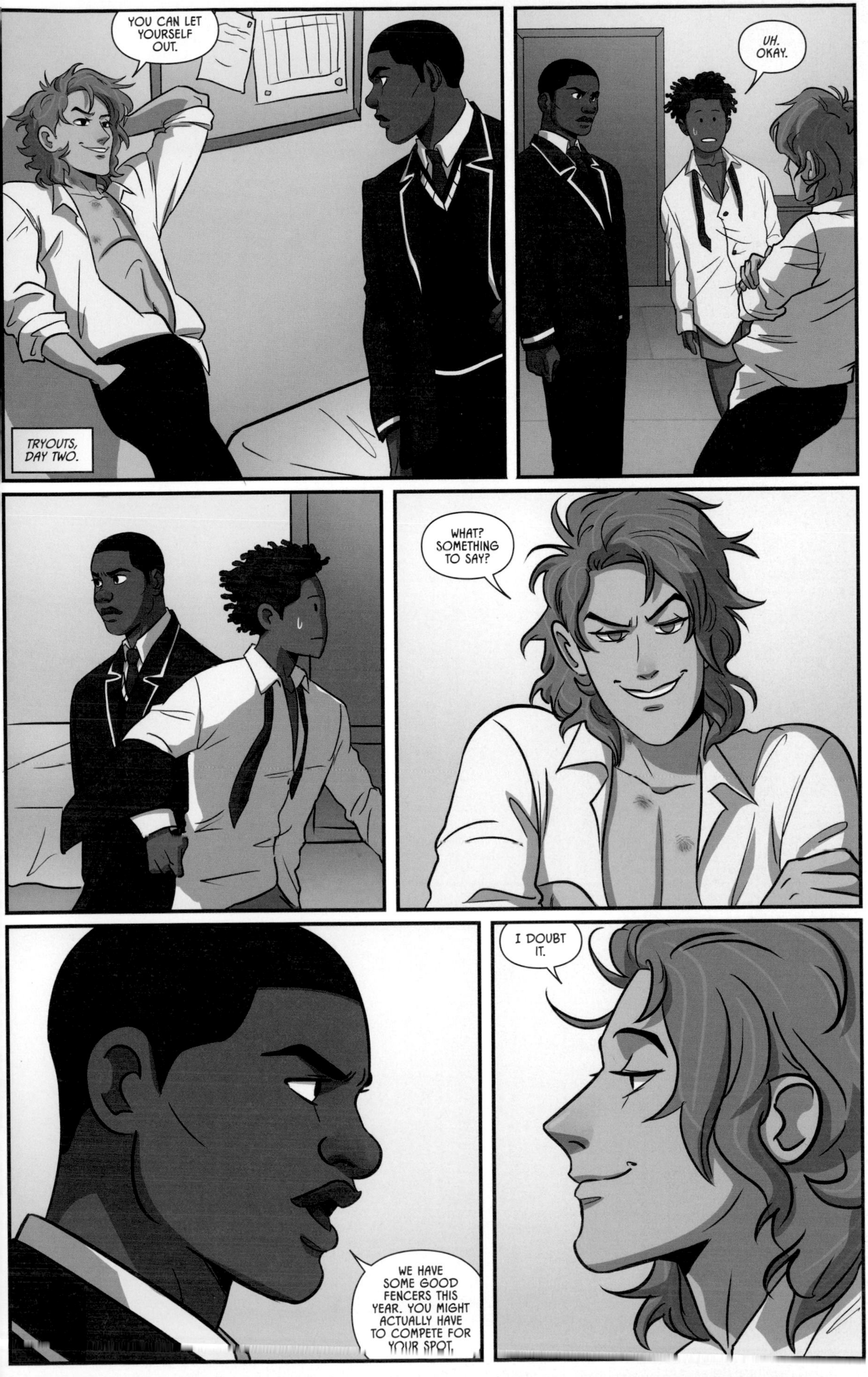
YOU CAN LET YOURSELF OUT.
TRYOUTS, DAY TWO.
UH. OKAY.
WHAT? SOMETHING TO SAY?
WE HAVE SOME GOOD FENCERS THIS YEAR. YOU MIGHT ACTUALLY HAVE TO COMPETE FOR YOUR SPOT.
I DOUBT IT.

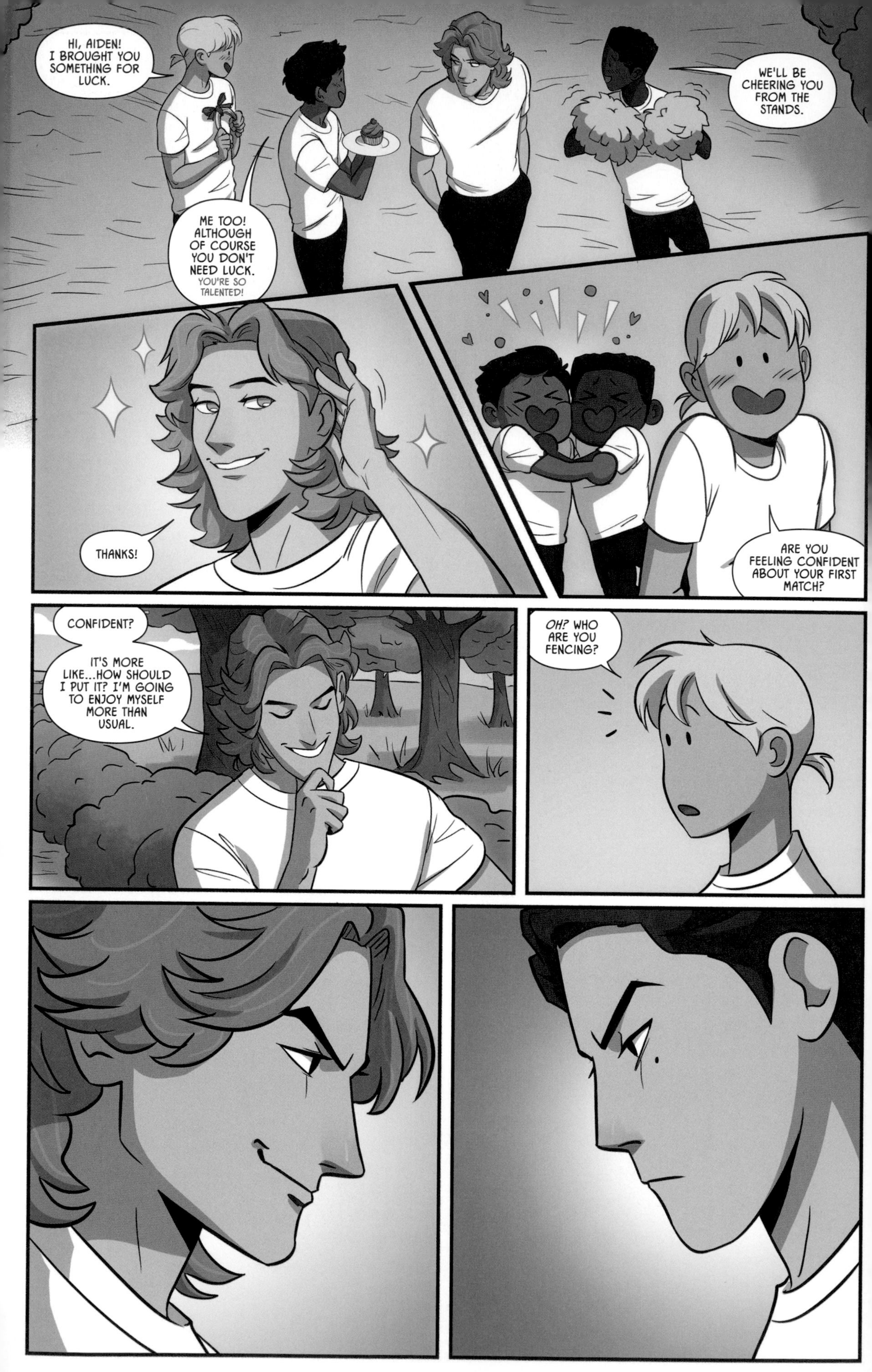
HI, AIDEN! I BROUGHT YOU SOMETHING FOR LUCK.
WE'LL BE CHEERING YOU FROM THE STANDS.
ME TOO! ALTHOUGH OF COURSE YOU DON'T NEED LUCK. YOU'RE SO TALENTED!
THANKS!
ARE YOU FEELING CONFIDENT ABOUT YOUR FIRST MATCH?
CONFIDENT?
IT'S MORE LIKE...HOW SHOULD I PUT IT? I'M GOING TO ENJOY MYSELF MORE THAN USUAL.
OH? WHO ARE YOU FENCING?

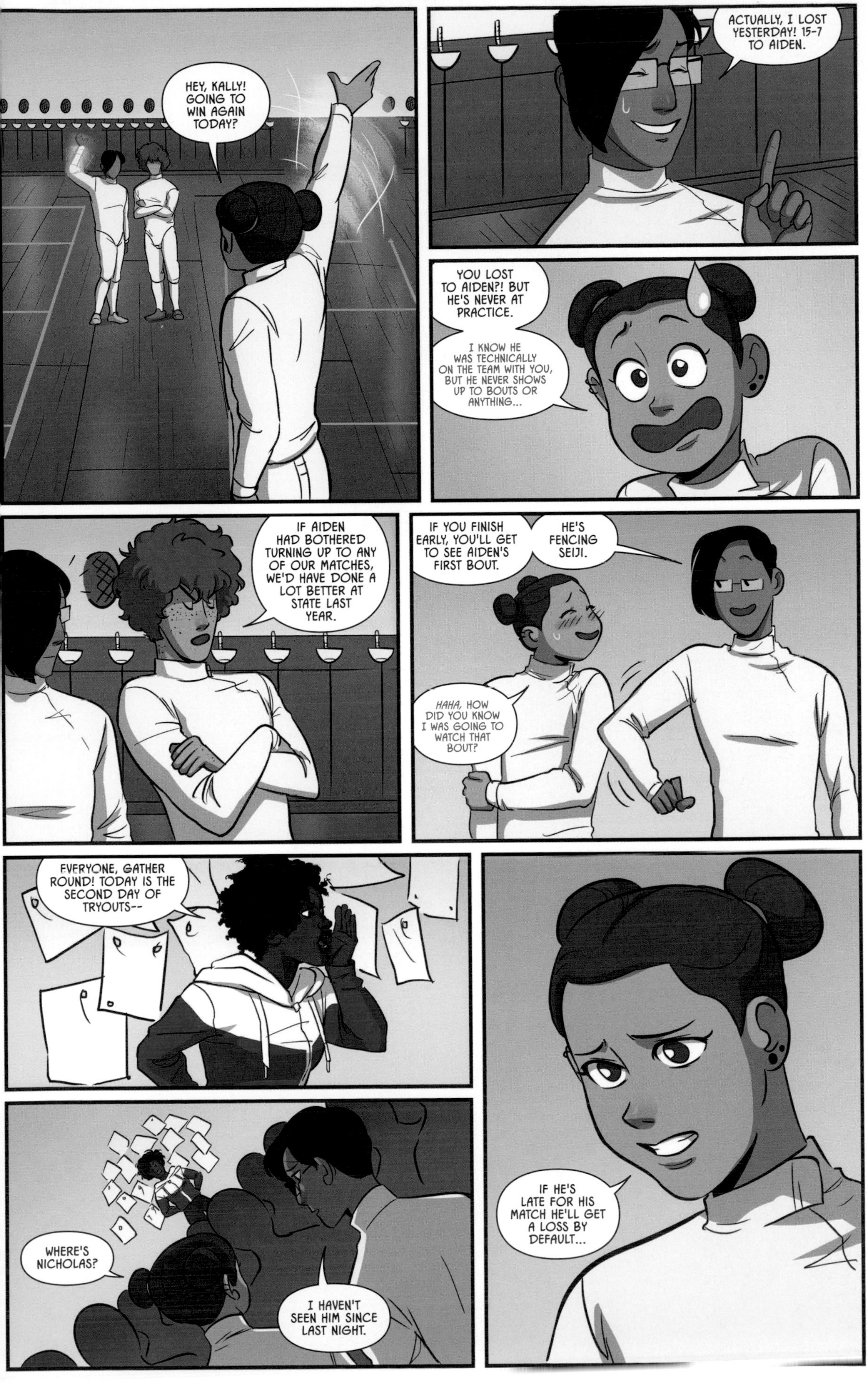
HEY, KALLY! GOING TO WIN AGAIN TODAY?
ACTUALLY, I LOST YESTERDAY! 15-7 TO AIDEN.
YOU LOST TO AIDEN?! BUT HE'S NEVER AT PRACTICE.
I KNOW HE WAS TECHNICALLY ON THE TEAM WITH YOU, BUT HE NEVER SHOWS UP TO BOUTS OR ANYTHING...
IF AIDEN HAD BOTHERED TURNING UP TO ANY OF OUR MATCHES, WE'D HAVE DONE A LOT BETTER AT STATE LAST YEAR.
IF YOU FINISH EARLY, YOU'LL GET TO SEE AIDEN'S FIRST BOUT.
HE'S FENCING SEIJI.
*HAHA,* HOW DID YOU KNOW I WAS GOING TO WATCH THAT BOUT?
EVERYONE, GATHER ROUND! TODAY IS THE SECOND DAY OF TRYOUTS--
WHERE'S NICHOLAS?
I HAVEN'T SEEN HIM SINCE LAST NIGHT.
IF HE'S LATE FOR HIS MATCH HE'LL GET A LOSS BY DEFAULT...

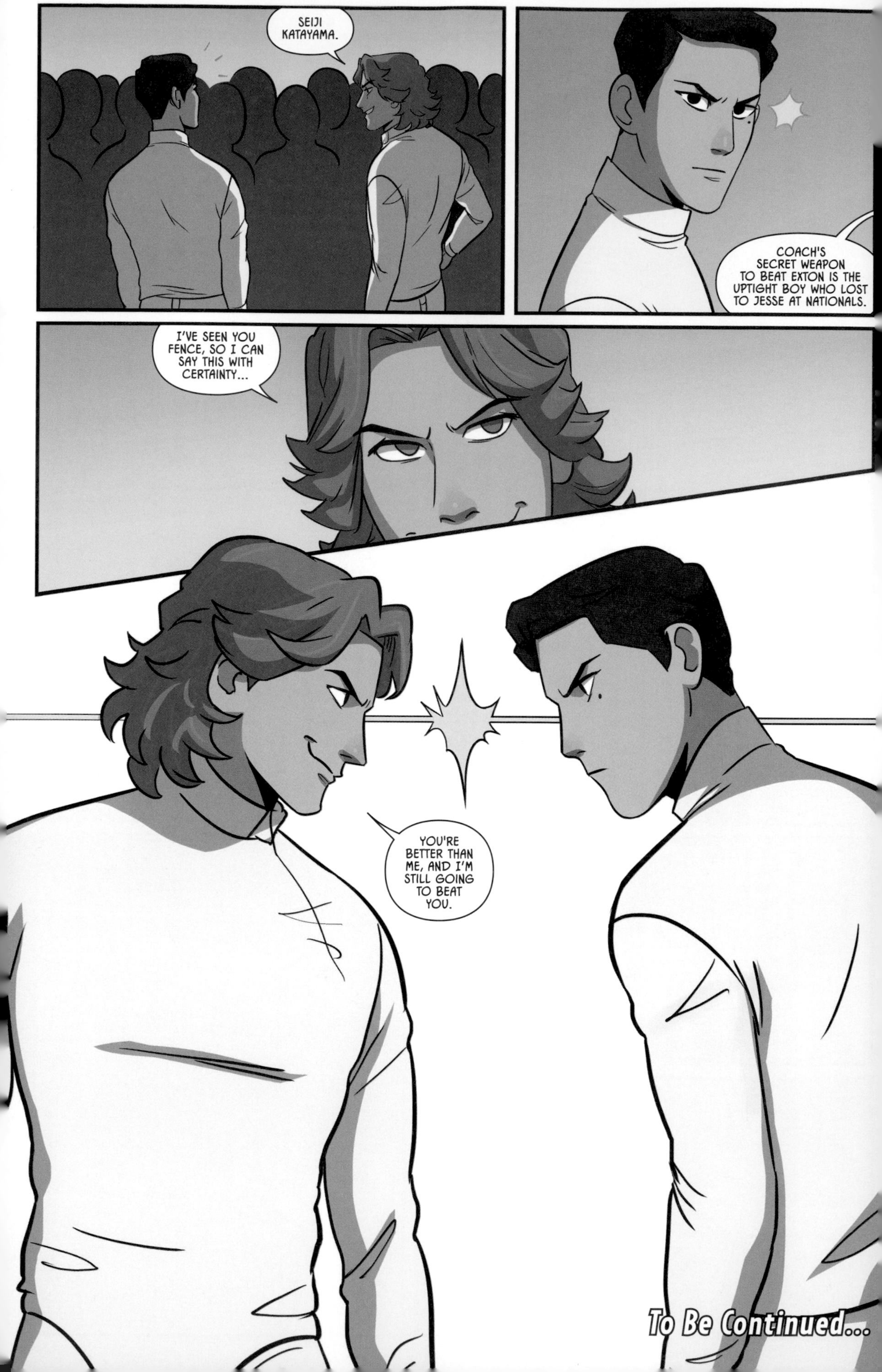
SEIJI KATAYAMA.
COACH'S SECRET WEAPON TO BEAT EXTON IS THE UPTIGHT BOY WHO LOST TO JESSE AT NATIONALS.
I'VE SEEN YOU FENCE, SO I CAN SAY THIS WITH CERTAINTY...
YOU'RE BETTER THAN ME, AND I'M STILL GOING TO BEAT YOU.
To Be Continued...

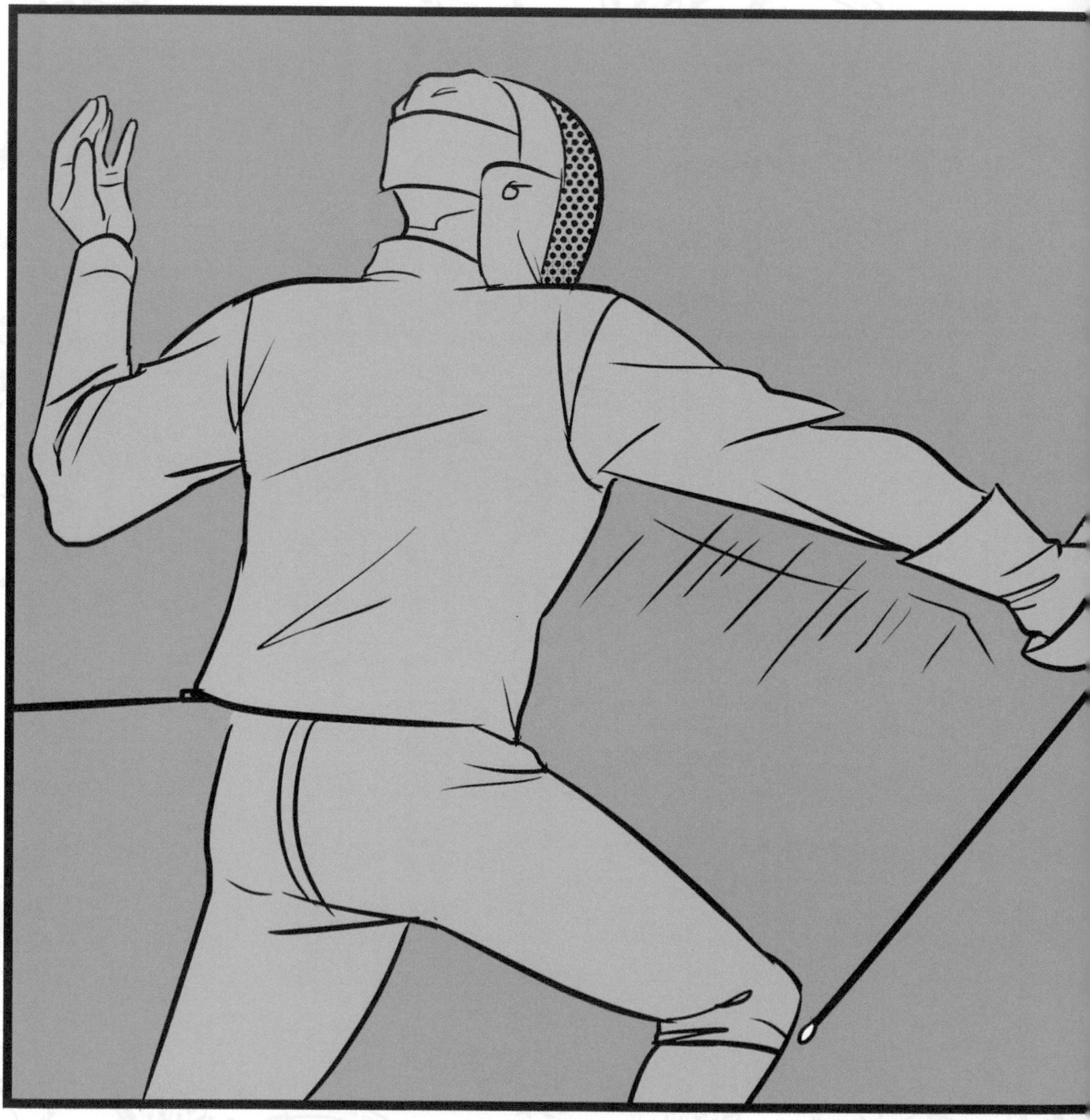

# COVER Gallery

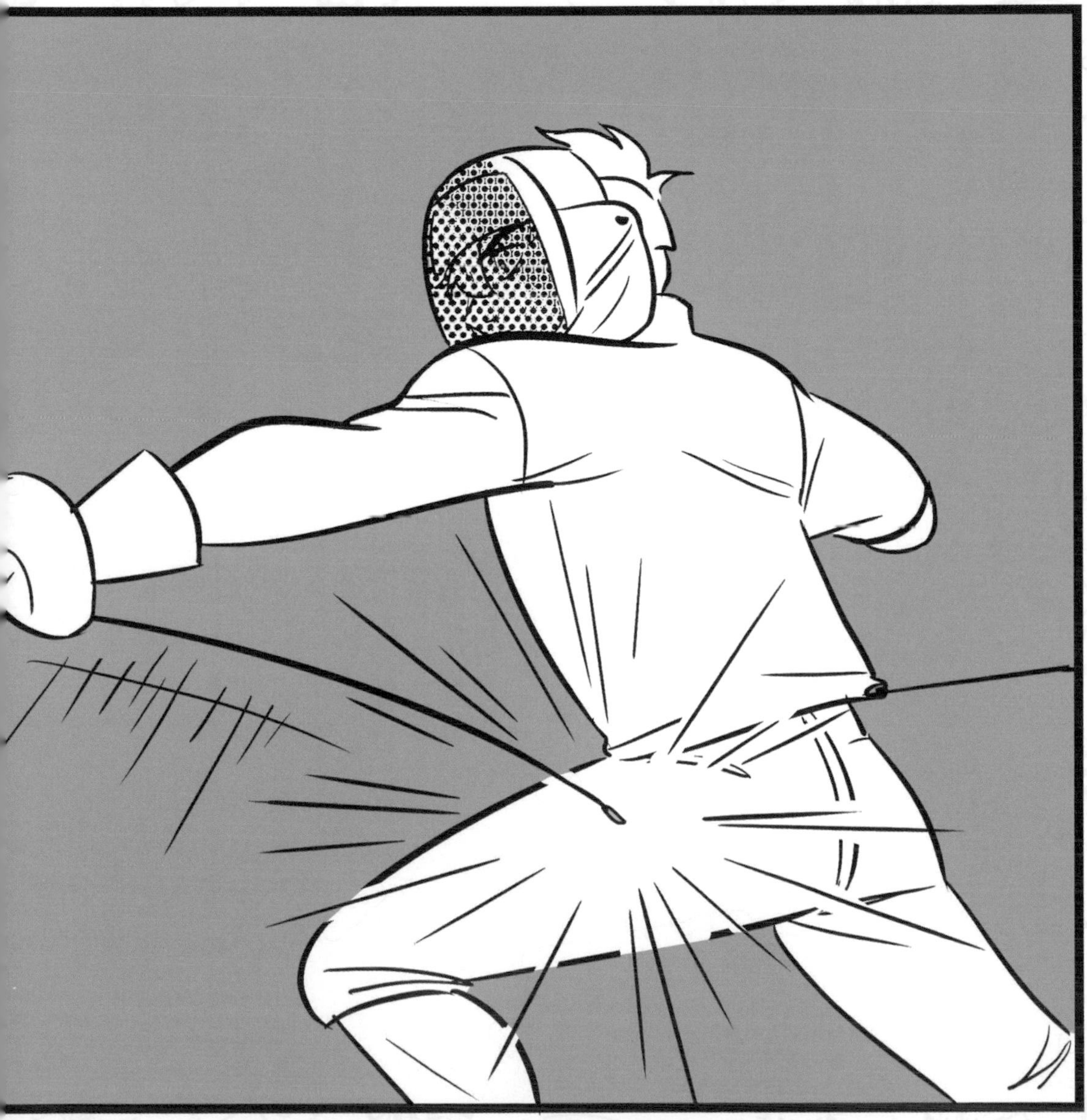

ISSUE 01 COVER BY

**Johanna the Mad**

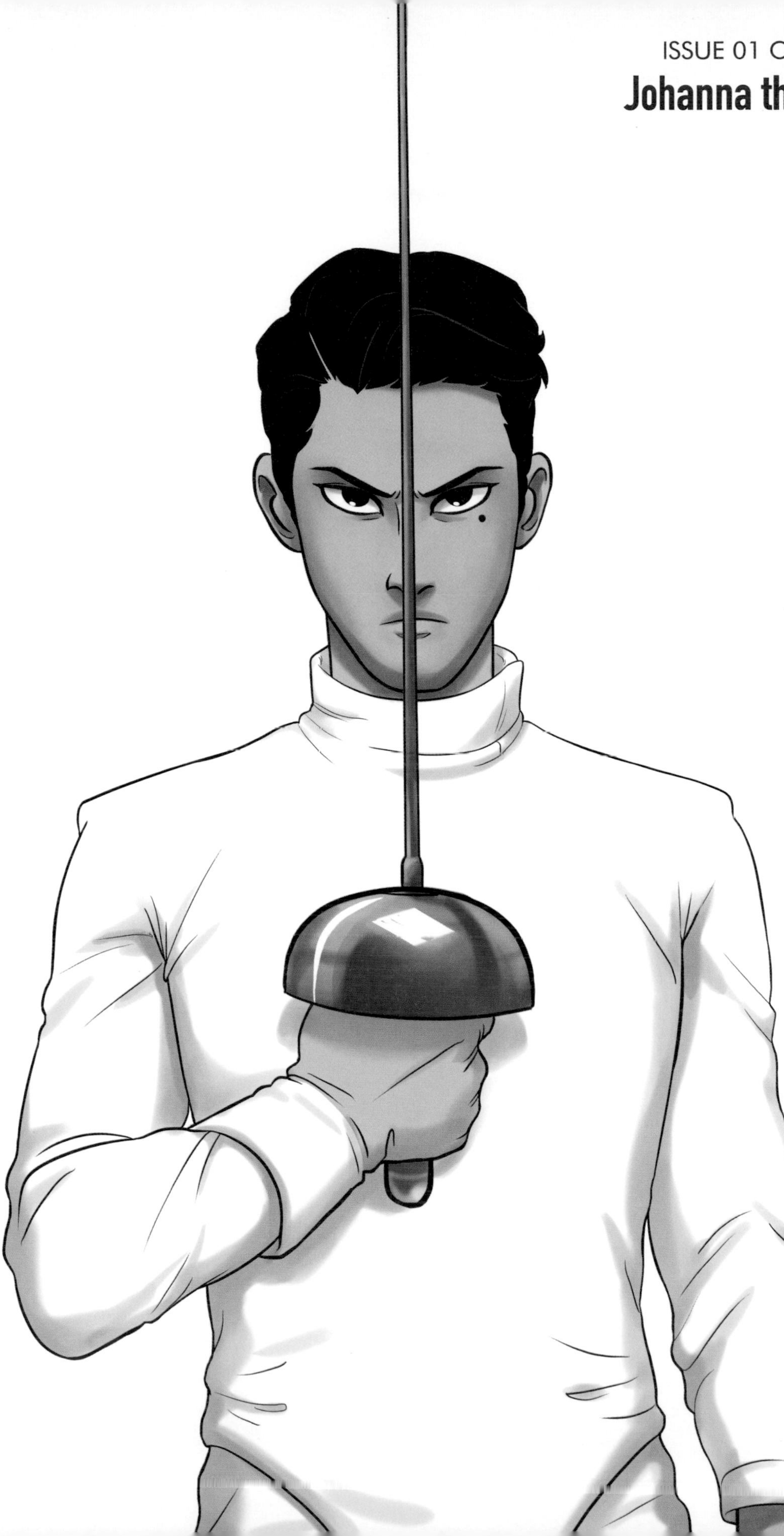

ISSUE 01 VARIANT COVER BY

**Kevin Wada**

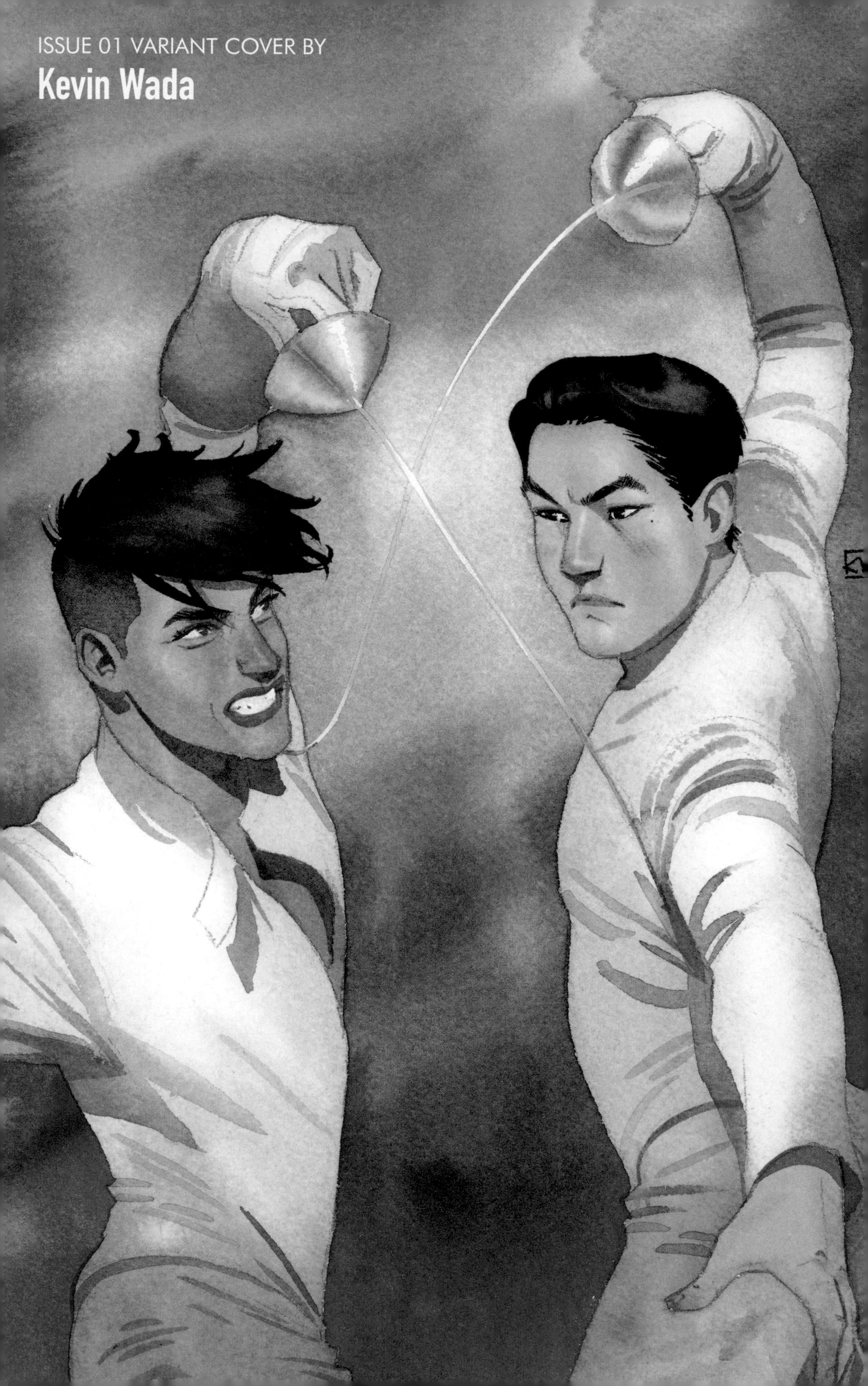

ISSUE 01 UNLOCKED RETAILER INCENTIVE COVER BY

**Shanen Pae**

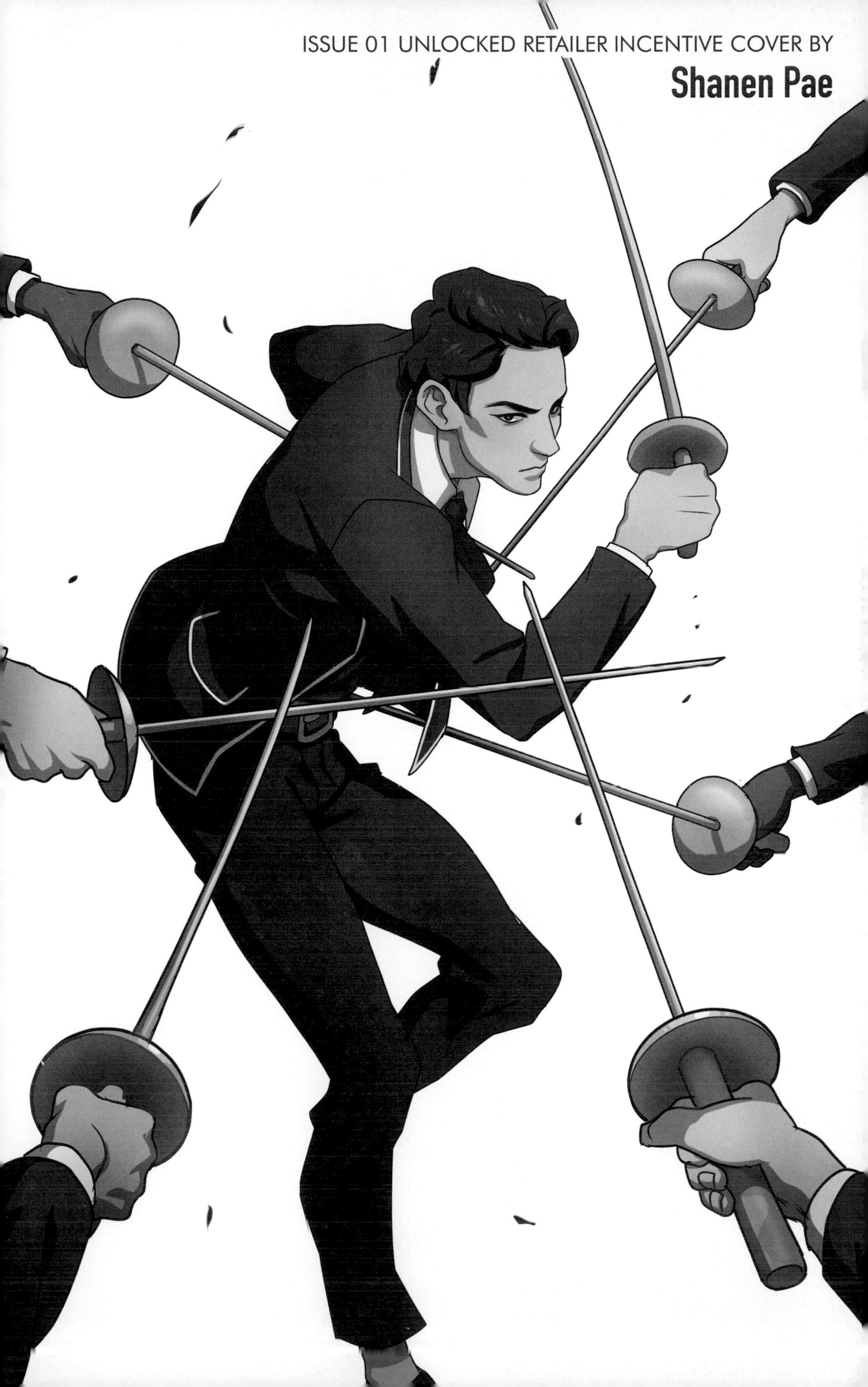

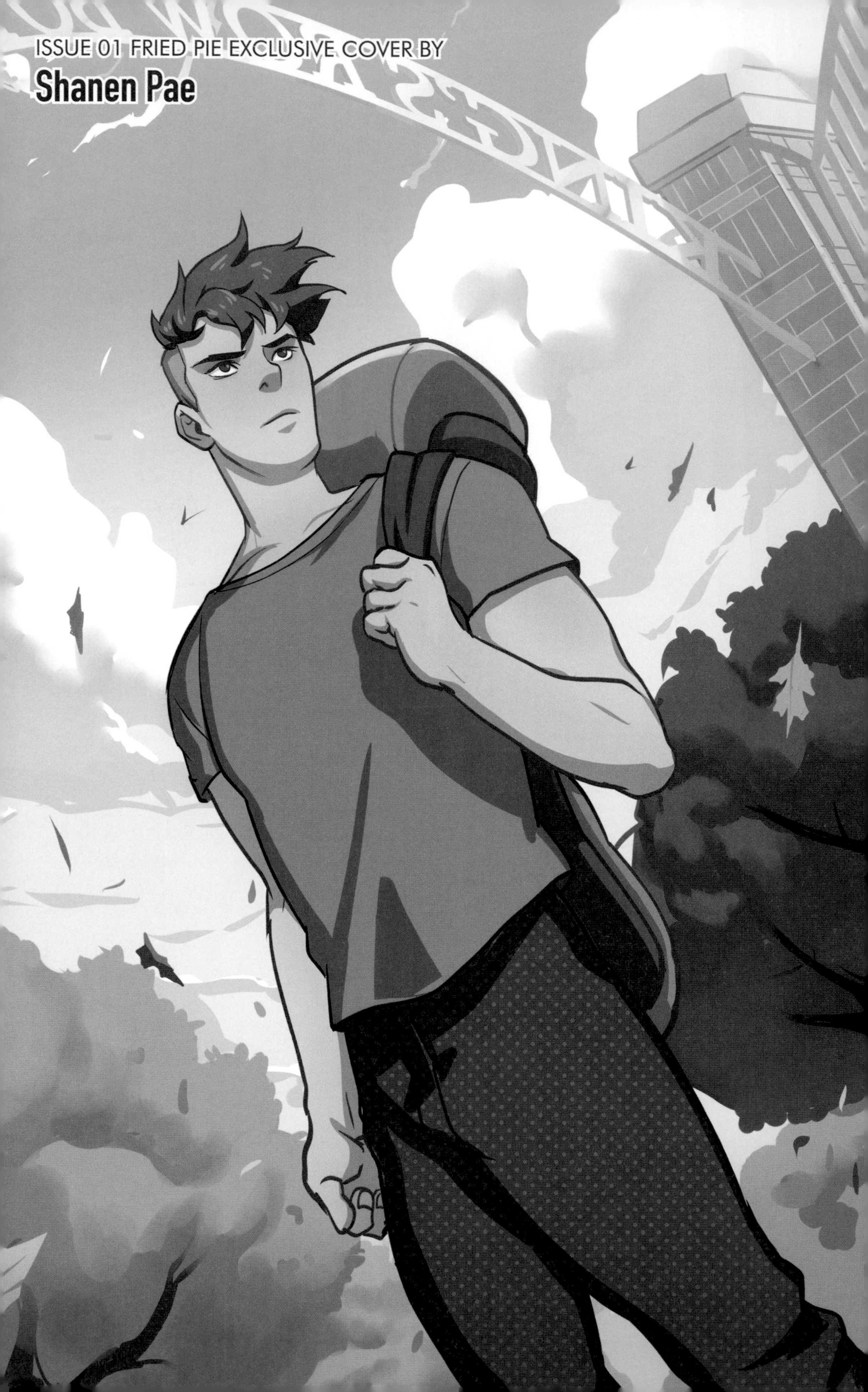

ISSUE 01 FRIED PIE EXCLUSIVE COVER BY
**Shanen Pae**

ISSUE 02 COVER BY

**Johanna the Mad**

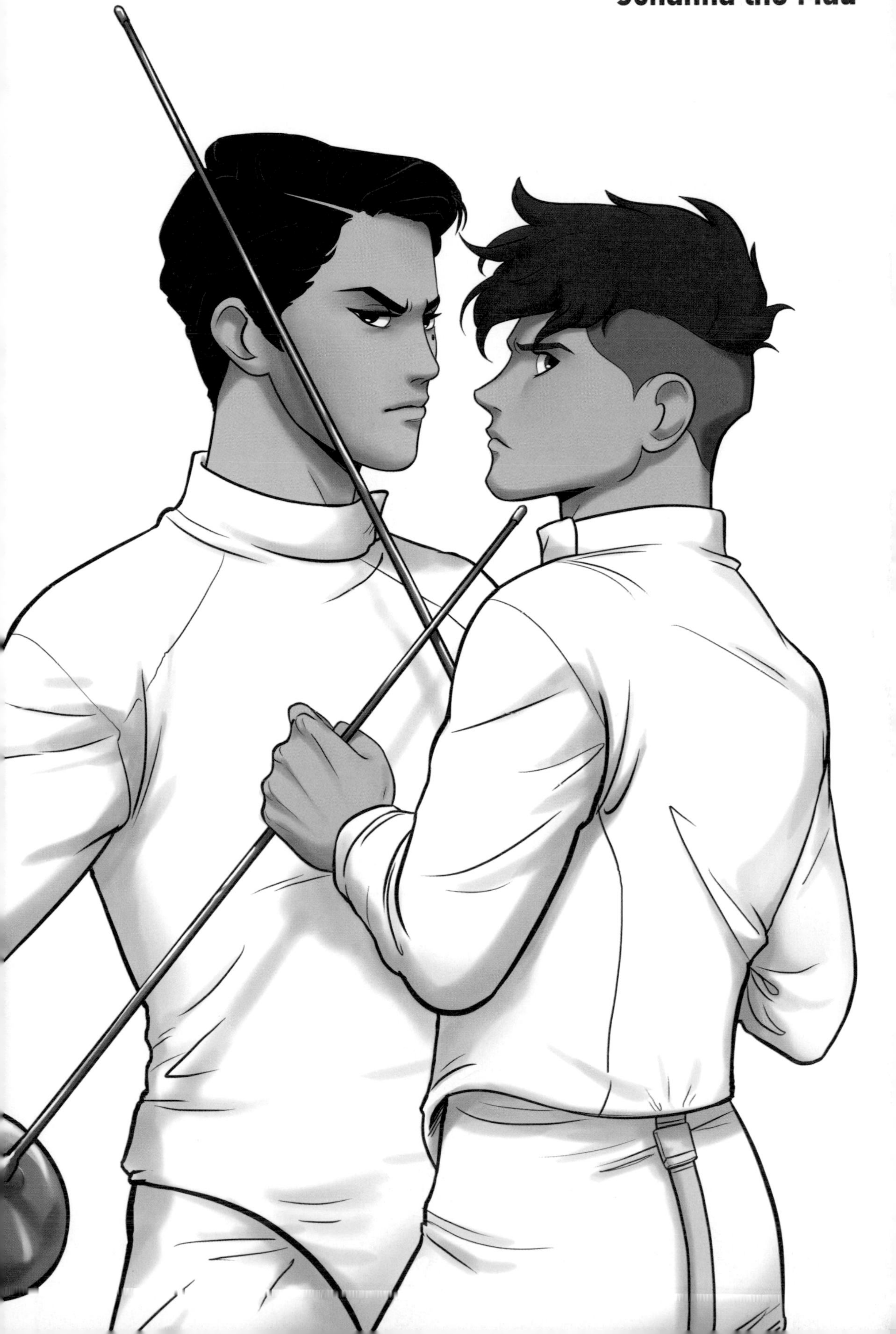

ISSUE 03 COVER BY

**Johanna the Mad**

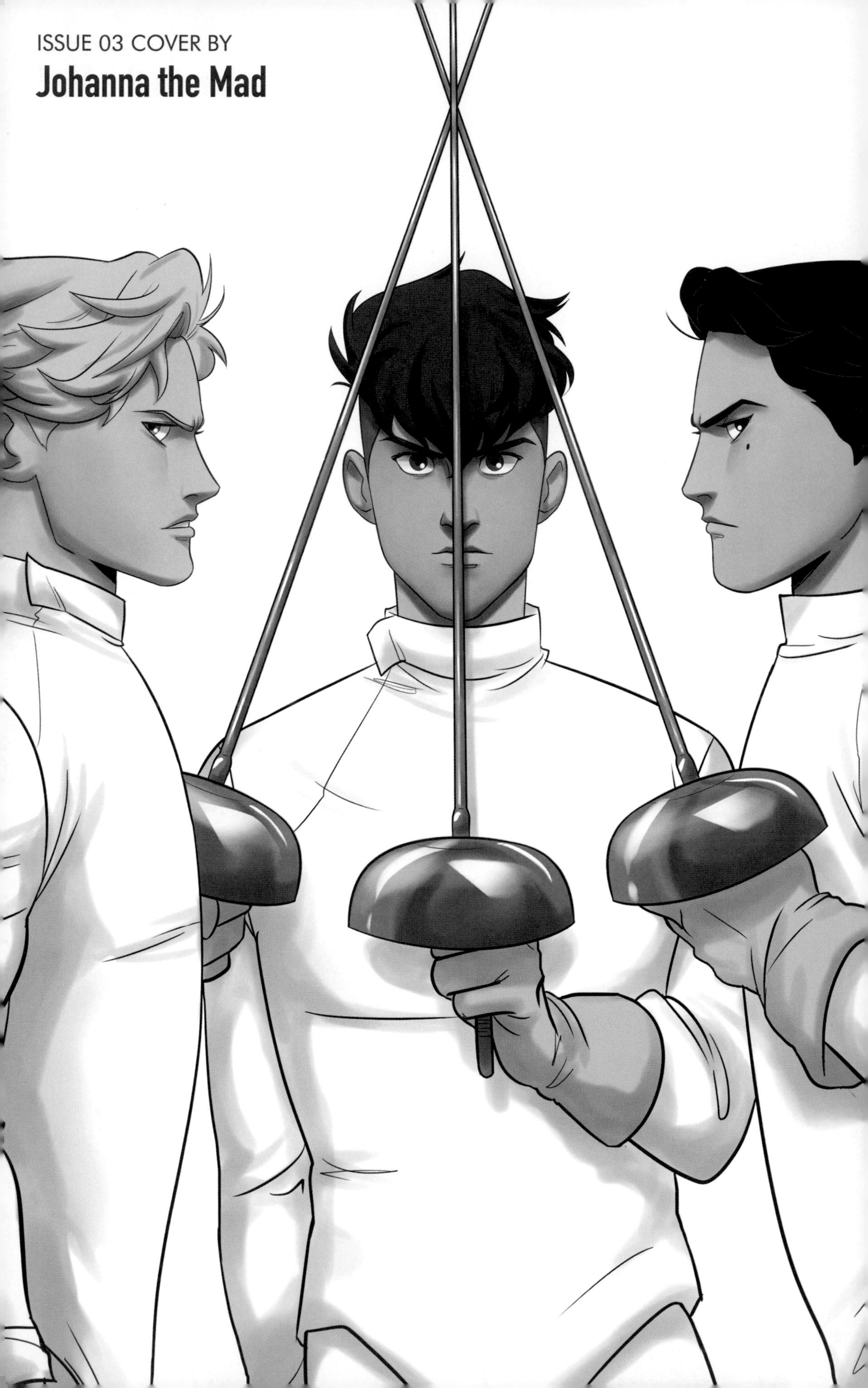

ISSUE 04 COVER BY

**Johanna the Mad**

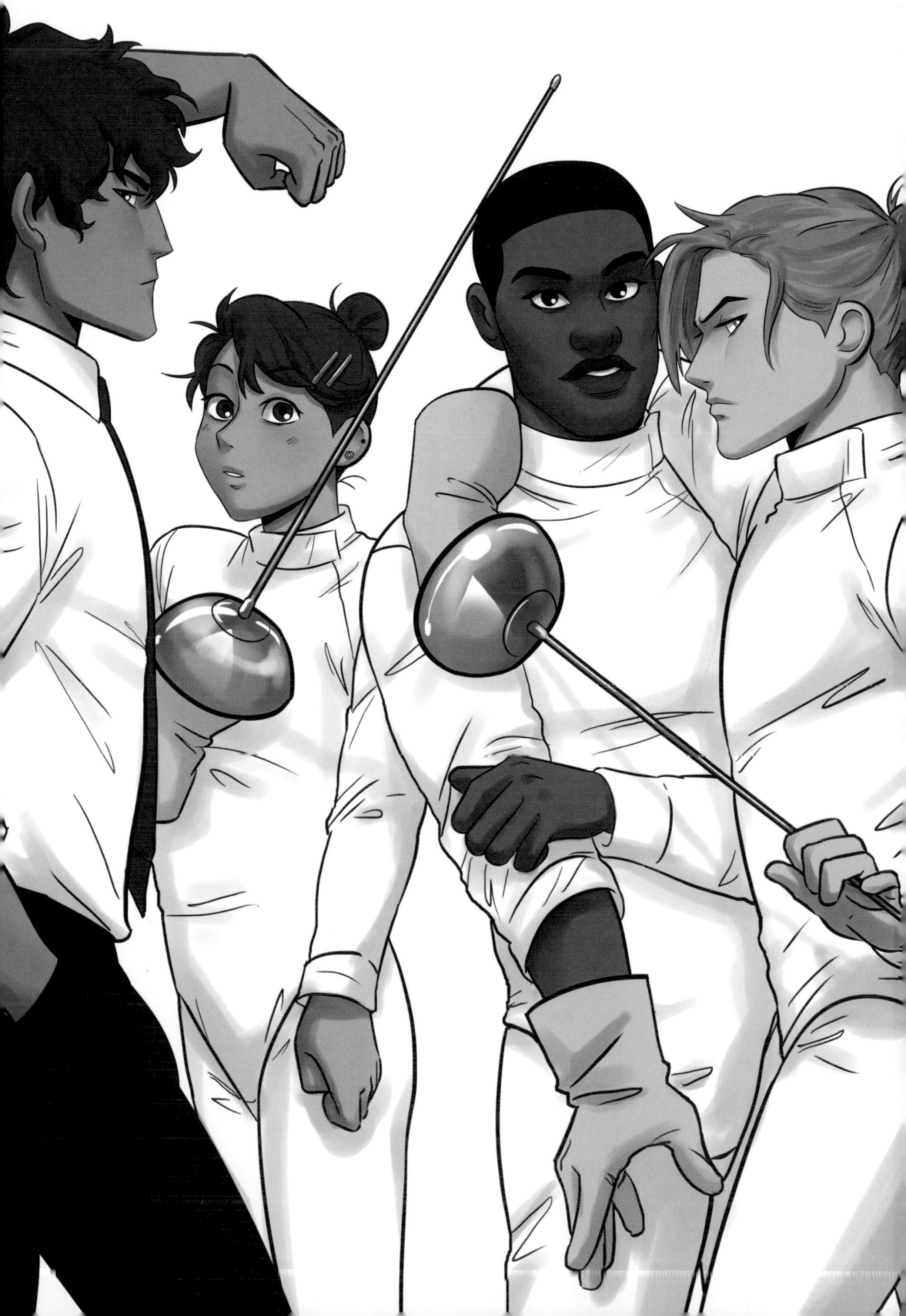